PRAISE FOR THE

"*The Moral Imagination* reminds u̲ ̲ ̲ ̲ ̲ ̲ ̲ Himmelfarb is our foremost historian of morality." —**Andrew Roberts**

"Beautifully written . . . a manual for modern statesmanship." —**Arnold Beichman**, *Washington Times*

"A complex, challenging book by one of the world's smartest and deepest scholars at the top of her game. . . . You must have your brain turned on every step of the way." —**David Gelernter**, *Weekly Standard*

"Crisp and judicious. . . . She has a marvelous grasp of the personal, historical, and intellectual features of her 'sitters.'" —**Peter Heinegg**, *America*

"Himmelfarb has a signal talent for bringing the figures and issues she discusses to life, which is to say that she has a signal talent for inhabiting history with the permanent passions of mankind." —**Roger Kimball**, *The New Criterion*

"A joy to read. . . . These thoughtful, perceptive, and calm essays are oases of reflection and concern in an age that screams and struts and points its fingers in all directions." —**Sam Coale**, *Providence Journal*

"Enlightening, infectiously enthusiastic." —**Ray Olson**, *Booklist*

The Moral Imagination

ALSO BY GERTRUDE HIMMELFARB

The People of The Book: Philosemitism in England from To Churchill (2011)

The Jewish Odyssey of George Eliot (2009)

The Roads to Modernity: The British, French, and American Enlightenments (2004)

One Nation, Two Cultures (2001)

The De-Moralization of Society: From Victorian Virtues to Modern Values (1995)

On Looking into the Abyss: Untimely Thoughts on Culture and Society (1994)

Poverty and Compassion: The Moral Imagination of the Late Victorians (1991)

The New History and the Old (1987)

Marriage and Morals Among the Victorians (1986)

The Idea of Poverty: England in the Early Industrial Age (1984)

On Liberty and Liberalism: The Case of John Stuart Mill (1974)

Victorian Minds (1968)

Darwin and the Darwinian Revolution (1959)

Lord Acton: A Study in Conscience and Politics (1952)

EDITOR OF:

Irving Kristol, *The Neoconservative Persuasion* (2011)

The Spirit of the Age: Victorian Essays (2007)

Milton Himmelfarb, *Jews and Gentiles* (2007)

Alexis de Tocqueville, *Memoir on Pauperism* (1997)

John Stuart Mill, *On Liberty* (1974)

John Stuart Mill, *Essays on Politics and Culture* (1962)

T. R. Malthus, *On Population* (1960)

Lord Acton, *Essays on Freedom and Power* (1948)

The Moral Imagination

From Adam Smith to Lionel Trilling

Second Edition

Gertrude Himmelfarb

ROWMAN & LITTLEFIELD PUBLISHERS, INC.
Lanham • Boulder • New York • Toronto • Plymouth, UK

Early versions of these essays appeared in the following journals or books: Disraeli, Knox, and Churchill, *The New Republic* (1983, 2000, 2001); Oakeshott and Eliot, *American Scholar* (1976, 1994); Burke, *American Enterprise* (1997); Bagehot, *New York Review of Books* (1965); Buchan, *Encounter* (1960); Trilling, *Weekly Standard* (2005); Dickens and Smith, in Himmelfarb, *The Idea of Poverty* (New York, 1984); Acton, *New Criterion* (2000); Marshall, in Himmelfarb, *Poverty and Compassion* (1991).

Published by Rowman & Littlefield Publishers, Inc.
A wholly owned subsidary of
The Rowman & Littlefield Publishing Group, Inc.
4501 Forbes Boulevard, Suite 200, Lanham, Maryland 20706
www.rowman.com

10 Thornbury Road, Plymouth PL6 7PP, United Kingdom

British Library Cataloguing in Publication Information Available

Library of Congress Cataloging-in-Publication Data
Himmelfarb, Gertrude.
  The moral imagination : from Adam Smith to Lionel Trilling / Gertrude Himmelfarb. — 2nd ed.
    p. cm.
  Includes bibliographical references and index.
  ISBN 978-1-4422-1829-1 (pbk. : alk. paper) — ISBN 978-1-4422-1830-7 (ebook)
  1. Philosophy, Modern 2. Political science—Philosophy. I. Title.
  B791.H56 2012
  190,—dc23
                                                                2012020626

∞™ The paper used in this publication meets the minimum requirements of American National Standard for Information Sciences—Permanence of Paper for Printed Library Materials, ANSI/NISO Z39.48-1992.

Printed in the United States of America

To my brother, Milton Himmelfarb

Contents

Introduction

～ Biographers do not often have the occasion to pay tribute to their subjects. They strive to be objective and dispassionate, describing and analyzing rather than praising or censuring. It is a great pleasure, therefore, to look back upon notable thinkers and writers who are eminently praiseworthy, and to find that the passage of time has shown them to be even more memorable and admirable than one might have thought.

Half of the essays in this volume were written within recent years: two go as far back as the 1960s, all have been substantially revised, some are new.* In rereading the originals, I was surprised to find a striking similarity of tone and theme in the discussion of people of such distinctive characters; of different times and places; of varied interests, occupations, and dispositions. I should not have been surprised. My own sense of history has obviously been shaped by some of these figures. Edmund Burke introduced the term "moral imagination" into political discourse. He was also the subject of the first of my published essays. (That is not the essay that appears here; when I reprinted that early essay many years later, I accompanied it with another recanting much of the first.) And Lionel Trilling, the subject of the last of these essays, popularized

---

*This edition contains three additional essays, on Adam Smith, Lord Acton, and Alfred Marshall.

that expression for our time. "The free play of the moral imagination"—this is what Trilling sought in literature and what he displayed so brilliantly in his own work.

The echo of that theme, and sometimes of Trilling himself, may be found in each of these essays. The great "problem" for scholars of Adam Smith has been the apparent disjunction between the political economist and the moral philosopher. It was no problem for his contemporaries, however—nor for Trilling, who referred to him, in his very first book, as one of "the best of the middle-class prophets."[1] Describing Walter Bagehot, I remark upon the "subtleties, complications, and ambiguities" that he saw everywhere, without realizing that I was echoing Trilling, for whom those words were at the heart of his own literary criticism. Trilling would have sympathized with Lord Acton, whose great work, "The History of Liberty," never got written because of his obsession with history as a moral enterprise. When I said that John Buchan's work was "inimical to what Lionel Trilling called the 'liberal imagination'," Buchan's son misinterpreted me as implying that his father was critical of Trilling, whereas, he assured me, his father had great admiration for him. Writing about Michael Oakeshott, Trilling's contemporary and a prominent English conservative, I could hardly resist opening that essay with the famous statement by Trilling about the conspicuous absence of conservatism in the United States. And the literary figures who appear in this volume—Jane Austen, George Eliot, Charles Dickens, even Benjamin Disraeli in his persona as novelist—are perfect exemplars of the title Trilling chose for his anthology, *The Experience of Literature.* For them, as for Trilling, the novel was a social and moral experience as much as a literary or esthetic one.

Other of my subjects are interrelated in ways I had not consciously intended. Using terms immortalized by William James, I present Bagehot as the typical "twice-born" soul, complicated, ambivalent, sometimes tormented, incapable of the easy, comfortable, optimistic demeanor of the "once-born." But that term applies as aptly to other of my characters: Buchan, the Knox brothers, even Dickens. The two women novelists, Jane Austen and George Eliot, are remarkably complementary, especially if one reverses the chronological order, as I have done, thus "humanizing *Middlemarch* and moralizing *Emma*." Disraeli and Churchill are not so much complementary as kindred spirits; Disraeli would surely have endorsed the tribute to Churchill as "quite simply, a great man," and Churchill's initiation into political life came as a schoolboy when he joined the Primrose League named in honor of Disraeli (the primrose presumed to have been his favorite flower). While Marshall was receiving the tributes of his colleagues and the public for his seminal work on economics, he himself, not in modesty but in all sincerity, insisted, "It's all in Adam Smith." And Buchan's insistence upon calling himself a Tory recalls Disraeli's use of the same word to distinguish himself from the Conservative leader of his party, Robert Peel.

"Conservative" is a term that recurs in several of the essays, but each time connoting a different kind of conservatism. Burke's conservatism was not Disraeli's, still less Oakeshott's; and Churchill's was quite his own, a synthesis of ideas and sentiments reflecting his unique personal and political experiences. Smith, a great friend of Burke and the inventor, so to speak, of classical economic liberalism, is now hailed by conservatives as one of their own, eighteenth-century liberalism having become twentieth-century conservatism. So, too, Lord Acton, the preeminent liberal Catholic of his day who resisted the doctrine of papal infallibility, is now known as the author of that aphorism, "Power tends to corrupt and absolute power corrupts absolutely," which conservatives quote (and misquote) as a rebuke to those seeking to expand the state. And then there is the great liberal, John Stuart Mill—in the person of the "other Mill"—who (paraphrasing his own epigraph on Coleridge) was not "wholly a liberal," reminding liberals of truths that they had forgotten and that the prevailing school of Tories never knew.

Finally, and most important, what the essays have in common is that they are all "appreciations"—not "untimely," like Buchan (although even he resonates today as a noble, if thoroughly romantic, spirit), and not, I trust, excessively adulatory, but simply appreciative of a sense and sensibility, a moral imagination, as pertinent now as it was then.

February 2012

The Moral Imagination

Adam Smith

Political Economist cum *Moral Philosopher*

❧   "*Das Adam Smith Problem*"—that problem was put to us a century-and-a-half ago by a German economist (August Oncken, little known today except for that memorable phrase), and we are still wrestling with it. At issue is the apparent contradiction between *The Wealth of Nations* and *The Theory of Moral Sentiments*—between the political economist and the moral philosopher.

This is not a case of an early and a late Smith (as with the early and late Marx). *The Theory of Moral Sentiments*, published in 1759, antedated *An Inquiry into the Nature and Causes of the Wealth of Nations*, published in 1776. But as Smith himself pointed out, the principal ideas of *The Wealth of Nations* appeared in his lectures in Edinburgh as early as 1750, again in a paper he delivered in Glasgow in 1755 (where he occupied the chair of Moral Philosophy at the university), and in drafts of the book that he worked on for almost two decades, to the despair of his friends who regretted the delay and feared that its length would discourage readers. Moreover, *The Theory of Moral Sentiments* was reprinted in 1774, only two years before the publication of *The Wealth of Nations*, so that he himself evidently perceived no disparity between the two.

One reason why this was not a "problem" for Smith—or for his contemporaries—was because he was not merely an economist, as we now understand that word. He was known at the time as a "political economist."* "Political economy" had a dimension larger than economics, focusing not so much on individual transactions in the marketplace as on the political and social consequences of those transactions. This was in keeping with the mercantilist idea of the *dirigiste* state, in which trade—foreign trade primarily but also domestic—was deemed to be the proper province of government, reflecting the strength and prosperity of the state in relation to other states; trade was, in effect, war by other means. Smith may have been deliberately provocative when he gave his book a title, *The Wealth of Nations*, that would seem to place it within the mercantilist tradition—and then proceeded to reinterpret both "wealth" and "nations" so as to create a political economy that was the very antithesis of mercantilism.

If Smith's political economy was in sharp contrast to the prevailing mercantilist doctrine, his moral philosophy was no less opposed to the idea of a "moral economy"—the pre-industrial, pre-capitalist, Christian ideal based on the principles of equity and justice. The Victorian moralist, John Ruskin, had something like that in mind when he inveighed against Smith, that "half-bred and half-witted Scotchman" who deliberately perpetrated the blasphemy, "Thou shalt hate the Lord thy God, damn His laws, and covet thy neighbor's goods."[2] A century later the socialist historian E. P. Thompson explicitly invoked the idea of a moral economy in describing the "crowd" in eighteenth-century England—the food rioters, for example, protesting against the high price of corn. That idea was the "legitimizing notion" that

*The term political economist originated in France as *"oeconomie politique"* early in the sixteenth century and in its English equivalent toward the end of the century. Not until late in the nineteenth century did it begin to be replaced by "economics," most notably in Alfred Marshall's *Principles of Economics* in 1890.[1]

inspired the poor—a traditional, paternalist view of the economy that respected social norms, obligations, and, most notably, fixed or low prices for food ("just prices," in the Catholic tradition). *The Wealth of Nations,* arguing against the corn laws and in favor of free trade, had the effect of "de-moralizing" that moral economy, replacing it with a new political economy "disinfested of intrusive moral imperatives"—not, Thompson hastened to add (unlike Ruskin), because Smith himself was immoral or unconcerned for the public good, but because that was the objective effect of his doctrine.[3]

When *The Wealth of Nations* was finally published, David Hume consoled Smith that while it required too close a reading to become quickly popular, it would, by its "depth and solidity and acuteness" and its "curious facts," eventually attract the public.[4] The publisher was less optimistic. The first edition, in two volumes and over a thousand pages, consisted of five hundred copies selling for the standard price of £1 16s., for which Smith received the grand sum of £300—this for the author of the well-known and highly regarded *Theory of Moral Sentiments* that had appeared in a new edition only two years earlier. Those five hundred copies sold out in six months, a second edition was published two years later, and three others followed in the dozen years before his death in 1790. The book was translated during his lifetime into French, German, Italian, Danish, and Spanish, and received the imprimatur of success in the form of a lengthy abridgement. Some of the most eminent men of the time, across the political spectrum, declared themselves his disciple: Edmund Burke and Thomas Paine, Edward Gibbon and Richard Price, William Pitt and Lord North.

Part of the success of *The Wealth of Nations* has been attributed, ironically, to the fact that it was not altogether original. The term *laissez faire,* like political economy, was an import from

France dating from the reign of Louis XIV, when a merchant is said to have pleaded with the king's minister, Louis-Baptiste Colbert, "Laissez-nous faire." Later popularized by the Physiocrats protesting against the highly regulated economy, it was imported into England where it retained its French form. (The term itself does not appear in *The Wealth of Nations,* although the concept obviously does.) Similarly, the "division of labor," the subject of the first chapter of the book, had its antecedents in Chambers's *Cyclopaedia* in 1728 (complete with the pin-factory example publicized by Smith); in the French *Encyclopédie* decades later (which borrowed it, with the same example); and in a book by Smith's friend, Adam Ferguson, *Essay on the History of Civil Society,* published only a few years before *The Wealth of Nations.*

The Victorian economist, Walter Bagehot, an admirer of Smith, conceded that these terms and concepts were not novel and that the idea of free trade was "in the air," although not generally accepted or established. "On the contrary, it was a tenet against which a respectable parent would probably caution his son; still it was known as a tempting heresy and one against which a warning was needed."[5] A later economic historian, Joseph Schumpeter (less well disposed to Smith), agreed that there was little original in *The Wealth of Nations*—not "a single *analytic* idea, principle, or method that was entirely new in 1776." It was a "great performance" deserving of success, Schumpeter conceded, but that success came, paradoxically, from Smith's limitations. "Had he been more brilliant, he would not have been taken so seriously. Had he dug more deeply, had he unearthed more recondite truth, had he used difficult and ingenious methods, he would not have been understood." But those were not his intentions or aspirations. "In fact he disliked whatever went beyond plain common sense. He never moved above the heads of even the dullest readers." He spoke their language, made them feel comfortable, and, most important, was "thoroughly in sympathy with the humors of his time."[6]*

Among the "humors of his time" that endeared Smith to his readers (but not to Schumpeter) was the moral philosophy that infused his political economy. So far from seeing *The Wealth of Nations* as a refutation of *The Theory of Moral Sentiments* (as some later commentators have), contemporaries welcomed the new book as a complement to the old. Edmund Burke, having reviewed the first book glowingly when it appeared, was as admiring in his review of the second. Nor did the new book displace or supersede the old. The appreciative memoir of Smith by Dugald Stewart, written three years after Smith's death, devoted twenty-six pages to *The Theory of Moral Sentiments* and only seventeen to *The Wealth of Nations*.

The favorable reception of both books is all the more remarkable because their subjects are different and on the surface, at least disjunctive, if not contradictory. The animating spirit of *The Wealth of Nations* is "interest" or "self-love"; that of *The Theory of Moral Sentiments* is "sympathy" or "fellow-feeling." The memorable dictum that highlights the contrast between the two appears early in *The Wealth of Nations*: "It is not from the benevolence of the butcher, the brewer, or the baker, that we expect our dinner, but from their regard to their own interest." This sentence is often quoted out of context. The preceding passage is less stark—indeed, it might well have appeared in the earlier book.

---

*Schumpeter did not intend these comments in a complementary sense. On the contrary, he had little respect for Smith personally and less for his doctrines— and precisely for the opposite reasons that Thompson held against him. Where Thompson criticized him for de-moralizing political economy, Schumpeter accused him of being so steeped in the moral traditions derived from scholasticism and natural law that he could not conceive of economics per se, as a discipline divorced from ethics and politics.

> In civilized society, he [man] stands at all times in need of the
> cooperation and assistance of great multitudes. . . . In almost
> every other race of animals, each individual, when it is grown
> up to maturity, is entirely independent, and in its natural
> state has occasion for the assistance of no other living crea-
> ture. But man has almost constant occasion for the help of his
> brethren, and it is in vain for him to expect it from their
> benevolence only.[7]

Only then, after placing man firmly in society, dependent on the
"cooperation" and "help of his brethren," does Smith invoke the
idea of interest—not to deny the idea of benevolence, but rather to
supplement "benevolence only" by another more dependable idea.
The butcher, brewer, and baker are appealed to on the basis of their
interests, because that would be more effective to achieve the same
end—the good of others, their "brethren."

Another memorable phrase, the "invisible hand," is often cited
as the attempt to reconcile self-love and the public good. By engaging in industry, man "intends only his own security . . . [and]
his own gain, and he is in this, as in many other cases, led by an invisible hand to promote an end which was no part of his intention.
. . . By pursuing his own interest he frequently promotes that of
the society more effectually than when he really intends to promote
it."[8] This phrase appears only once in *The Wealth of Nations,* late in
the book, as well as in *Moral Sentiments* in quite a different context.
There the issue is not industry but luxury, the disparity between
the rich and the poor.

> In spite of their natural selfishness and rapacity, though they
> [the rich] mean only their own convenience, though the sole
> end which they propose from the labors of all the thousands
> whom they employ, be the gratification of their own vain and
> insatiable desires, they divide with the poor the produce of all

their improvements. They are led by an invisible hand to make nearly the same distribution of the necessaries of life, which would have been made, had the earth been divided into equal portions among all its inhabitants, and thus without intending it, without knowing it, advance the interest of society, and afford means to the multiplication of the species.[9]

The "invisible hand" has been given a teleological interpretation, as if some benevolent agent is active in bringing about that benevolent end.* For Smith the hand is simply a metaphor for a free market, a "system of natural liberty," in which individuals exchange their goods and services without the intervention of any supervising hand or authority.[10] Only in such a system could the division of labor produce the "opulence" that would distribute the "necessaries of life" for the benefit of all. "By necessaries" *The Wealth of Nations* explains "I understand, not only the commodities which are indispensably necessary for the support of life, but whatever the custom of the country renders it indecent for creditable people, even of the lowest order, to be without."[11]

Society, the rich and the poor, employers and workers, even unto the "lowest order"—this is the "nation" in *The Wealth of Nations*. It is not the nation-state in the mercantilist sense, but the people who constitute society. And not the "people," as contemporaries

---

*Smith's "invisible hand" may be reminiscent of Hegel's "cunning of reason," but it is profoundly different, precisely because Hegel's "reason" is teleological. For Hegel, the ends that are unwittingly furthered by the exercise of individual wills and interests are those of a providential History and Reason. There is no evidence that Hegel was inspired by Smith when he coined that phrase in the *Philosophy of History*. Yet he had read Smith and there are echoes of him in the *Philosophy of Right*, especially the concept of "civil society," the realm intermediate between the individual and the state where individuals pursue their private interests.

often used that word—those who play an active part in politics—but the "common people" as well, including the lower and even the lowest orders. By the same token, the "wealth" in the title is not the wealth of the state (again, as the mercantilist understood it), but the wealth, or well-being, of all the people. Only a "progressive"—that is, a free and industrious—economy, could bring about "a universal opulence which extends itself to the lowest ranks of the people, . . . a general plenty [which] diffuses itself through all the different ranks of society."[12] To those who complain that if the poor shared in the "general plenty," they would no longer be content with their lot in life, Smith put the question: "Is this improvement in the circumstances of the lower ranks of the people to be regarded as an advantage or an inconvenience to the society?" His answer is unequivocal—and very much in the spirit of *Moral Sentiments*:

> Servants, laborers and workmen of different kinds, make up the far greater part of every great political society. But what improves the circumstances of the greater part can never be regarded as an inconvenience to the whole. No society can surely be flourishing and happy, of which the far greater part of the members are poor and miserable. It is but equity, besides, that they who feed, clothe and lodge the whole body of the people should have such a share of the produce of their own labor as to be themselves tolerably well fed, clothed and lodged.[13]

Smith's critics often assume that his political economy was designed not only to further the interests of businessmen (not yet named "capitalists"), but also to vindicate and even exalt them. In fact, the rhetoric of *The Wealth of Nations* is more often deprecatory and even hostile. Of the three "orders" in society—landlords, laborers, and merchant-manufacturers—the first two are seen as acting in accord with the public interest and the last in conflict with it.

The proposal of any new law or regulation of commerce which comes from this order ought always to be listened to with great precaution, and ought never to be adopted till after having been long and carefully examined, not only with the most scrupulous but with the most suspicious attention. It comes from an order of men whose interest is never exactly the same with that of the public, who have generally an interest to deceive and even to oppress the public, and who accordingly have, upon many occasions, both deceived and oppressed it.[14]

People of the same trade seldom meet together, even for merriment and diversion, but the conversation ends in a conspiracy against the public, or in some contrivance to raise prices.[15]

Deception and oppression, conspiracy and contrivance are only part of this indictment. Elsewhere the merchants and manufacturers are accused of "clamor and sophistry," "impertinent jealousy," "mean rapacity," "mean and malignant expedients," "sneaking arts," "interested sophistry," and "interested falsehood."[16] There are surely enough "intrusive moral imperatives" in *The Wealth of Nations* to satisfy an ethical socialist like Thompson and to distress a "scientific" economist like Schumpeter.

If Smith's moral rhetoric belies the conventional view of him, his political economy does so even more. His opposition to mercantilism is generally read as a criticism of government regulation and a defense of laissez faire.[*] It is that, and much more, for

---

[*]It is by now generally accepted that Smith is not the rigorous laissez fairist that some of his disciples, and critics, made him out to be. The final book of *The Wealth of Nations*, on the duties and functions of government, testifies to that, as does Smith's own life. As Commissioner of Customs for Scotland (a post he sought and conscientiously fulfilled—it was not a sinecure), he supervised the collection of revenue to be used for the proper functions of the state: defense, justice, public works, and education.

his objection to mercantilism is not only that it inhibits a progressive economy by interfering with the natural processes of the market; it is also unjustly biased against workers. "Our merchants and manufacturers complain much of the bad effects of high wages. . . . They say nothing concerning the bad effects of high profits. . . . They are silent with regard to the pernicious effects of their own gains."[17]

According to the mercantilist doctrine, low wages are both natural and necessary: natural because the poor would not work except out of dire need, and necessary in order to maintain a favorable balance of trade. As the popular writer and economist Arthur Young put it: "Everyone but an idiot knows that the lower classes must be kept poor, or they will never be industrious."[18] Even Hume, not a mercantilist, believed that in years of scarcity, when wages are low, "the poor labor more, and really live better, than in years of great plenty, when they indulge themselves in idleness and riot."[19] Excessively low wages, they agreed, would be counterproductive, providing no incentive to work. But this was an argument for subsistence wages, not high wages.

Smith, on the other hand, took a positive view of high wages, defending them as in the best interests of society as well as the laborer.

> The liberal reward of labor, as it encourages the propagation, so it increases the industry of the common people. The wages of labor are the encouragement of industry, which, like every other human quality, improves in proportion to the encouragement it receives. A plentiful subsistence increases the bodily strength of the labourer, and the comfortable hope of bettering his condition and of ending his days perhaps in ease and plenty animates him to exert that strength to the utmost. Where

wages are high, we shall always find the workmen more active, diligent, and expeditious, than where they are low.[20]

High wages encouraging the "propagation," as well as the "industry," of people—in effect, Smith was refuting in advance Malthus's "principle of population." For Malthus, high wages leads to an increase of population, and because population grows "geometrically" and the food supply only "arithmetically," the result is the inevitable "misery and vice" of the lower classes. In Smith's expanding, "progressive" economy, high wages have the opposite effect. There the demand for labor keeps abreast of the supply, and wages remain high even as the population increases. So far from "misery and vice," the laborer enjoys a "plentiful subsistence" and the reasonable expectation of "bettering his condition."

This benign view of the condition and prospects of the laboring poor extends to the indigent as well—the "lowest ranks" of society. England was the first country—and for a long time the only country—to have a public, secular, national (although locally administered) system of poor relief. Unlike some of his successors—again, Malthus, most notably—Smith had no quarrel with poor relief as such. What he did vigorously oppose were the "settlement laws" that established residency requirements for the poor, thus limiting their mobility and opportunities for improvement, as well as depriving them of the liberty enjoyed by other Englishmen.[21] In the same spirit, he argued for proportional taxation and taxes on luxuries rather than necessities, so that "the indolence and vanity of the rich is made to contribute in a very easy manner to the relief of the poor."[22]

Smith's optimism failed him at one point. Toward the end of *The Wealth of Nations*, in what has come to be known as the "alienation" or "immiseration" passage, he described the effects of the division of labor on a man who has spent his life performing a few simple operations, with no opportunity to "exert his understanding" or "exercise his invention."

> He naturally loses, therefore, the habit of such exertions, and generally becomes as stupid and ignorant as it is possible for a human creature to become. The torpor of his mind renders him, not only incapable of relishing or bearing a part in any rational conversation, but of conceiving any general, noble, or tender sentiments, and consequently of forming any just judgment concerning many even of the ordinary duties of private life. Of the great and extensive interests of his country he is altogether incapable of judging; and unless very particular pains have been taken to render him otherwise, he is equally incapable of defending his country in war. The uniformity of his stationary life naturally corrupts the courage of his mind, and makes him regard with abhorrence the irregular, uncertain, and adventurous life of a soldier. It corrupts even the activity of his body, and renders him incapable of exerting his strength with vigor and perseverance, in any other employment than that to which he has been bred. His dexterity at his own particular trade seems, in this manner, to be acquired at the expense of his intellectual, social, and martial virtues.[23]

This is a damning portrait—and a surprising one, because these are the laboring poor whom Smith earlier praised and for whom he held out such high promise. It also contradicts the opening sentence of the book: "The greatest improvement in the productive powers of labour, and the greater part of the skill, dexterity, and judgment with which it is any where directed, or applied, seem to have been the effects of the division of labor."[24] Yet toward the end of the book, that "skill, dexterity, and judgment"—and much else—seem to be belied by the division of labor. An explanation for this apparent contradiction may be found in the final sentence of that passage: "But in every improved and civilized society this is the state into which the labouring poor, that is, the great body of the people, must necessarily fall, unless government takes some pains to prevent it."[25]

"Unless government takes some pains . . . ." Smith went on to suggest just how this might be done: by means of a state-administered, state-supported, state-enforced system of education. A school would be established in every district where children, including those "bred to the lowest occupation," would be instructed in reading, writing, and arithmetic. The burden of the cost of this system would be borne by the state, although parents would be charged a fee so modest that even the common laborer could afford it. The schools themselves would not be compulsory (there were already pauper schools and varieties of private schools), but some form of schooling would be. To ensure a proper level of instruction, the student would have to pass an examination in the "three R's" before entering a guild or setting up in a trade.[26]*

Marxists have made much of this "alienation" theme (as they have christened it), without, however, attending to Smith's proposal to "prevent," or at least mitigate, it. Marx himself, after quoting that passage in *Capital*, referred to this proposal as providing "education of the people by the state, but prudently, and in homoeopathic doses."[28] The alternative measure he himself put forward

*At one other point, the industrial worker is compared with the agricultural laborer, to the advantage of the latter—the agricultural laborer having to perform many tasks in the course of the day, unlike the factory worker who is confined to one. Here too the context is interesting, for the paragraph appears in the course of his criticism of manufacturers and tradesmen who find it easy to "combine together" to further their own interests against those of the public, and of the workers, whereas farmers are too dispersed to engage in such practices.[27]

might strike a modern reader as not so much prudent or homoeopathic as simply regressive. Writing almost a century after Smith,
only a few years before the Forster Act of 1870 that established the
principle of free, compulsory public education, Marx took as his
model for educational reform the Factory Act of 1864, which permitted children under the age of fourteen to work only if they
spent part of the day at schools provided by the employer. Although he criticized that measure as "paltry," he approved of the
principle of combining education with work, accepting the claim
of factory inspectors that these children, in far fewer hours, learned
as much or more than day-school children. His own proposal was
heavily weighted toward work. "When the working class comes
into power, as inevitably it must, technical instruction, both theoretical and practical, will take its proper place in the working class
schools," making workers fit for a "variety of labors, ready to face
any change of production."[29] This was no passing thought on
Marx's part. Almost twenty years earlier, in *The Communist Manifesto,* he derided the "bourgeois claptrap" about education, proposing instead free education with the proviso: "combination of
education with industrial production."[30]*

---

*One is reminded of Hannah Arendt's observation that no thinker ever reduced
man to an *animal laborans* as totally as Marx did. Locke, she pointed out, made
of labor the source of property; Smith made of labor the source of wealth; Marx
made of labor the very essence of man.[31] If Marx's solution to the problem of
alienation was different from Smith's, so was his concept of the problem itself.
For Smith, it was not capitalism that was flawed but the division of labor inherent in modern industry. This was close to the position of the "early Marx,"
for whom alienation arose in the earliest stages of society, with the separation of
man from physical nature and the division of labor in the family. The "mature
Marx," on the other hand, located the problem in capitalism—the divorce of
workers from the means of production. Communism, to be sure, did not solve
that problem because it was as much dependent upon industrialism, hence upon
the division of labor, as capitalism itself.

Apart from the belated appearance of this pessimistic theme, the tone of *The Wealth of Nations* is notably optimistic. A flourishing economy is not only the precondition for the material improvement of the people; it also fulfills their natural desire for "betterment," a desire that "comes with us from the womb, and never leaves us till we go into the grave."[32] Perhaps more important, it promotes liberty and good government. "Commerce and manufactures gradually introduced order and good government, and with them, the liberty and security of individuals, among the inhabitants of the country, who had before lived almost in a continual state of war with their neighbors and of servile dependency upon their superiors." Smith credited Hume with calling attention to this beneficent aspect of industrialism: its civilizing, moderating, and pacifying effect on the people, on society, and on government itself.[33]

Beyond material improvement, beyond even liberty, security, and tranquility, perhaps the most remarkable aspect of *The Wealth of Nations* is its democratic character. Smith used the conventional words to describe what we now call the "working classes": "lower ranks (or orders)," "the common people," "the laboring poor," or, simply, the "poor." But it is the functional, rather than the hierarchic, nature of the three orders of society that concerned him. His classes are defined by the source of their income: rent, wages, and profit. And wage earners, or laborers, constitute not the third order, as was customary at the time (and still is in general discourse), but the second order, taking precedence over merchants and manufacturers who are the third order.[34] The laborer is a full partner in the economic enterprise, indeed, the most important partner, because labor is the source of value. Moreover, labor, like rent and profit, is a "patrimony," a form of property entitled to the same consideration as any other kind of property.

The patrimony which every man has in his own labour, as it is the original foundation of all other property, so it is the most sacred and inviolable. The patrimony of a poor man lies in the strength and dexterity of his hand; and to hinder him from employing this strength and dexterity in what manner he thinks proper without injury to his neighbor is a plain violation of this most sacred property.[35]

Democratic, too, is the concept of human nature implicit in Smith's political economy. The much quoted phrase, "the propensity to truck, barter, and exchange one thing for another," appears early in the book in the section on the division of labor. Smith refused to speculate about the origin of that "certain propensity in human nature"—whether it is innate in human nature or a consequence of the "faculties of reason and speech."[36] In either case, it is a basic trait "common to all men"—just as the "moral sentiments," in the earlier book, are common to all men. These are the modest attributes that make the laborer a fully moral being, capable and desirous of bettering himself, of exercising his interests, passions, and virtues, and of enjoying the liberty that is his right as a free individual and a responsible member of society. No enlightened despot, not even an enlightened philosopher or legislator, is required to activate these qualities or to regulate and harmonize them for the general good.

This common human nature has even more dramatic implications, for it means that all men share not only these modest virtues, but also the "natural talents" that make for a distinctive "genius and disposition."

The difference of natural talents in different men is, in reality, much less than we are aware of; and the very different genius which appears to distinguish men of different professions, when grown up to maturity, is not upon many occasions so much the cause as the effect of the division of labour. The difference between the most dissimilar characters, between a philosopher and a common street porter, for example, seems to arise not so much from nature, as from habit, custom, and education. . . . By nature a philosopher is not in genius and disposition half so different from a street porter, as a mastiff is from a greyhound, or a greyhound from a spaniel, or this last from a shepherd's dog.[37]

Even today this stands as a bold assertion of the priority of nurture over nature, an affirmation of the natural equality of all people—not, to be sure, political, economic, or social equality, but a basic equality of human nature. Hume had earlier made a similar observation: "How nearly equal all men are in their bodily force, and even in their mental power and faculties, till cultivated by education."[38]* This may be one of the defining differences between the British and French Enlightenments. One of the most eminent of the French *philosophes*, writing about the same time as Smith, rejected any notion of the natural equality of men. When Helvétius was bold enough to suggest that circumstance, education, and interest account for differences in *"l'esprit,"* Diderot rebuked him. "He has not seen the insurmountable barrier that separates a man destined by nature for a given function, from a man who only brings to that function industry, interest and attention."[40]

A philosopher "not so different from a street porter"—this does not have quite the ring of that "self-evident" truth, "All men are

*Locke, on the other hand, a generation earlier, had taken exactly the opposite position, asserting, in effect, the natural inequality of men. He did not presume to judge the reason for the enormous difference, as he saw it, in men's capacity to understand and reason, but he did not hesitate to say that there was "a greater distance between some men and others in this respect than between some men and some beasts."[39]

created equal." Yet it does seem providential that the *Wealth of Nations* should have been published only months before the American Declaration of Independence. For its time and place, without the provocation of revolution or radical dissent, Smith's statement is memorable, all the more because it comes from one of England's most eminent philosophers—a political economist who was truly a moral philosopher.

Edmund Burke

Apologist for Judaism?

❧ One of the most moving experiences in my teaching career occurred after a seminar discussion of Edmund Burke's *Reflections on the Revolution in France*. A student came up to me to explain that she had missed the previous session because it was a Jewish holiday (a little-observed one, which I had quite forgotten), but she wanted to assure me that she had borrowed another student's copious notes. She also took the opportunity to tell me how much she valued the course and especially how affected she was by Burke's book, for it gave her a new understanding and appreciation of Judaism— of *her* Judaism, which was a rigorous form of orthodoxy (so rigorous that she had had to get a special dispensation to attend a secular university).

I confess that I had never thought of Burke as an apologist for Judaism in any form. Of Catholicism, yes, in France—and in England, according to Conor Cruise O'Brien, who sees Burke as a crypto-Catholic, a "slumbering Jacobite," whose attack on the French revolutionaries was really a polemic against the English who had illegitimately (so he thought) imposed the Protestant ascendancy on Ireland.[1*] But no one had ever accused Burke of being

---

*Burke's father, born a Catholic, had been converted to Anglicanism before Burke's birth, and his son was brought up as an Anglican and remained one. Burke's

21

a crypto-Jew. Indeed, some students had been disturbed by the references in the *Reflections* to "Jew brokers" and "money-jobbers, usurers, and Jews," the classic expressions of anti-Semitism.[2] They also noted that in his diatribe against the anti-Catholic agitator Lord George Gordon, Burke made a point of the fact that Gordon was a "public proselyte to Judaism," heir to "the old hoards of the synagogue, . . . the long compound interest of the thirty pieces of silver." And they were only slightly mollified by Burke's suggestion that this convert "meditate on his Talmud, until he learns a conduct more becoming his birth and parts, and not so disgraceful to the ancient religion to which he has become a proselyte."[3] But the student who found in Burke a rationale for her faith was less troubled by these lapses. What impressed her was his defense of tradition and religion—and of religion *as* tradition. This is what spoke to her, as an Orthodox Jew, so directly and powerfully.

Tradition is, indeed, one of the main motifs of the *Reflections*—the crucial distinction, as Burke saw it, between the French Revolution and the English "Glorious Revolution" a century earlier. Where the French sought to create a society *de novo*, based upon principles dictated by reason, the English, even in the midst of their revolution, had tried to retain as much of the past as possible. The English revolutionaries, he explained, wanted nothing more than "to preserve our *ancient* indisputable laws and liberties, and that *ancient* constitution of government which is our only security for law and liberty." To make of the revolution itself *"an inheritance from our forefathers,"* they sought precedents in "our histories, in our records, in our acts of parliament and journals of parliament," going back to that "ancient charter," the Magna Charta, and beyond

---

mother and wife, although converted to Anglicanism after their marriages, were thought to have been privately practicing Catholics. Burke himself was suspected of being a Catholic and was sometimes caricatured as a Jesuit.

that to "the still more ancient standing law of the kingdom." This, Burke emphasized (the italics were his), was the "pedigree," the "patrimony," the "*hereditary title*," the "*entailed inheritance*" of England's liberties.[4]

Burke conceded that the English lawyers citing those ancient documents might have got some of the details wrong. But this made their motive, their "powerful prepossession towards antiquity," all the more evident. Moreover, the past served not only to validate the revolution; it validated the future as well. "People will not look forward to posterity, who never look backward to their ancestors." And the past itself was not fixed and immutable; on the contrary, as the revolution itself proved, the past was the only security for reform. "The idea of inheritance furnishes a sure principle of conservation, and a sure principle of transmission, without at all excluding a principle of improvement. It leaves acquisition free; but it secures what it acquires."[5]*

The French revolutionaries, on the other hand, in destroying whatever of the past they could, also tried to destroy that most venerable of institutions, the church, thus denying the most basic of human impulses, religion. We know, Burke declared, that "man is by his constitution a religious animal; that atheism is against, not only our reason but our instincts; and that it cannot prevail long."

---

*The idea that the principle of transmission contains within it the means of improvement is obviously congenial to an Orthodox Jew, whose reverence for the Talmud, the accretion over the ages of oral law, is second only to a reverence for the Bible. Had my student been of the Reform denomination, she would also have been impressed by such evidence of "reformism" or "progressivism" as Burke's defense of John Wilkes against the parliamentary "cabal" that expelled him from the House of Commons for libeling the king, or his long-standing criticism of the British government and East India Company for misrule in India, or his ardent support of the American colonies in their pursuit of liberty and independence.

If the French Revolution succeeded in subverting Christianity, he predicted, the void would be filled by "some uncouth, pernicious, and degrading superstition."[6] (This prediction was borne out three years later, with the inauguration of the "Worship of Reason," complete with new Temples of Reason, a new calendar, new festivals, and new saints.)

As religion was rooted in human nature, Burke reasoned, so the church was in human society. For the church was one of the institutions that reflected "the rational and natural ties that connect the human understanding and affections to the divine," helping to sustain "that wonderful structure, Man." And the best kind of religious institution was a church establishment that was part of the state and yet, by virtue of its independent property, independent of the state. Such a religious establishment consecrated church and state alike. This was especially important in a parliamentary regime, for it imbued free citizens with a "wholesome awe," reminding them that they were not entirely free, that they were only "temporary possessors and life-renters" in the commonwealth and were accountable to "the one great master, author and founder of society."[7] Such an establishment, moreover, did not preclude the toleration of other religions. On the contrary, unlike unbelievers who tolerate other religions out of neglect or contempt, an establishment like that of the English tolerates them out of respect. The English "reverently and affectionately protect all religions, because they love and venerate the great principle upon which they all agree, and the great object to which they are all directed."[8]

My student could have found a vindication of her faith elsewhere. Certainly she could have found it, or something very like it, in Maimonides or other Jewish authorities. But Burke gave her a more universal, less parochial justification of her faith as well as a better understanding of it in relation to her own time and place. Where

Burke challenged an Enlightenment that, in the name of reason, threatened Christianity, she saw Jewish orthodoxy not threatened, to be sure, but demeaned by the enlightened secular ideology of her own age. And where he defended the idea of an established yet tolerant church, she recognized such a de facto establishment in her own dominantly Christian yet tolerant society—and, indeed, in the de jure yet tolerant Jewish establishment in Israel.

More important was the role Burke attached to tradition, in religion as in society. Burke has been criticized for being overly deferential to tradition and history and insufficiently respectful of both reason and revelation. If this is so, it is less a problem for Judaism than for Christianity. No religion is as tradition-bound and history-centered as Judaism. And Orthodox Judaism is all the more so. Of the 613 commandments prescribed for devout Jews, some are universal moral principles binding on all civilized human beings. But others are unique to Judaism; they are what distinguish it from all other faiths and peoples. To nonobservant Jews, some of these commandments seem arbitrary and irrational, relics of primitive customs and superstitions. For the Orthodox they carry the weight of law and morality because they have the mandate of authority—that of revered although not divinely ordained rabbis—and the sanction of tradition, of generations of ancestors.

Burke has also been criticized for having too utilitarian a view of religion, valuing it as an instrument of social cohesion and moral edification rather than as a personal, emotional spiritual experience. For Judaism, however, there is no dichotomy between the utility and the spirituality of religion. The observance of law and participation in the community of worshippers are so much a part of the religious faith that they enhance rather than diminish the spiritual experience, giving that experience a depth and a dimension it might otherwise lack. The idea that there is something spiritually demeaning or impoverishing in such an ethical, communal, "utilitarian" (as is said invidiously) religion is itself a product of the French Enlightenment, which denied the need for any transcendent basis for morality or community because it deemed reason to be self-evident and self-sufficient.

For most readers of Burke's *Reflections*—and for most of my students—the most disturbing passages in the *Reflections* were his vindication of "prejudice" and "superstition." These words were as provocative then as now, and deliberately so, for Burke used them purposefully to dramatize his differences with the French Enlightenment. For this Enlightenment, prejudice and superstition tainted all those aspects of life—habit, custom, convention, tradition, and religion—that were offensive because they seemed to violate the principle of reason. For Burke it was precisely those qualities that were the saving graces, so to speak, of civilized society—and, ultimately, of reason itself. Prejudice and superstition, he insisted, were not arbitrary or irrational. On the contrary, they existed in a continuum with wisdom and virtue, having in them the "latent" wisdom and virtue that had accumulated over the ages.

It was in the spirit of enlightenment—although not that of the Enlightenment as the French understood it—that Burke framed his defense of prejudice. The church establishment itself was a form of prejudice: "the first of our prejudices, not a prejudice destitute of reason, but involving in it profound and extensive reason."[9] And all the other manifestations of prejudice had the same complementary relation to reason.

> We are afraid to put men to live and trade each on his own private stock of reason; because we suspect that this stock in each man is small, and that the individuals would do better to avail

themselves of the general bank and capital of nations, and of ages. Many of our men of speculation, instead of exploding general prejudices, employ their sagacity to discover the latent wisdom which prevails in them. If they find what they seek, and they seldom fail, they think it more wise to continue the prejudice, with the reason involved, than to cast away the coat of prejudice, and to leave nothing but the naked reason; because prejudice, with its reason, has a motive to give action to that reason, and an affection which will give it permanence. Prejudice is of ready application in the emergency; it previously engages the mind in a steady course of wisdom and virtue, and does not leave the man hesitating in the moment of decision, sceptical, puzzled, and unresolved. Prejudice renders a man's virtue his habit; and not a series of unconnected acts. Through just prejudice, his duty becomes a part of his nature.[10]

So, too, superstition, for Burke, existed in a continuum with reason—and with religion as well. In excess, Burke granted, superstition was a great evil. But, like all moral subjects, it was a matter of degree, and in moderate forms it was a virtue. Superstition was "the religion of feeble minds," which had to be tolerated in a mixture with religion, in some shape or other, "else you will deprive weak minds of a resource found necessary to the strongest."[11] Burke was not arguing, as some have claimed, that superstition was necessary *pour les autres,* for the lower classes, still less that religion was necessary *pour les autres.* It was not particular men but "man" generically who was "by his constitution a religious animal."[12] And it was all men, the strongest as much as the weakest, who had need of religion. Indeed, the strong required it even more than the weak, because they were more exposed to temptation, pride, and ambition, therefore more needful of the "consolations" and "instructions" of religion.[13]

Finally, even more repugnant to the modern temper was Burke's paean to Marie Antoinette. "History will record," he promised, that momentous day, the 6th of October 1789, when "a band of cruel ruffians and assassins" descended upon Versailles, rushed into the queen's chamber, killing the guard and forcing the queen, "almost naked," to flee to her husband, where they were seized and taken to Paris, leaving behind a palace "swimming in blood, polluted by massacre, and strewed with scatterd limbs and mutilated corpses."[14] That gory scene was followed by Burke's rhapsodic memory of his sight of the queen, then a dauphiness, sixteen or seventeen years earlier, "glittering like the morning star, full of life, and splendor, and joy." Little did he then dream that he would live to see such disasters fall upon her in a nation of "gallant men," "men of honour." Surely ten thousand swords would have leaped from their scabbards to avenge her. "But the age of chivalry is gone," he lamented. "That of sophisters, economists, and calculators has succeeded; and the glory of Europe is extinguished for ever."[15]

"The age of chivalry is gone." And with it those sentiments—honor, reverence, loyalty, gallantry—that not only protected kings and queens but "kept alive, even in servitude itself, the spirit of an exalted freedom." This was the meaning of ancient chivalry in modern times. "Without confounding ranks, [it] had produced a noble equality, and handed it down through all the gradations of social life. It . . . mitigated kings into companions, . . . raised private men to be fellows with kings, . . . subdued the fierceness of pride and power, . . . obliged sovereigns to submit to the soft collar of social esteem, compelled stern authority to submit to elegance, and gave a dominating vanquisher of laws to be subdued by manners." But all of this was being destroyed by the Enlightenment.

All the pleasing illusions, which made power gentle, and obedience liberal, which harmonized the different shades of life, and which, by a bland assimilation, incorporated into politics the sentiments which beautify and soften private society, are to be dissolved by this new conquering empire of light and reason. All the decent drapery of life is to be rudely torn off. All the super-added ideas, furnished from the wardrobe of a moral imagination, which the heart owns, and the understanding ratifies, as necessary to cover the defects of our naked shivering nature, and to raise it to dignity in our own estimation, are to be exploded as a ridiculous, absurd, and antiquated fashion.[16]

It took a bold and original mind, like Burke's, to make so radical a critique of the Enlightenment of his day—and of much of modernity today. And it took a brave and mature mind, like my student's, to see in that critique an explanation and appreciation of her own religion, which draws upon all the resources of history and humanity to sustain and invigorate itself: ancient traditions, the origins of which may have been lost in time; institutions and establishments, sanctified by age and experience, which bind people together in the common existence of daily life; prejudices and superstitions that betoken the larger truths of virtue and wisdom; and, not least, the "moral imagination" that gives heart and soul, as well as mind, to a living faith.

George Eliot
The Wisdom of Dorothea

George Eliot is a great novelist and *Middlemarch* is, by common consent, her greatest novel. The English critic F. R. Leavis, who was no slouch at pronouncing novels great or less than great, opened *The Great Tradition* with a long account of George Eliot, in which *Middlemarch* appears as the culmination of her "mature genius." (*Middlemarch* was "late Eliot," the sixth of her seven novels, followed by *Daniel Deronda.*)

Leavis was also a great moralist, which is perhaps why he was so well disposed to Eliot. He rebuked Henry James who disparaged Eliot for precisely the reasons that Leavis found her so admirable. For Eliot, James complained, the novel was not, as it was for most novelists, a "picture of life" but rather a "moralized fable, the last word of a philosophy endeavoring to teach by example."[1] Virginia Woolf, on the other hand, who was herself not much of a moralist, indeed was profoundly distrustful of moralists (and of Victorian moralists especially), was somewhat redeemed in Leavis's eyes by her description of *Middlemarch* as "the magnificent book which, with all its imperfections, is one of the few English novels written for grown-up people."[2]

Virginia Woolf, in turn, cited Lord Acton, himself no mean moralist, who pronounced Eliot greater than Dante. She might also have quoted Acton's tribute to her as "a great moral teacher," "a consummate expert in the pathology of conscience," who managed to make of atheism a worthy moral rival of Christianity.[3] "You cannot think how much I owed her," Acton wrote to Mary Gladstone after Eliot's death. "Of eighteen or twenty writers by whom I was conscious that my mind has been formed, she was one."[4] When one considers the other writers—philosophers, theologians, historians—who formed the mind of one of the most learned men of the time, that is no small tribute.

In view of such encomia, it may seem strange to pose, as the central moral issue in *Middlemarch*, Why does Dorothea marry Ladislaw? It seems a simpleminded question to ask of a book that has been given so much moral weight by so many high-minded thinkers. It is also an odd question to ask of a book that has been so highly praised, because it suggests that there may be a serious flaw at the very heart of it. This was, indeed, the way it appeared to some contemporary critics—to Henry James, for example, who protested that, midway in the book, after the death of Dorothea's first husband, the reader's attention is focused on the "relatively trivial" and "slightly factititous" question, "Will she or will she not marry Will Ladislaw?"[5]

In the prelude to the novel, Eliot, with obvious reference to her heroine, invokes the image of Saint Theresa, whose "passionate ideal nature demanded an epic life," perhaps even martyrdom.[6] In Dorothea's case, we soon discover, it is not a religious vocation but a secular one that the young woman seeks, a desire to lead a life that transcends her personal interests and happiness, a purposeful, elevated, moral life. It is for this reason that she rejects her first suitor, Sir James Chettam, an amiable but irresolute young man, choosing instead to marry the Reverend Edward Casaubon, an unprepossessing and unsuitable mate (he is more than forty-five years old and she is not quite eighteen), but who has for her the great attraction of being dedicated to a large intellectual enterprise, a work that will provide a comprehensive key to all mythologies. It is a tragic marriage even before Casaubon's untimely death (they had been married only eighteen months), for he turns out to be something of a fraud as a scholar, so that Dorothea, who had thought to find her own salvation in his work, is bereft spiritually, morally, and intellectually as well.

The young Dr. Lydgate, a newcomer to Middlemarch, has a different but no less powerful sense of vocation. He aspires to make a great scientific discovery (the "primitive tissue" that is the basis of life), which will serve not only his community but all of mankind. As he puts it, he hopes to do "good small work for Middlemarch, and great work for the world."[7] Lydgate would seem to meet all of Dorothea's requirements of a husband. Many readers of *Middlemarch* in its serial form, including Henry James, expected her to marry Lydgate after Casaubon died. Even today this is a constant reproach to Eliot. Shortly after an adaptation of the novel was televised, a letter in the *New York Times Book Review* commented on an earlier article by the novelist Mary Gordon, who had described *Middlemarch* as a "tragic and ironic" novel. The writer of the letter recalled her own professor, many years earlier, using exactly the same words. Asked to explain them, he had said, "Because Dorothea belonged with Lydgate and vice versa."[8]

To be sure, Lydgate is already married at the time that Dorothea is widowed—unhappily married because his wife Rosamond is as frivolous as Casaubon was pompous. His marriage, however, need not have been an impediment to the union of Dorothea and Lydgate. Eliot might have killed off Rosamond, in childbirth or a cholera epidemic. Or she could have had Lydgate and Rosamond divorced; divorce was difficult but not impossible at the time. Or Dorothea and Lydgate might have entered into the kind of extramarital relationship that Eliot herself had with George Lewes.

The plot does not take any of these turns because Dorothea is attracted not to Lydgate but to the young artist Will Ladislaw. And Ladislaw, judged by her own standards (and by comparison with Lydgate), is a rather pathetic character—"dilettantish and amateurish," another artist, a friend, describes him. Even if he were a serious artist, that would not have endeared him to Dorothea, who confesses that art is "a language I do not understand."[9] More important, he is something of a sensualist and hedonist. "The best piety," he tells her, "is to enjoy."[10] (His flirtation with Rosamond very nearly leads to his downfall.) When he does, finally, embark upon a political career, it is not as an idealist but as a pragmatist. He will be a reformer, we are given to believe, but not a zealous one.

Why, then, does Dorothea marry Ladislaw—a "light creature," Henry James describes him—and then, in a damning phrase, "a woman's man"?[11] Dorothea cannot explain it even to her sister. "You have to feel for me," she tells her.[12] The most obvious explanation, for the modern reader at least, is sex. Dorothea, one may reasonably assume, has been starved of sexuality with Casaubon; there are critics who find in the novel intimations of his impotence. This interpretation, however, presents several difficulties. Eliot was quite capable of expressing this sexual attraction had she so wished (as she did in *Adam Bede*). Moreover, this does not explain why Dorothea chooses Ladislaw over Lydgate, who is no less attractive sexually. More important is the fact that this interpretation vitiates the essential theme of the book, depriving it of its moral dimension and its moral tension.

Dorothea marries Ladislaw, according to her own account, because she loves him and he loves her. In this respect *Middlemarch* is a classic Victorian love story, with the woman giving up her estate to marry the man she loves, and the man giving up his inheritance to gain the respect of his beloved. But it is also, as Henry James said, a "moralized fable." Ladislaw attracts Dorothea precisely because he is morally flawed, an imperfect human being. It is her love for him and faith in him that will make him a better human being, so that he can be worthy both of her and of society. His is not an exalted mission; Ladislaw in Parliament is not going to be a heroic character aspiring to transform society. But he will be a sensible, moderate reformer. To paraphrase Lydgate, he will do "good small work for the country" rather than "great work for the world." By helping him achieve that small mission, Dorothea will redeem him—and herself as well.

For Dorothea to marry Lydgate, on the other hand, would have been too easy, lacking in moral drama. Lydgate needed no redeeming; he knew exactly what he wanted to do and was entirely capable of doing it. He did not even need a wife to help him—only not to hinder him, as Rosamond did. With Lydgate, there would have been no moral tension to resolve, no conflict between pleasure and work; his pleasure was his work. And his ambition—discovering the basis of life—was even greater than Casaubon's; his work was real and realizable; his subject, after all, was science, not mythology.

The parallel between Casaubon's search for the "key" to all mythologies and Lydgate's for the "single tissue" as the basis of life is obvious. One commentator points to a passage in the novel intimating that Eliot believed the tissue theory to be mistaken; he cites the notes she made on an essay by T. H. Huxley supporting the cell rather than tissue theory. But, as Huxley said in that essay, even a false hypothesis may further science. And Eliot clearly differentiated Casaubon's thoroughly futile work, which was ignorant of an earlier generation of German scholars, from Lydgate's, which was to be disproved only later. (The final irony, this critic points out, is that the tissue theory is more in keeping with present-day biochemistry than is the cell theory.)[13]

A different turn of the plot, making for a quite different kind of moral drama, would have been an illicit love affair between Dorothea and Lydgate—an out-of-wedlock relationship like that of Eliot and Lewes. But this, too, was not what Eliot had in mind, for it would have been to countenance, even to romanticize and idealize, an arrangement that she regarded, in her own case, as an unfortunate and regrettable necessity. Some modern feminists look up to her as a "role model" for the liberated woman, praising her for defying the bourgeois, patriarchal convention of marriage by living with the man she loved without benefit of clergy. But she did not willfully choose that role; she had no alternative, since Lewes was already married and could not get a divorce. (A divorce was unobtainable because, after fathering three children with his wife, he condoned her affair with his friend, Thornton Hunt, with whom his wife had another three children, while Hunt himself was married to another woman.)

Although Eliot lived with Lewes in that "irregular relationship," as the Victorians delicately put it, she tried to "regularize" it by making it as much like a proper marriage as possible, and their twenty-four years together were spent in perfect domesticity and fidelity. She referred to Lewes as her "husband" and to herself as his "wife"; she dedicated *Mill on the Floss* to "my beloved husband, George Henry Lewes"; she signed her letters "Marian Lewes," asked her friends to address her as "Mrs. Lewes," and had the satisfaction of having the real Mrs. Lewes do just that. (This was also one of the reasons she adopted the pseudonym "George Eliot." She would have preferred to go under the name of Lewes but could hardly do so officially, so she compromised by assuming his first name and adopting a fictitious surname.)* After Lewes died, she married John

*The usual feminist interpretation is that a woman writing under her own name would not be taken seriously. In fact, many women did so with no ill effect: Mary Shelley, Elizabeth Browning, Frances Trollope, Harriet Martineau, Elizabeth

Cross, with all the trappings of a proper marriage: a trousseau, a church wedding, and a honeymoon. No, an out-of-wedlock relationship with Lydgate was not the moral Eliot wished to convey and not the fate she sought for her heroine (any more than she had sought it for herself).

Nor was Dorothea to be a Saint Theresa, ascetic and self-abnegating. The mature Dorothea (not much older in years but much older in experience and wisdom) comes to terms with reality, without, however, succumbing to cynicism or egoism. She loves Ladislaw, knowing that for all his weaknesses he is nevertheless capable of true "good small work," which, for her, is the true meaning of morality. At one point, while she is still married to Casaubon, she explains to Ladislaw the belief that sustains her: "That by desiring what is perfectly good, even when we don't quite know what it is and cannot do what we would, we are part of the divine power against evil—widening the skirts of light and making the struggle with darkness narrower." That is mysticism, Ladislaw protests. No, she replies, "It is my life. I have found it out and cannot part with it. I have always been finding out my religion since I was a little girl. I used to pray so much—now I hardly ever pray."[14]

"Now I hardly ever pray." That, for Eliot, was the great problem of morality in the modern secular age. How, in the absence of religion, can morality—a purely secular morality—prevail? Having herself lost her religious faith, she was haunted, as many of her generation were, by what in *Middlemarch* she called "moral chaos":[15] the fear that religious skepticism would lead to moral lax-

---

Gaskell, Christina Rossetti, Beatrice Webb, and dozens of others little known today but best-selling authors in their own time. Throughout the nineteenth century, more novels were published by women writers, under their own name, than by men.

ity, or worse, nihilism, and that the disbelief in immortality would result in immorality. One recalls her much quoted remark: Asked how morality can subsist in the absence of religious faith, she replied that God is "inconceivable," immortality "unbelievable," but duty nonetheless "peremptory and absolute."[16]

Eliot never explained what would sustain that secular idea of duty. But her novel implies that if it were to replace religion, it had to be available to everyone, just as religion was. It had to be a democratic morality, as it were, a morality fit not for heroes or saints or geniuses but for ordinary people—not just for a Lydgate who could aspire to great work but for a Ladislaw who, like most human beings, was capable only of good work. That is a large "only," for to Eliot it meant all the difference between an immoral and a moral society, between one that knows no higher values than hedonism and egoism and one imbued with altruism and a sense of duty. "We are all of us," Eliot wrote in one of the most memorable sentences in *Middlemarch*, "born in moral stupidity, taking the world as an udder to feed our supreme selves."[17] To overcome that state of "moral stupidity" we have to wean ourselves of our infantile egoism and become morally mature adults, responsible and dutiful. In Ladislaw we witness precisely that maturation, the coming to moral adulthood.

This brings us to an even more difficult problem. Why does Dorothea, who carries the moral burden of the book and who, more than any other character, has attained a state of moral maturity, have to find her own moral purpose in being a wife, first to Casaubon and then to Ladislaw, both of whom are clearly her moral inferiors? Why does she have to marry at all? Or if she does choose to marry, why does she have to be merely the helpmate in that marriage? Surely she is capable of "good work," if not "great work," on her own. In the Finale, Dorothea intimates as much when she wonders whether there was "something better which she might have done." Her friends are more forthright. They "think it a pity that so substantive and rare a creature should have been absorbed into the life of another, and be only known in a certain circle as a wife and mother."[18]

For some of Eliot's contemporaries who could not but see the figure of Eliot herself behind Dorothea, this thought is no less troublesome. Eliot was not only the creator of great works; she was also an independent spirit. Why could she not create an equally independent spirit in Dorothea, a woman who would not be "absorbed into the life of another" and was not merely "a wife and mother"? Florence Nightingale, confronting this question, suggested that there was someone "close at hand, in actual life," whom Eliot personally knew, whom she might have taken as a model for such an independent woman.[19] She was referring to Octavia Hill, the Victorian housing reformer and philanthropist, whose sister was married to Lewes's son. But Nightingale might have had herself in mind as well.

Today that question is even more urgent. Why could Eliot not have given us a Dorothea more congenial to a modern feminist? The simple answer is that Eliot herself was not a feminist in the modern sense. She did not flaunt her defiance of convention by living with Lewes without marrying him; on the contrary, she tried to observe the forms of marriage as much as possible. Nor did she subscribe to one of the elementary tenets of feminism, women's suffrage. In 1867, five years before *Middlemarch*, a group of women, knowing of Eliot's interest in women's education (she was a charter subscriber to Girton College, Cambridge, the first college for women), called upon her to sign a petition supporting the amendment proposed by John Stuart Mill that would have enfranchised women. Eliot refused, explaining that she favored any reform that would give the sexes "an equivalence of advantages . . . as to education and the possibilities of free development," but she did not believe the vote would further that purpose. The fact that women have "the worse share in existence," she said, should inspire "a sublimer resignation in woman and a more regenerating tenderness in man."[20]

If this explanation seems unpersuasive to us today, we should remember that other prominent women writers shared her opposition to women's suffrage: Charlotte Bronte, Mrs. Gaskell, Elizabeth Barrett Browning, Christina Rossetti, and Florence Nightingale, who lent her name to the cause only reluctantly, after she was personally solicited by Mill. They did so for various reasons: because it would distract from more important issues (such as the reform of the divorce or property laws); or because they believed that women's education should precede the vote; or because it would undermine what was felt to be the uniquely feminine quality of women; or because (this on the part of some Liberals) women were more likely to vote Conservative. "Surely," one well-known woman wrote, when the issue came up again later in the century, "we need some human beings who will watch and pray, who will observe and inspire, and above all, who will guard and love all who are weak, unfit or distressed? Is there not a special service of woman, as there is a special service of man?"[21] This was the formidable intellectual and socialist Beatrice Webb speaking. Eliot would have agreed with Webb about little else, but she would have agreed with her about this.

There is no discussion of the suffrage or any other overtly feminist subject in *Middlemarch*.* But the book is undeniably a challenge to

---

*In the original four-volume edition, one passage might have lent itself to a feminist interpretation; this was the suggestion that society was responsible for ill-suited marriages and for the failure to educate women. When one reviewer objected that this allusion to the "woman's question" fell short of the imaginative power of the rest of the book, Eliot deleted it from the next edition.[22]

modern feminists. The idea that only in marriage can Dorothea find her personal happiness as well as her moral mission seems peculiarly Victorian. And so it is. For the Victorians, even for Victorian feminists, marriage and family were the primary human relationships, so that the champions of women's suffrage, university education for women, divorce reform, property rights, or birth control had to demonstrate (and did so in all honesty) that their proposals were compatible with marriage and family. Victorian families, recent scholarship has shown, were not nearly as oppressive or patriarchal as was once thought. But the idea of the family was very nearly sacrosanct, as was the idea that men and women had distinctive natures and virtues which bound them together in a complex relationship of rights, duties, and, if they were fortunate, love.

Early in the novel, we are told, Dorothea has a "childlike idea about marriage." She thinks that "the really delightful marriage must be that where your husband was a sort of father, and could teach you even Hebrew, if you wished it."[23] Casaubon disillusions her of that idea. But he does not disillusion her of the idea of marriage. At the end of the novel, Dorothea sees marriage as "a great beginning," although fraught with difficulties. "It is still the beginning of the home epic—the gradual conquest or irremediable loss of that complete union which makes the advancing years a climax, and age the harvest of sweet memories in common."[24] The Lydgates' marriage is a failure because Rosamond does not understand the nature of marriage; she thinks her discontent is with her husband, whereas it is with "the conditions of marriage itself, . . . its demand for self-suppression and tolerance."[25] Dorothea never makes that mistake. Even when she is most displeased with Casaubon, she does not rebel against marriage itself. "Permanent rebellion," we are told, "the disorder of a life without some loving reverent resolve, was not possible to her."[26]*

Love and reverence, that is the message of *Middlemarch*. And that is the motto engraved on Eliot's memorial stone in Westminster Abbey. It is a quotation from one of her earliest stories, "Janet's Repentance": "The first condition of human goodness is something to love: the second something to reverence."[28] If the modern feminist finds it difficult to accept that message, she may prefer to find the moral of *Middlemarch* in the fact that Dorothea, not Ladislaw, is the hero of the book. In fact, all the women characters, for good or bad, are more interesting and powerful than the men. It is the women who make their men what they become: decent, worthy, happy citizens like Ladislaw and Fred Vincy, or embittered failures like Lydgate, who, so far from making his great scientific discovery about the basis of life, settles for writing a book on gout— "a disease," Eliot wryly comments, "which has a good deal of wealth on its side."[29]

Dorothea is no Saint Theresa. But she is an unsung hero— unsung, that is, to everyone except Eliot, and, Eliot hoped, to the reader of *Middlemarch*. The last words of the book are Eliot's tribute to Dorothea:

> Her finely-touched spirit had still its fine issues, though they were not widely visible. Her full nature . . . spent itself in channels which had no great name on the earth. But the effect of her being on those around her was incalculably diffusive: for the

---

*But some readers have made just that mistake. Virginia Woolf, in her essay on "Women and Fiction," said that in *Middlemarch* as in *Jane Eyre*, "we are conscious not merely of the writer's character . . . but we are conscious of a woman's presence—of someone resenting the treatment of her sex and pleading for its rights."[27]

growing good of the world is partly dependent on unhistoric acts; and that things are not so ill with you and me as they might have been, is half owing to the number who lived faithfully a hidden life, and rest in unvisited tombs.[30]

This is not a tragic ending, not even a "tragic irony." It is, as Eliot meant it to be, eminently moral, even heroic—an appropriate conclusion to a novel that, as Virginia Woolf said, was "written for grown-up people."

Jane Austen
The Education of Emma

~ Reading, or rereading, Jane Austen's *Emma* after George Eliot's *Middlemarch* is an exhilarating experience, perhaps even more so than reading them in their proper chronological order. To read *Emma* first would be to make *Middlemarch* intolerably solemn, didactic, moralistic, while at the same time making *Emma* frivolous, superficial, trivial. The reverse order has a leavening effect upon both books, humanizing *Middlemarch* and moralizing *Emma.*

In fact, the two have much in common. Each has been judged the greatest work of the greatest English novelists of the century. (Austen has been compared, by Macaulay among others, to Shakespeare.) Each is a work of maturity; *Emma* (1815) was the last novel of Austen's novels published in her lifetime; *Middlemarch* (1871–1872) the next to the last in Eliot's. And each is, in its own way, a moral fable. In *Middlemarch* the moral message is overt and insistent, from the opening page preparing us for a Saint Theresa–like heroine, and throughout the novel in which every character and episode bears a moral imprint. In *Emma* the moral lesson emerges slowly, tentatively, lightened with humor and irony. Where *Middlemarch* is a tale of moral fulfillment, *Emma* is a tale of moral education. And each puts marriage at the center of the moral drama. If in the case of *Middlemarch* one asks, Why does Dorothea

marry Ladislaw? so in *Emma* one may ask, Why does Mr. Knightley marry Emma?

The gender in that question is reversed because Emma is the
very antithesis of Dorothea. "Emma Woodhouse," the opening sentence informs us, "handsome, clever, and rich, with a comfortable
home and happy disposition, seemed to unite some of the best
blessings of existence; and had lived nearly twenty-one years in the
world with very little to distress or vex her." By the end of the page
we are told that Emma, the mistress of the house (her mother having died long before), has the habit of "doing just what she liked,"
has things "too much her own way," and has "a disposition to think
a little too well of herself."[1] These qualities, it is implied, are about
to be exacerbated with the marriage of her governess, Miss Taylor,
who has long since ceased to exercise even the nominal authority of
her position and is now a dear friend. With her departure, Emma
will be deprived of even that constraining influence—another self
to temper her own. Nor will her father be of much help. Elderly,
good-natured, well intentioned, but utterly occupied with his own
physical comfort, he can only project his own anxieties upon others, seeing in them only what he sees in himself and caring for
them only to the extent that it does not inconvenience him.

The counterpoint to these two self-absorbed characters, father
and daughter, is "a sensible man about seven or eight-and-thirty,"
an old friend of the family who also happens to be related to them
by marriage. Mr. Knightley is "one of the few people who could see
faults in Emma Woodhouse, and the only one who ever told her of
them."[2] At the moment, the fault he finds in her, and in her father
as well, is their selfish reaction to Miss Taylor's marriage, their regret at losing a friend and companion rather than pleasure at her
gaining a husband and family. It is a small premonition of the
other occasions when he will find fault with Emma, the first of her
many lessons in moral education.

Having introduced us to the protagonists in this moral drama, the opening scene also establishes the motif that dominates that drama, marriage. In response to Mr. Knightley's charge that she is insufficiently concerned with Miss Taylor's happiness, Emma says that she herself was responsible for that marriage. "I made the match myself," she boasts, for she alone predicted that Mr. Weston, a widower, would marry again. Pleased with her success, she promises to continue this "greatest amusement" of matchmaking. Again, it is Mr. Knightley who rebukes her, pointing out that she had, in fact, done nothing to promote the marriage except to think idly, now and again, that it would be a good thing for them to marry. Her "success," he says, is nothing more than a "lucky guess."[3]

All of Emma's matchmaking efforts prove to be disastrous—or would be if she succeeded in them. And all of them reveal, in one way or another, her moral failings: an arrogance, pride, impetuosity, and, above all, a self-preoccupation that blinds her to reality. Her first exercise in matchmaking, or rather un-matchmaking, involves a young woman whom she has taken up as a protégé. Harriet Smith is a pretty, amiable girl, a boarder at the local school, with no family and few friends—"the natural daughter of somebody," it was said, which Emma takes to mean that she is of good, if not high, birth.[4] Harriet is pleased to receive a proposal of marriage from Mr. Martin, a farmer whom Emma might have seen on his many trips to town. Emma's response is withering.

> A young farmer, whether on horseback or on foot, is the very last sort of person to raise my curiosity. The yeomanry are precisely the order of people with whom I feel I can have nothing to do. A degree or two lower, and a creditable appearance might interest me; I might hope to be useful to their families in some way or other. But a farmer can need none of my help, and is therefore in one sense as much above my notice as in every other he is below it.[5]

This passage, and a subsequent one in which Emma warns Harriet against such a misalliance, as she sees it, have been much cited as evidence of the cruel class system that can inspire such merciless snobbery. Because of the "misfortune" of her birth, Emma explains, Harriet must be wary of an association with someone her inferior. "There can be no doubt of your being a gentleman's daughter, and you must support your claim to that station by every thing within your own power, or there will be plenty of people who would take pleasure in degrading you."[6] But if that class system produces a callous, and callow, Emma, it also produces a Mr. Knightley, who rebukes Emma for discouraging a marriage that would be to Harriet's advantage and to her happiness. Mr. Knightley, to be sure, is not at all unmindful of considerations of class. Harriet, he observes, is "the natural daughter of nobody knows whom, with probably no settled provision at all, and certainly no respectable relations." More important, she has been taught nothing useful, has no experience and little wit; she is not a "sensible girl." "Sensible," connoting both sense and sensibility, is the highest praise Austen can bestow upon a character. And Mr. Martin, like Mr. Knightley, is sensible, thus much the superior, in character if not in class, to Harriet, in spite of her putatively higher birth. When Emma protests that it would be a "degradation" for Harriet to marry him, Mr. Knightley retorts: "A degradation to illegitimacy and ignorance, to be married to a respectable, intelligent gentleman-farmer!"[7]

"Illegitimacy and ignorance," "respectable [and] intelligent"—for Mr. Knightley, class is always counterbalanced by character. And there is no necessary correspondence between the two; class is not at all a reliable indicator of character. Where Emma—at this stage of her moral education, at any rate—consistently misinterprets both, Mr. Knightley gives each its proper due. He understands and respects the realities of class, but he understands and respects even more the realities of character. He has a higher regard for the farmer Mr. Martin than for the vicar Mr. Elton. And he is very critical of the dashing gentleman Frank Churchill, the adopted heir to a large estate and fortune. (Mr. Martin, like Mr. Knightley, is always referred to as "Mr." Only Frank Churchill is deprived of that title.) When Emma defends the "amiable" young Churchill, who has repeatedly delayed visiting his father in order to curry favor with his imperious aunt (and potential benefactor), Mr. Knightley once again is obliged to take her to task. "Your amiable young man," he informs her, "is a very weak young man. . . . It ought to have been a habit with him by this time, of following his duty, instead of consulting expediency." Even his good manners—or what Emma takes to be such—do not redeem him. "No, Emma, your amiable young man can be amiable only in French, not in English. He may be very '*aimable*,' have very good manners, and be very agreeable; but he can have no English delicacy towards the feelings of other people: nothing really amiable about him."[8]

A critical episode in Emma's moral education involves Miss Bates, a good-natured, garrulous, impoverished, and pathetic old maid. At a picnic, Frank Churchill, seeking to enliven the occasion, suggests (attributing the idea to Emma) that each person contribute "one thing very clever, be it prose or verse, original or repeated—or two things moderately clever—or three things very dull indeed." Miss Bates, somewhat uneasy in their company, comments, "'Three things very dull indeed.' That will just do for me, you know. I shall be sure to say three dull things as soon as ever I open my mouth, shan't I?" Whereupon Emma, not to be outdone, adds: "Ah! ma'am, but there may be a difficulty. Pardon me—but you will be limited as to number—only three at once."[9] This provokes Mr. Knightley to his sharpest rebuke yet.

> Emma, I must speak to you as I have been used to do: a privilege rather endured than allowed, perhaps, but I must still use it. I cannot see you acting wrong, without a remonstrance. How could

you be so unfeeling to Miss Bates? How could you be so insolent in your wit to a woman of her character, age, and situation? . . . Were she a woman of fortune, I would leave every harmless absurdity to take its chance, I would not quarrel with you for any liberties of manner. Were she your equal in situation—but, Emma, consider how far this is from being the case. She is poor; she has sunk from the comforts she was born to; and, if she live to old age, must probably sink more. Her situation should secure your compassion. It was badly done, indeed![10]

Emma, it should be said, is not always so thoughtless. Indeed, a modern reader might be impressed by her admirable forbearance in listening to the many long, rambling monologues by Miss Bates, or coping with her father's endless, petty anxieties about drafts and colds, or making the perpetual round of duty-calls expected of her, or observing the many proprieties and courtesies that must often have tried her patience. Occasionally she even gives evidence of a wisdom beyond her years. In the unfortunate episode at the picnic, Mr. Knightley chastises her for lacking compassion for Miss Bates. But earlier, describing her visit to a poor and sick family, Austen tells us, not ironically, that Emma is "very compassionate," giving generously of her attention, kindness, and money. Emma herself then makes an observation that is worthy of Mr. Knightley. "I hope it may be allowed that if compassion has produced exertion and relief to the sufferers, it has done all that is truly important. If we feel for the wretched, enough to do all we can for them, the rest is empty sympathy, only distressing to ourselves."[11]

This kind of compassion, real and unsentimental—"doing good" rather than "feeling good"—may well seem to Mr. Knightley testimony of Emma's essentially good nature and, despite her lapses, good character. And it helps resolve a question similar to that we put to *Middlemarch*—not, why does Emma marry Mr.

Knightley, but why does Mr. Knightley marry Emma? On the surface, it is an unlikely match. He has done little but find fault with her, and she has persistently given him occasion to do so. Older and wiser than she, he has been a surrogate father to her (more a father, certainly, than her own)—not, it would seem, a suitor or lover. Yet, like Dorothea and Ladislaw, Emma and Mr. Knightley are a good match because they need and complement each other. They marry for love, but also out of a kind of moral urgency. Mr. Knightley is charmed by Emma, as Dorothea is by Ladislaw. And, like Dorothea, he has no illusions about his beloved. He knows Emma to be frivolous and willful, often thoughtless and foolish. Yet he loves those qualities in her—her vitality, spontaneity, spiritedness—that are lacking in himself, and he has confidence that, under his tutelage, she can realize her better self.

Emma, for her part, who, after all her mismatches, finally discovers that it is Mr. Knightley, not Frank Churchill, whom she loves, also comes to terms with herself, with the self-love that has been so mischievous. "With insufferable vanity had she believed herself in the secret of everybody's feelings; with unpardonable arrogance proposed to arrange everybody's destiny."[12] Her moral education has been completed.

It is sometimes said, in criticism of Austen, that the moral import of her novels is diminished by the small stage upon which the drama plays itself out. In a letter to her niece, who was starting to write fiction, Austen praised her for "collecting your people delightfully, getting them exactly into such a spot as is the delight of my life—three or four families in a country village is the very thing to work on."[13] Highbury, the setting of *Emma,* is such a village, "large and populous" as such villages go, but not quite a town— large and populous enough so that Emma is acquainted with varieties of individuals and classes, and small enough so that the

Woodhouses can be "first in consequence there," and Emma herself can play a starring role.[14] (London, only sixteen miles away, is off on the horizon. An enterprising young man like Frank Churchill might make the trip occasionally, but not Emma or her father. Emma's sister, living in London after her marriage, returns for a visit only on Christmas and important family occasions.)

One of the highlights of the novel is the ball initiated by Frank Churchill. Mr. Knightley demonstrates his gallantry (and moral sensitivity) by dancing with Harriet; Emma confesses her willfulness in trying to match Harriet with an altogether unworthy mate; and Emma and Mr. Knightley find themselves congenial dance partners—not "brother and sister," as she supposed.[15] That ball takes place in the Crown, the local inn, but it was originally planned as a more modest dance to be held in the home of Frank's uncle, which could accommodate only ten couples. Emma worries that ten couples in a small room would be overly crowded. "Nothing can be farther from pleasure," she objects, "than to be dancing in a crowd—and a crowd in a little room." Frank Churchill takes up the idea: "I agree with you exactly. A crowd in a little room— Miss Woodhouse, you have the art of giving pictures in a few words. Exquisite, quite exquisite!"[16]

That "crowd in a little room" (the ball at the inn is only a somewhat larger version of that) is a metaphor for the small community in which Emma's moral education takes place—and, the implication is, the only place where such an education can occur. Again, one recalls *Middlemarch,* where Lydgate fails in his moral ambition to do "good small work for Middlemarch, and great work for the world," because he is inadequate to the small world in which he finds himself, whereas Dorothea is fulfilled as a moral being precisely because she is content to do good work in her small world, thus for the world as a whole.[17]

It is not only the smallness of Austen's world that some critics find fault with, but the nature of that world. Her novels, it is said, lack the transcendent power of Russian novels, for example, because they are so embedded in the particular class structure of her time and place. That class structure, accepted without question, makes for a narrow vision of society, and, more important, dehumanizes the individuals in it, thus vitiating the moral purpose of the novels.[18] Another reading of the novels would come to exactly the opposite conclusion: that Austen was not only extraordinarily conscious of the realities of class in her small world but used those realities to make her moral points—to humanize and moralize, as it were, her characters.

Emma is, in a sense, a comedy of manners—manners in the service of class. In a more important sense, however, it is a drama of manners, with manners in the service of morals. In Emma's world, manners mitigate class. Knightley chastises her not for being excessively class conscious but for being insufficiently well mannered, for failing to observe the proprieties that humanize and civilize social relations in a society where class is an indubitable fact of life. Writing soon after the French Revolution, Austen was neither a revolutionary nor a utopian; she had no illusions about a classless society or even a very mobile class society. But she was a moralist and thus an individualist. Her characters, of whatever class, are responsible moral agents. And the measure of their character is the way they conduct themselves toward others, above all toward those whom they regard as their social inferiors.

Moreover, this society (Emma's and Austen's as well) was not the crude class society that some historians and social critics envisage. It consisted not of two or even three classes but of a multitude of social gradations related to each other in subtle but perceptible ways. They were not, in fact, called "classes"; the contemporary terms, testifying to their multiplicity, were "ranks," "sorts," "degrees," "estates." And transcending these social distinctions were "characters" in all the meanings of that ambiguous word: eccentrics (some of almost Dickensian eccentricity), and individuals of varying moral natures and dispositions. (The word "character" was also used of the written reference or recommendation carried by a worker and presented to a potential employer.) It was in this context that manners were so important. For manners, even more than morals, lend themselves to the subtleties and nuances appropriate to the variety of classes and characters. And manners, more readily than morals, can be taught—as Emma was taught. "Jane Austen's 'principles,'" C. S. Lewis has said, "might be described as the grammar of conduct. Now grammar is something that anyone can learn; it is also something that everyone must learn."[19]

In 1796, almost twenty years before Jane Austen wrote *Emma*, Edmund Burke composed the perfect epigraph for that novel:

> Manners are what vex or soothe, corrupt or purify, exalt or debase, barbarize or refine us, by a constant, steady, uniform, insensible operation, like that of the air we breathe in. They give their whole form and colour to our lives. According to their quality, they aid morals, they supply them, or they totally destroy them.[20]

A century and a half before that, Hobbes explained that by manners he meant not "decency of behavior, as how a man should wash his mouth, or pick his teeth before company, and such other points of the *small morals*; but those qualities of mankind, that concern their living together in peace and unity."[21]

Small morals and large—that was Austen's forte, as it was also Eliot's. *Middlemarch* carries the burden of its moral message more weightily, as is appropriate to this high-Victorian fable. But *Emma* is no less a moral fable—a pre-Victorian one in the guise of a romantic tale.

POSTSCRIPT

If reading *Emma* after *Middlemarch* is an exhilarating—and edifying—experience, so is rereading *Emma* after seeing film versions of the novel. In the novel, class is kept in the background as an omnipresent and unquestioned part of the social reality. In the film *Emma*, it is so much in the foreground, visually as well as thematically, that it becomes the only reality—and a distorted reality. The elaborate attire and lavish dinner parties of the rich (in fact, too elaborate and lavish for the squirearchy of a village like Highbury) contrast starkly with the unkempt poor in their mean and dirty hovels. The effect is to obscure the many differentiations of class—of "ranks," "sorts," and "degrees"—portrayed in the novel, as well as the distinctions of manners and morals within each of these groups, which are the essence of the novel.

Paradoxically, the film version intended as a parody of the novel, *Clueless*, is more in keeping with the spirit of the novel, at least to the extent of retaining the sense of a comedy of manners, if not quite the comedy (or drama) intended by Jane Austen.

Charles Dickens
"A Low Writer"

꙳ To the social historian or the historically minded literary critic, Dickens offers a cornucopia of treasures: institutions (poorhouses and prisons, factories and schools, law courts and the civil service); social problems (poverty and crime, child labor and child abuse, housing and sanitation); ideologies (Malthusianism and utilitarianism, laissez-faireism and radicalism); and, of course, people of every rank, character, occupation, and disposition.

Contemporaries were as aware as we are of the need to approach these subjects with great caution, not to take Dickens's fictional accounts as literal truth. The *Westminster Review*, reviewing *Our Mutual Friend* in 1866, suggested that if Dickens were serious about the poor laws he should write a pamphlet or go into Parliament; to use the novel as an instrument of reform was as "absurd as it would be to call out the militia to stop the cattle disease." The very idea of the social novel was an anomaly; "like an egg with two yolks, neither is ever hatched."[1] Historians have good reason to endorse these sentiments, reminding us of the perils not only of fictionalized politics but also of fictionalized biography, of assuming that Dickens's own position on any particular issue could readily be deduced from his novels. One commentator on Dickens has pointed out that he was a prominent advocate of two educational institutions that were mercilessly satirized in his novels: training colleges (in *Hard Times*) and ragged schools (in *Our Mutual Friend*).[2]

Some literary critics have gone so far in the other direction as to warrant a different kind of cautionary note. In the effort to reconstruct the "imaginary universe" of the novels, they have virtually constructed that universe de novo, with little regard for the universe Dickens himself inhabited or for his own creative intentions. Divorced from the world of Victorian England, Dickens's novels are located in an imaginative universe cohabited by Dante, Dostoevsky, Kafka, D. H. Lawrence, and T. S. Eliot. Lionel Trilling, gently chiding his students who vied with each other in finding symbolic parallels between *Our Mutual Friend* and *The Waste Land*, recalled his own discovery of the historical reality, the "actuality," of what he himself had once thought of as pure symbols—the dust heaps in *Our Mutual Friend*, which were in fact, as in the novel, very large and remunerative, or the Thames, which actually served as a sewer for London.[3]

Dickens captured that actuality so successfully because he was not only a brilliant novelist but also an acute reporter and social critic. The imaginative world of his novels was part of the real world, reflecting that world but also helping create it. He did for the nineteenth century what Bunyan had done for the seventeenth, providing a common cultural denominator, a common stock of characters, situations, expressions, and witticisms for people of all classes, occupations, and persuasions. For countless Englishmen, Mrs. Gamp was more real than Mr. Gladstone, Scrooge as familiar as any skinflint of their own acquaintance. After his death, a costermonger girl was reported as saying, "Dickens dead? Then will Father Christmas die too?"[4] In his obituary of Dickens, Anthony Trollope predicted that his books would become staples, like "legs of mutton or loaves of bread," a sentiment echoed by the *Times* when it memorialized him as "the intimate of every household."[5]

It did not take Dickens's death to make people aware of his universal appeal. In 1837, G. H. Lewes reported that he often saw the butcher-boy with his tray on his shoulder avidly reading the latest number of *Pickwick*, while the maidservant, footman, and chimney sweep followed the *Sketches by Boz* with the same fascination.[6] One of Henry Mayhew's informants told him that Dickens had been a great favorite of the "patterers" (the street-sellers of songs, broadsheets, and ballads) until Dickens's journal, *Household Words*, offended them by publishing a piece attacking the professional begging-letter writers.[7] Reviewing *Great Expectations* in 1861, the *Times* was pleased to find that although it was addressed to a "much higher class of readers," a "better" class than that catered to by other penny journals, it was sensational enough to compete successfully with them.[8] Walter Bagehot explained that the phrase "household book" was peculiarly apt for Dickens, there being no other writer whose works were read throughout the house, giving "pleasure to the servants as well as to the mistress, to the children as well as to the master."[9] Dickens's son recalled that a walk with his father in the streets of London was a "royal progress, people of all degrees and classes taking off their hats and greeting him as he passed."[10]

The memoirs of the time are filled with accounts of poor people reading Dickens, and those who could not read listening to the latest installment read aloud in the servants' hall, lodging house, public house, or tea shop.[11] Most contemporary critics, whatever their other reservations, took it as a tribute to him that he was able to appeal to the literate and illiterate alike. An early review praised him for performing the function of "moral teacher" to the "millions who are just emerging from ignorance into what may be called reading classes."[12] Occasionally, however, his popular appeal was recorded with the snide overtone of Leslie Stephen's later comment: "If literary fame could safely be measured by popularity with the half-educated, Dickens must claim the highest position among English novelists."[13]

It was said at the time that Dickens was a "low writer" who wrote about low subjects, for a low audience.[14] A reviewer of *Bleak House* complained that it was "meagre and melodramatic, and disagreeably reminiscent of that vilest of modern books, Reynolds's *Mysteries of London*."[15] John Ruskin later defended Dickens against this charge by distinguishing him from another "low" writer, the Frenchman Eugène Sue. Unlike *The Mysteries of Paris*, a loathsome specimen of "prison-house literature," *Oliver Twist* was an "earnest and uncaricatured record of the state of criminal life, written with a didactic purpose, full of the gravest instruction."[16] Dickens himself was sensitive to this criticism. When he started his magazine *Household Words*, which might be thought to be competing with Reynolds's *Miscellany*, his introductory editorial denounced the periodicals that were "Bastards of the Mountain, draggled fringe on the Red Cap, Panders to the basest passions of the lowest natures."[17]

Those who accused Dickens of being a "low" writer generally had in mind his criminal characters and prison scenes. But this criticism did not usually extend to his depiction of the "lower classes," as distinct from the "dangerous classes." Lord Melbourne, to be sure, disliked both kinds of lowness. Persuaded to read *Oliver Twist* by Queen Victoria, he confessed he could not get beyond the opening chapters. "It's all among Workhouses, and Coffin Makers, and Pickpockets," he told her. "I don't like that low debasing view of mankind. . . . I don't like those things; I wish to avoid them; I don't like them in reality, and therefore I don't wish them represented."[18] Queen Victoria, on the other hand, reading the book over the objections of her mother (who disapproved not only of low books but of all "light books"), found *Oliver Twist* "excessively interesting."[19] Even Thackeray, who thought that the Fagin scenes pandered to the sensational tastes of the age, did not object to Dickens's other low themes and characters. "The pathos of the workhouse scenes in *Oliver Twist*, or the Fleet prison descriptions in *Pickwick*, is genuine and pure—as much of this as you please; as tender a hand to the poor, as kindly a word to the unhappy as you will; but in the name of common sense, let us not expend our sympathies on cut-throats, and other such prodigies of evil."[20] Dickens himself left no doubt of the villainy of his criminals. His compassion was reserved for those worthy of it—the poor woman in *Oliver Twist*, for example, who died gasping the names of her children. "O, ye scions of a refined age," his friend, Richard Horne, rebuked those who pronounced Dickens a "low writer": "Look at this passage—find out how low it is—and rise up from the contemplation chastened, purified—wiser, because sorrow-softened and better men through the enlargement of sympathies."[21]

Oliver Twist, the most Hogarthian of Dickens's novels, alternates between low characters of both kinds, and it is hard to say which fascinated readers the more. (Or, for that matter, Dickens himself; the murder of Nancy was his favorite reading piece.) Some critics see an intimate relationship between the two species of lowness, Fagin and Oliver being "alike if not identical" in their alienation from respectable society, a society in which "poverty was tantamount to crime."[22] The strongest support for this view comes from an autobiographical memoir in which Dickens recalled that unhappy period of his childhood in the blacking warehouse, when he was obliged to associate with "common men and boys." "I know that I lounged about the streets, insufficiently and unsatisfactorily fed. I know that, but for the mercy of God, I might easily have been, for any care that was taken of me, a little robber or a little vagabond." This passage appears almost verbatim—in *David Copperfield*, however, not *Oliver Twist*.[23]

In fact, David (like Dickens himself) never ran the risk of becoming "a little robber or a little vagabond." The streets of London he wandered through were perfectly respectable, and he never so much as encountered anyone like the Artful Dodger, let alone a Fagin or a Bill Sikes. Even young Oliver, thrown into the company of criminals, was never really in danger of becoming one of them. Throughout the novel he is sharply distinguished from the others, in character and appearance. When he runs away from the undertaker to whom he is apprenticed, he is shabbily clothed, but he manages to include in his little bundle a spare shirt and two pairs of stockings. Ragged, hungry, and footsore after a week of wandering, he is still not peculiar or strange-looking. The Artful Dodger, on the other hand, even in the eyes of Oliver, accustomed to the ragged children in the poorhouse, is "one of the queerest looking boys" he had ever seen.[24]

The gulf between pauperism and criminality, in the novel as in reality, was large though not unbridgeable. If some pauper children, like Noah Claypole, join the community of thieves, others, like Oliver, do not. So far from Fagin and Oliver being "alike if not identical" in their alienation from society, Dickens made them utterly unlike. Oliver is entirely at home in the respectable company of Mr. Brownlow and Mrs. Maylie. What he is alienated from, indeed repelled and terrified by, is the dark, dirty, dangerous underworld of the criminal. Fagin is not an outcast from society, as a pauper might be; he is an outcast from humanity. He has no redeeming qualities because he is not human. A "loathsome reptile, engendered in the slime and darkness through which he moved," he is like that primordial creature, evil incarnate, a "villainy perfectly demoniacal."[25] He is as quintessentially vicious as the dying pauper child, who bids farewell to Oliver when he flees the workhouse, is quintessentially virtuous.[*]

---

[*]Fagin may have been inspired by Ikey Solomons, a notorious fence, but his name derived from the Bob Fagin who befriended the young Charles Dickens in the blacking warehouse. That Dickens should have attached the name of that good and kindly child to that evil old man has been a source of much speculation. The historian is reminded once again of the treacherous gap between fiction and reality.

Fagin and the saintly pauper child are extreme types; they are what makes *Oliver Twist*, as one critic says, a morality play more than a social novel.[26] For Dickens, morality always trumped class. While some of his pauper children are too good to be true (indeed, too good to live), others (like Noah Claypole) are clearly "bad 'uns." Even the poor-law officials are not all of a kind; the magistrate who prevents Oliver from being apprenticed to the odious chimney sweep is kindly and humane, if also somewhat senile; indeed, his senility saves the boy from the cruel rationality of the other authorities. It is not the matron but another inmate of the workhouse who robs Oliver's mother on her deathbed. And Oliver's half-brother, Monks, better born and bred than Oliver, is a bad man who comes to a bad end, while Oliver, an illegitimate child born and raised in the workhouse, is the true, natural gentleman.

The social message of the novel is also more complicated than might be thought. Published in 1837–1838, *Oliver Twist* was a powerful indictment of the New Poor Law passed a few years earlier, a law that gave the poor, as Dickens said in a much-quoted sentence, the alternative "of being starved by a gradual process in the [poor]house, or by a quick one out of it."[27] In more subtle ways, however, the book affirmed and validated the essential principle of that law: the separation of the pauper from the working poor so as to prevent the "pauperization" of the poor. By the same token, the pauper was to be separated from the criminal to prevent the working class from becoming a "dangerous class." The workhouse may have seemed to Dickens and others like a prison. But it was meant to keep the pauper out of prison, to give him an alternative to a life of crime. For all of Dickens's hatred of the workhouse and the New Poor Law, he was as insistent as any poor law reformer on the need to distinguish the pauper from the criminal, to separate, physically and conceptually, the unfortunate victim of circumstances from the willful villain, an Oliver from a Fagin.

In his provocative, oddly querulous essay on Dickens, George Orwell mocked G. K. Chesterton's characterization of Dickens as "the spokesman of the poor." Chesterton had called Sam Weller "the great symbol in English literature of the populace peculiar to England." But Sam Weller, Orwell protested, is "a valet!" Orwell suspected that Dickens knew as little about the poor as Chesterton did. "He [Dickens] is vaguely on the side of the working class, has a sort of generalised sympathy with them because they are oppressed—but he does not in reality know much about them; they came into his books chiefly as servants, and comic servants at that." And not even "modern" servants. Sam Weller is so much the "feudal" type of servant that he offers to work without wages and deliberately gets arrested in order to serve his master in jail. For Dickens, Orwell says, human equality is not only practically impossible; "it is not imaginable either."[28]

Dickens had, in fact, no difficulty imagining equality; he simply refused to make it the measure of human worth and dignity. Though the servants in his novels are not the social equals of their masters, this in no way degrades or dehumanizes them. Sam Weller has a powerful sense of his own dignity and a lively, indeed peculiarly modern, sense of his rights. When Pickwick proposes to engage him, Weller insists on spelling out carefully the terms of employment, a parody of a businessman negotiating a contract. He puts the questions to his prospective employer:

> "Wages?" inquired Sam.
> "Twelve pounds a year."
> "Clothes?"
> "Two suits."
> "Work?"
> "To attend upon me; and travel about with me and these gentlemen here."

"Take the bill down," said Sam emphatically. "I'm let to a single gentleman, and the terms is agreed upon."[29]

Only later, when Weller has come to respect Pickwick as a human being as well as a generous employer, does he offer to work without wages in jail. He does this in a spirit of friendship rather than servitude; there is little or no service required of him in jail, except to initiate Pickwick into the strange mores of prison life. (There was nothing odd about having a servant in jail; Dickens's own family took a servant girl with them when they were committed to Marshalsea prison for indebtedness.)

So far from being a caricature of the feudal servant who knows his place, Sam Weller is a caricature of the independent, irreverent servant who does not know his place, who can even fancy himself a gentleman. Shortly after their acquaintance, Sam tells Pickwick something of his background. Before being a bootboy, he had been a waggoner's boy and before that a carrier's boy. "Now I'm a gen'l'm'n's servant. I shall be a gen'l'm'n myself one of these days, perhaps, with a pipe in my mouth, and a summer-house in the back garden. Who knows? I shouldn't be surprised, for one."[30] Nor would "jolly" Mark Tapley, in *Martin Chuzzlewit*, have been surprised at his own reversal of class. First a hostler at the Blue Dragon Inn, then Martin Chuzzlewit's servant, he returns from America to marry the innkeeper and become the proprietor of the inn, renamed the Jolly Tapley. If Sam and Mark are caricatures, it is of a type rather than a class, just as some of Dickens's upper-class characters are caricatures—Lord Decimus Tite Barnacle, for example, the high official in the Circumlocution Office in *Little Dorrit*, who is entirely defined and satirized in terms of his occupation.

The presence of all those servants in Dickens's novels is itself a reflection of the social reality. By the middle of the century no fewer than one million people, of a total population of eighteen million, were domestic servants; they were the largest single group of employed people after the agricultural laborers. And there were many more who had been in service for part of their lives or had parents, children, and other relatives in service. Even some working-class families, themselves barely above the servant class, managed to keep a much overworked and underpaid skivvy, a maid-of-all-work. At a time when, as Orwell said, the slavey drudging in the basement kitchen was "too normal to be noticed,"[31] Dickens did notice her—as an individual, not merely a member of a class. Apart from Sam Weller, Mrs. Peggotty, and Mark Tapley, there are a host of memorable minor characters in his novels: Sloppy, the "love-child," brought up in the poorhouse, given a home by Betty Higden, the washerwoman, and then sent into service with the Boffins; the "orfling" girl who works for the Micawbers and is distinguished chiefly by her habit of snorting; Susan Nipper, Florence Dombey's maid, who boldly stands up to the master of the house and then marries the rich, amiable, dotty Mr. Toots.

The conventional image of the model Victorian servant resembles that of the model Victorian child, silent, invisible, and dutiful. He enters rooms without knocking as if his presence is unnoticeable, and conversation goes on in his hearing as if he were deaf. Dickens's servants are of another species. They are visible, vocal, and frequently "uppity," fully conscious of themselves as others are conscious of them. So far from living in the shadow of their masters, they live lives of their own, sometimes even overshadowing their masters. And so far from trivializing the subject of the poor by creating so many servants, Dickens may be said to have rescued from oblivion those who, as Orwell rightly said, were too often out of sight and out of mind.

Orwell complained that there was no proletariat in Dickens's novels, that if a reader were asked which "proletarian characters" he remembered, he would almost certainly mention Bill Sikes, Sam Weller, and Mrs. Gamp—a burglar, a valet, and a drunken midwife.[32] The complaint was an old one, going back at least to George Gissing in the late nineteenth century, who found many "poor people" but not a single "representative wage-earner" outside of *Hard Times*, the least successful, he thought, of Dickens's novels. "The working class," Gissing concluded, "is not Dickens's field, even in London."[33] A few years later Louis Cazamian, in what is still one of the best books on the English social novel, addressed the same question. "If Dickens could make his poor characters alive, and give them a striking realism even while he romanticized them, precisely who were these representatives of the poor?" Cazamian's answer was that the poor whom Dickens found most attractive, whom he celebrated as the glory of England, came from the "lower middle class." It was they who practiced the "philosophy of Christmas"—love, charity, generosity, warmth, good humor.[34]

Typical of that class, according to Cazamian, are the Cratchits. As Scrooge's clerk, Cazamian says, Cratchit belongs to the lower middle class. Yet the family, with eight mouths to feed and an income of little more than a pound a week, is "poor and needy," below the level of most working-class families of the time. They live "in a very small way" in a four-room house in Camden Town, suffering their privations cheerfully and making the best of their world. Nor does the Nubbles family in *The Old Curiosity Shop* comfortably fit in that class. The reader is introduced to Mrs. Nubbles, a widow with three children, at midnight when she is still hard at work as a laundress, having been at it, we are told, since morning; the oldest child, Kit, just returned from work as an errand boy, is having his supper. After Kit loses his job (through no fault of his own), he earns some pennies minding horses, in the course of which he meets the Garlands, who take him in as a servant, giving him board, lodging, and the munificent sum, it seems to him, of £6 a year. Delighted with his new home, a little thatched cottage in Finchley, he is still prouder of his own family's much more modest home, where there was as much "comfort in poverty" as could be found anywhere.[35] Eventually, after many misfortunes (including the memorable death of Little Nell) and some simple pleasures (an outing to the circus), Kit marries the Garlands' other servant and leaves their service for a "good post," presumably another domestic position.

So, too, some of the other supposedly lower-middle-class characters. Clara Peggotty, Mrs. Copperfield's servant, not a pampered lady's maid but a maid-of-all-work, becomes "independent" when she marries Mr. Barkis, but after his death returns to her post as servant. Her brother, a hardworking fisherman, "rough but ready," as he describes himself, owns his own boat, but that does not make him less poor, any more than it did his partner, Mr. Gummidge, who "died very poor."[36] To Orwell the Peggottys "hardly belong to the working class."[37] But Emily, their niece, has a different sense of it. "Your father," she tells David Copperfield on their first meeting, "was a gentleman, and your mother is a lady; and my father was a fisherman, and my mother was a fisherman's daughter, and my uncle Dan is a fisherman."[38]* Or there is Polly Toodle, Paul Dombey's nurse, whose husband, a stoker on steam engines, can neither read nor write and is pleased to be offered the job of engine-fireman on the railroad. Or Charley, the thirteen-year-old girl in *Bleak House*, who does washing to earn a few "sixpences and shillings" to support her younger brother and sister, before she has the good fortune

*David Copperfield's mother—a "lady," Emily calls her—was an orphan who had worked as a nursery governess before her first marriage. The governess had an anomalous position in Victorian society, a servant in one sense, but a very special kind of servant, since this was one of the few occupations open to the well-bred lady fallen upon bad times. Even after her marriage, Mrs. Copperfield was a rather impoverished lady, employing only one servant when she was widowed and living on an annuity of £105 a year.

to be taken on as a maid and taught to write (which she does with the greatest difficulty).

Perhaps social critics elevate these families to the "lower middle class" because they think of the Victorian working class as a "social problem," and these families are clearly not problematic—not for themselves and not for society; they are not oppressed, miserable, "alienated" (as we might say), or "pauperized" (as a Victorian would say). Dickens loves them because they are warm, spontaneous, cheerful, devoted to their families, respectful and respected by others, making their way, in their own way, in the society in which they find themselves (hence Dickens's famous happy endings)—all this while being "poor and needy."

A social reformer like Edwin Chadwick may not have approved of the Nubbles' outing to the circus or the Cratchits' Christmas "feasting." But even he could not have asked more of them by way of hard work, independent spirit—and cleanliness, the epitome of virtue. It is with the eye of a superior housewife that Dickens is pleased to note that Cratchit's threadbare garments are "darned up and brushed" in readiness for the Christmas dinner, and that after the feast, "the cloth was cleared, the hearth swept."[39] The old barge in which Daniel Peggotty and his assorted dependents live is "beautifully clean inside and as tidy as possible."[40] When Susan Nipper, in *Dombey and Son*, finally locates Polly Toodle in her new home, she is ushered into a "clean parlour full of children."[41] Little Charley, in *Bleak House*, has the compulsive habit of "folding up everything she could lay her hands on," and is complimented on the exemplary state of the sickroom, "so fresh and airy, so spotless and neat."[42] The Nubbles live in a house that is "an extremely poor and homely place, but with that air of comfort about it, nevertheless, which—or the spot must be a wretched one indeed—cleanliness and order can always impart to some degree."[43]

The repeated refrain, "cleanliness and order," may seem to come oddly from Dickens, not quite in keeping, one might think, with the joyousness and spontaneity he valued so highly. Yet if Dickens, like those reformers and do-gooders whom he derided, harped on these traits, it was because they were the prerequisites for a good and happy life. In the Victorian version of the Puritan ethic, cleanliness was, if not next to godliness, at least next to industriousness and temperance. In their mean and cramped houses, it was only by the greatest effort of cleanliness and orderliness that the poor could make their homes livable. The symbol of the hearth in Dickens's work has often been commented on; it was the symbol of the family, of warmth and brightness, intimacy and devotion. Poverty might sometimes extinguish the fire in the hearth, but the hearth remained as the center of the family. And a clean hearth meant that it was being tended, that someone cared enough to make that effort, so that whatever other misfortunes might strike (and misfortunes were all too common), the family was united and sustained.

For contemporaries, these people did not constitute a "lower middle class" or even a "lower class"; they were the "lower classes" or "lower orders" (pluralized to signify the many differences within them), or simply the "poor" or "deserving poor."* If one does not think of Dickens as celebrating the "deserving poor," it is because "deserving" has been given a bad name, as if to be deserving is to be calculatingly, grudgingly, joylessly virtuous. His deserving poor were hardworking, sober (but not teetotalers—theirs was the time-honored drink of the poor, beer or ale, not gin), honest, chaste,

---

*"Lower orders" had become less common by the 1840s, but it was by no means unusual. The reviewer of "The Chimes" in 1844 praised Dickens who "first drew those admirable portraits of the poor—called lower orders—which have rendered his name so truly dear to every lover of his country."[44]

clean, orderly, and at the same time lively, spirited, and good-humored. In Dickens's moral economy, these virtues were domesticated and socialized, serving the welfare of family and friends rather than of the individual, and exercised naturally and spontaneously, not dutifully and self-righteously.

"It is Dickens's delight in grotesque and rich exaggeration which has made him, I think, nearly useless in the present day." This was John Ruskin writing to his friend Charles Eliot Norton just after Dickens's death.[45] Much of the exaggeration Ruskin complained of had to do with Dickens's portraits of another group of poor, neither the admirable Cratchits and Nubbles nor the despicable Sikes and Fagin but an assortment of bizarre characters, strange looking, strange speaking, and above all engaged in strange occupations—sometimes grotesque in their strangeness, sometimes picturesque or quaintly amusing.

Almost all his novels have such types, but none in such profusion as *Our Mutual Friend*. The powerful opening scene tantalizingly introduces one of the more memorable characters, a boatman, we are told, who is neither fisherman, nor waterman, nor lighterman, nor river-carrier, a man who is not rowing the boat (a girl is doing that) but only holding the rudder, staring intently at the river, trying to penetrate below the "slime and ooze" on its surface. The man is "half savage," bare-chested, his hair matted, his dress seemingly made of the same mud that begrimes the boat. A sudden flash of light dimly illuminates, in the bottom of the boat, a "rotten stain" resembling a human form. The boatman is finally identified as Gaffer Hexam, a dredgerman, and the object in the boat as a dead man fished out of the Thames. The horror of the scene is highlighted by the matter-of-fact argument between Gaffer and another dredgerman about the morality of robbing a dead man compared with robbing a live one. Gaffer reminds his daughter Lizzie, who is terrified by the body and by the river that yielded it, that the river is her best friend. It provided the wood for the fire that warmed her when she was a baby, and the basket she slept in and the rockers of her cradle were made of the flotsam picked out of the water.

It has been said that the main character in *Our Mutual Friend* is the Thames, and much has been made of the symbol of the river coursing through the city, carrying with it the filth and refuse of London, the remains of all the dirty secrets and criminal acts that tainted the lives of everyone coming in contact with it. When Lionel Trilling discovered the "actuality of the symbols" in Dickens's work, he cited the sewage in the Thames, which was so compellingly present in the consciousness of Londoners.* What they were also conscious of were the men who made their living out of that "slime and ooze," hauling out the pieces of wood that might be used for firewood or a baby's cradle, or the occasional corpse that could be turned in for a reward after the pockets had been picked.

Some of Dickens's more bizarre characters had their counterpart in Henry Mayhew's nonfictional *London Labour and the London Poor*, suggesting to some scholars that Dickens may have borrowed them from Mayhew.[47] (*Our Mutual Friend* appeared serially, in 1864–1865, at the same time as the reprinting of Mayhew's work.) There is no hard evidence of this, no reference to Mayhew in Dickens's

---

*In June 1858 the stench from the river was such as to cause a rapid evacuation of the houses of Parliament. The *Times*, whose offices must have been afflicted by the same malodor, described the men rushing out of a committee room, "foremost among them being the Chancellor of the Exchequer [Disraeli], who, with a mass of papers in one hand and with his pocket handkerchief clutched in the other, and applied closely to his nose, with body half bent, hastened in dismay from the pestilential odour, followed closely by Sir James Graham, who seemed to be attacked by a sudden fit of expectoration." A fortnight later Disraeli introduced a bill for the financing of new sewage drains—eleven years after the establishment of the Metropolitan Commission of Sewers for that purpose.[46]

writings, and no copy of *London Labour and the London Poor* in his library (which did contain other books on London). Indeed, the reverse may have been possible; it may have been Mayhew who borrowed from Dickens.[48] In fact, both drew upon the wealth of contemporary literature exposing the seamier parts of London life. If there are dozens of Mayhewian characters in *Our Mutual Friend*— Noddy Boffin, the rich dustman; Mr. Venus, the seller of stuffed animals and birds; Jenny Wren, the doll's dressmaker; Betty Higden, the laundress whose fear of the workhouse makes her take to the road and become an itinerant seller; the professional begging-letter writers who besiege Boffin with their importunities—it is because such characters were a conspicuous part of the London scene, quite out of proportion to their actual numbers.* The newspapers regularly reported on the recovery of dead bodies from the Thames, together with the amount of the reward and details about the clothing and state of the body. Dickens's Gaffer had a worthy confrere in the dredger interviewed by Mayhew, who also insisted that there was nothing strange or repulsive in his job and nothing dishonest in rifling the pockets of a dead man. But Gaffer was more poetic than Mayhew's dredger, who merely claimed that he had a better right to the money than the police who would otherwise appropriate it. Gaffer's defense has the distinct echo of Shylock: "What world does a dead man belong to? T'other world. What world does money belong to? This world. How can money be a corpse's? Can a corpse own it, want it, spend it, claim it, miss it?"[50]

Long before *London Labour and the London Poor*, even before the *London Charivari* (better known as *Punch*), Dickens had established

---

*Henry James criticized Dickens for making so outlandish a character as Jenny Wren. But he could have made her even more outlandish by giving her the occupation of two of Mayhew's real-life characters who specialized in making doll's eyes.[49]

himself as the chronicler and celebrant of the streets of London. Most of the *Sketches by Boz* deal with some aspect of London street life: costermongers, cab drivers, old-clothes dealers, street vendors, street performers, street laborers, and street walkers (in both senses). Cruikshank's illustrations include a breakfast cart in the street in the early morning, a quarrelsome crowd at Seven Dials, clothes strung along the shop fronts on Monmouth Street, a First-of-May street festival. The most prominent street character is Boz himself, the indefatigable wanderer, observer, and commentator, who refers to himself in the first-person plural but who puts his singular stamp upon this vista of London street life.

> We have a most extraordinary partiality for lounging about the streets. Whenever we have an hour or two to spare, there is nothing we enjoy more than a little amateur vagrancy-walking up one street and down another, and staring into shop windows, and gazing about as if, instead of being on intimate terms with every shop and house in Holborn, the Strand, Fleet-street and Cheapside, the whole were an unknown region to our wandering mind.[51]

There are echoes of Boz in all of Dickens's work, even in a novel like *Dombey and Son* which takes place in the dark and gloom of the countinghouse. The house is on a street that every morning witnesses a procession of street-folk: "the water-carts and the old-clothes men, and the people with geraniums, and the umbrella-mender, and the man who trilled the little bell of the Dutch clock as he went along."[52] One of the more dramatic episodes involves the odious "Good Mrs. Brown," the ugly, old, ragged woman carrying rabbit skins over her arm, who accosts little Florence, takes her to her home (a hovel crammed with rags, old clothes, bones, dust, and cinders), robs her of her clothes, and refrains from cutting off her hair only because of the memory of her own long-lost daughter.[53] This fictional character was all too real: in 1860 ninety-seven such cases were reported.[54]

Much has been written about Dickens's image of himself as a poor, undernourished, neglected child roaming the streets of London at night, making his way, like the thieves in *Oliver Twist*, through the "cold wet shelterless midnight streets," or following David Copperfield in his daily walk from the warehouse in Blackfriars to Micawber's prison in Southwark.[55] But there is another London celebrated by Dickens, a familiar and friendly country where men embark on adventures knowing they will turn out well and where even misadventures are more often comic than tragic. *Pickwick Papers* is not usually regarded as a "social novel" because it is not usually identified with the "social problem" or the working classes. In one sense it is the most middle class of Dickens's novels. Samuel Pickwick, Esq., Augustus Snodgrass, Esq., Nathaniel Winkle, Esq., and the other members of the club are not rich, certainly not "upper class," but their means are sufficient to support them in retirement and permit them to indulge their hobby of travel. The description of Pickwick as a retired businessman and a "gentleman of considerable independent property" is probably an exaggeration (it is provided by his defense counsel to establish his respectability).[56] He lives modestly in a small apartment in Mrs. Bardell's house in Goswell Street, not a fashionable part of London, and is attended to by her and, later, by Sam Weller.

Yet some contemporary reviewers associated the book with the lower classes, and specifically with the lower classes of London (although much of the action takes place on the open road and in country inns and houses). The *Quarterly Review* attributed its success to Dickens's felicity in conveying "the genuine mother-wit and unadulterated vernacular idiom of the lower classes of London." Another reviewer praised him for depicting the "humours of the lower orders of London."[57] It is, of course, Sam Weller who dominates the book and gives it its lower-class London character. Until his arrival in the fourth number, the serial, in spite of an extensive publicity campaign, had sold poorly, and reviews had been less than enthusiastic. After Weller's appearance, sales dramatically improved, and by the end of the serial in 1837, forty thousand of each number were being sold. Where Orwell saw Weller as a parody of a feudal servant, contemporaries saw him as the epitome of the Cockney, the Londoner born and bred within the sound of Bow Bells who was the true urban aborigine. Accompanying the Pickwickians on their travels, he puts the impress of London on all of England, making the entire country a provincial outpost of the metropolis. The relationship of Pickwick and Weller is not that of benevolent master and obsequious servant—Weller is independent to the point of impertinence—but that of the naive, bumbling, genial master and the shrewd, articulate, worldly-wise (streetwise, we would now say) servant.

"It is fun," a woman reviewer wrote of *Pickwick Papers*, "London Life—but without anything unpleasant: a lady might read it all aloud; and it is so graphic, so individual, and so true, that you could curtsey to all the people as you met them in the streets."[58] Yet even here there are intimations of the "dark side" of Dickens, in the tragic stories of the dying clown and his destitute family, the convict who broke his mother's heart and then killed his father, the man ruined by a long legal suit, the debtor in prison watching his child and wife die in poverty and later cruelly exacting his vengeance. These bitter tales presage an unhappy turn in the plot when Pickwick is imprisoned and discovers what Weller and his kind have always known: that even in prison there are vast differences between the classes, some enjoying prison as a "regular holiday . . . all porter and skittles," while others pine away in misery and despair. Weller, as usual, delivers the final word: "'It's unekal,' as my father used to say wen his grog warn't made half-and-half; 'It's unekal, and that's the fault on it.'"[59]

This was not, however, the message most readers took from the book. It was not read as a social novel, as an exposé of the unequal conditions in prison or the inequities of the legal system. These dark episodes function as tragic relief in an otherwise comic tale. The Pickwickian world is "unekal," often unjust, sometimes tragic, but basically decent, hopeful, and humane. What makes it a place of good cheer, for the Wellers of that world as well as the Pickwicks, is the promise of freedom rather than equality. As the Thames casts its malignant spell over the London of *Our Mutual Friend*, so the road is the dominant and benign symbol of *Pickwick Papers*—and not, as one might think, because it permits men to escape from the evil city. When the coach makes its way through the streets of London, they are not the dark, treacherous alleys that terrify Oliver Twist nor the gloomy back streets that oppress David Copperfield; they are well-lit, cheerful thoroughfares where a lady might well curtsey to everyone she meets. For Pickwick and his friends, the open road is a release not from the prison of the city but from the bonds of a prosaic, routinized, if comfortable and decent, existence.

Today Pickwickians of both classes—Pickwick and his friends, Sam Weller and his—may be seen by literary critics as picaresque characters, romantic fantasies, "quasi-mythical" creatures representing a vision of the "ideal possibilities of human relations."[60] At the time they appeared as perfectly ordinary people of middle and low rank, of no special distinction except their great goodwill and good humor. Reviewers spoke of them as "droll," "comic," "original," "curious," "whimsical," and at the same time as "realistic," "true," "natural," "veritable," "actual." "All of it," one said, "is real life and human nature. It is not a collection of humorous or pathetic dialogues about people who have no tangible existence in mind; but it is a succession of actual scenes, the actors of which take up a place in the memory."[61] Even Thackeray, who was not always generous to his rivals, praised it for portraying "true characters under false names," and for giving a "better idea of the state and ways of the people than one could gather from any more pompous or authentic histories."[62]

One does not know what the butcher-boy, the footman, the maidservant, or the chimney sweep—those whom George Lewes saw reading the latest issue of *Pickwick Papers*—made of it, whether they too thought Sam's wit and dialect true to life. If they did not, if they enjoyed it as fantasy, it was evidently a fantasy much to their liking, which is itself a social fact of some importance. At least as important is the fact that other readers thought that Dickens captured the idiom and image of the lower classes, perhaps, one reviewer conceded, in a slightly "heightened" but still realistic and "veritable" form.[63] Throughout this period, when melodramatic and sensationalist novels were popular, *Pickwick Papers* continued to be reissued and reread, as if to provide an antidote to other more forbidding images of the poor.

In a sense, *Pickwick Papers* is an antidote to Dickens himself. All of his earlier novels have "dark" overtones, but none is as unrelievedly dark as *Hard Times*. Coketown is representative of England, not in the sense that industrialism is typical of England (it was not, of course) but in the sense that industrialism magnifies all the other aspects of modernity—the cold, calculating rationality, the impersonality and lack of community—that threaten the congenial world of *Pickwick Papers*. It was a familiar criticism of Dickens in his own time (and is still more today) that in this novel, when he finally confronted the industrial problem, he was distracted by such extraneous issues as utilitarianism, education, marriage, and divorce.[64] To Dickens, these were not extraneous. For him the problem of industrialism was not that of an oppressed or exploited class, of inadequate wages or intolerable working and living conditions. What was at issue was the way people felt and thought about themselves and one another, their ability to understand, sympathize, suffer, enjoy, love, work. If the factory was oppressive, it was because it was destructive of these natural human emotions and experiences. And the factory itself reflected the more grievous faults of society—of a system of education designed to transform children into reasoning machines, of marriages held together by unjust laws and calculations of interest, and, more grievously, of a utilitarian philosophy that had little room for pleasure or love.

While he was working on the novel, Dickens considered two other titles, "A Mere Question of Figures" and "The Gradgrind Philosophy," either of which would have made utilitarianism, not industrialism, the main theme.[65] The opening words of *Hard Times* proclaim the utilitarian catechism.

> "Now, what I want is, Facts. Teach these boys and girls nothing but Facts. Facts alone are wanted in life. Plant nothing else, and root out everything else. You can only form the minds of reasoning animals upon Facts; nothing else will ever be of any service to them. This is the principle on which I bring up my own children, and this is the principle on which I bring up these children. Stick to Facts, sir!"[66]

Mr. Gradgrind, the headmaster who delivers this speech, dominates the opening chapters. The industrialist, Josiah Bounderby, is introduced only later, when he is identified not as the local mill owner but as a "rich man: banker, merchant, manufacturer, and, what not." And he makes his first appearance not in his factory in Coketown but in Gradgrind's house a mile or so out of town.[67] Coketown comes into view only later, as Gradgrind and Bounderby make their way into town.

It was a town of red brick, or of brick that would have been red if the smoke and ashes had allowed it; but as matters stood it was a town of unnatural red and black like the painted face of a savage. It was a town of machinery and tall chimneys, out of which interminable serpents of smoke trailed themselves for ever and ever, and never got uncoiled. It had a black canal in it, and a river that ran purple with ill-smelling dye, and vast piles of buildings full of windows where there was a rattling and a trembling all day long, and where the piston of the steam-engine worked monotonously up and down like the head of an elephant in a state of melancholy madness.[68]

This is the familiar description of a textile town—dark, dirty, noisy, smoky, smelly—an obvious prelude to a critique of the factory system. The emphasis soon shifts, however, and the great evil of the town, as of the factory (which is described only once, and then briefly), becomes not the physical pollution of the atmosphere but the pall of utilitarianism that hangs over it. Everything is "severely workful." The chapel resembles the warehouse, the jail looks like the infirmary, the town hall and the school are indistinguishable from the rest. The factory itself appears more as a monument to fact than to industry, less a means of production than an attitude of mind, routinized, rationalized, materialized. "Fact, fact, fact, everywhere in the material aspect of the town; fact, fact, fact, everywhere in the immaterial."[69]

When Gradgrind and Bounderby walk to town, their destination is the public house where Sissy, one of the pupils, lives with her father. There they meet some of the members of the circus troupe to which Sissy's father belongs—this before the reader has met a single factory worker. The circus folk are yet another variety of "streetfolk"—"vagabonds," "strollers," "comers and goers," "queer," "rakish and knowing," "not at all orderly in their domestic arrangements," peculiarly dressed, and speaking a language so strange as to be almost incomprehensible to the townsman.[70] What disturbs Gradgrind and Bounderby is the troupers' attitude to work. It is not that they are idlers; like the other street-folk, the circus people work as hard as ordinary folk. But they are workers of another species, working outdoors, at their own pace, at activities of their own choice, in keeping with their own instincts and skills. Bounderby explains the difference between them: "We are the kind of people who know the value of time, and you are the kind of people who don't know the value of time." One of the circus men amends this: "If you mean that you can make more money of your time than I can of mine, I should judge from your appearance, that you are about right."[71] The trouper's point is well taken. It is not that the circus people have no regard for time; on the contrary, time for them is of the essence. (Sissy's father has to leave the circus because he is "missing his tip," his timing is off.) It is only that they do not "value" their time, as Bounderby and his kind do, in terms of money.

The circus is obviously a counterpoint to the factory, the natural, graceful, spontaneous rhythm of the performers contrasting with the artificial, rationalized, mechanized rhythm of industry. But the circus is a supplement, not an alternative, to the factory; it is a traveling circus set up temporarily on the outskirts of town, on the periphery of the workaday world. The circus people are "deserving": "deserving often of as much respect, and always of as much generous construction, as the everyday virtues of any class of people in the world."[72] Not, however, more deserving; ordinary folk have their "everyday virtues." Nor are the circus folk meant to be a model for everyone. Sissy's father, who loves her and wants the best for her, deliberately removes her from the circus and places her in Gradgrind's school, not knowing the exact nature of that school but knowing that some schooling, some education and maturation (the circus people are "childish") will be good for her. When Sissy briefly considers rejoining the circus, she is persuaded by the kindly circus owner to return to school until she is old enough to go to work—in the factory, not in the circus.

The more dramatic counterpoint to the circus is not Bounderby's factory but the school, which tries to turn children into fact-grinding machines. The disaster is compounded when the adult world, adopting the same utilitarian philosophy, commits itself to a regimen of "facts, facts, facts," opposing anything that smacks of the childish—pleasure, fantasy, imagination, playfulness, spontaneity, sentiment, love. The circus helps relieve this utilitarian sameness, the deadly monotony of workaday life. It is a transient, marginal affair, but that is enough to make it an essential part of society, recalling adults to the pleasures of childhood and keeping alive in them the spark of innocence without which adulthood would be unendurable.[73]

It is interesting that this idea of pleasure should appear in the context of an attack on utilitarianism, for "pleasure" was one of the key words in the Benthamite vocabulary, the maximization of pleasure and minimization of pain being the basis of the "felicific calculus." Bentham's pleasure, however, was the very antithesis of Dickens's; it was a measure of utility or interest, not of joy or playfulness. Disraeli had made just this point in his early, little-known tale, "The Voyage of Captain Popanilla," explaining the logic by which the utilitarian deduced that "pleasure is not pleasant."

> He did not imagine that the most barefaced hireling of corruption could for a moment presume to maintain that there was any utility in pleasure. If there were no utility in pleasure, it was quite clear that pleasure could profit no one. If, therefore, it were unprofitable, it was injurious; because that which does not produce a profit is equivalent to a loss; therefore pleasure is a losing business; consequently pleasure is not pleasant.[74]

In Freudian terms, one might say that, paradoxically, Bentham's "pleasure" corresponded to the "reality principle" and Dickens's to the "pleasure principle." Mr. Gradgrind is introduced as a "man of realities."[75] And "reality," like "fact," is repeatedly invoked to describe the material, mechanical, utilitarian world of Gradgrind and Bounderby. Even the rich members of that world (Miss Gradgrind, later Mrs. Bounderby) are spiritually impoverished by a reality devoid of pleasure. For the poor, for whom reality is not merely joyless but oppressive, that deprivation is fatal.

> Utilitarian economists, skeletons of schoolmasters, Commissioners of Fact, genteel and used-up infidels, gabblers of many little dog's-eared creeds, the poor you will have always with you. Cultivate in them, while there is yet time, the utmost graces of the fancies and affections, to adorn their lives so much in need of ornament; or, in the day of your triumph, when romance is utterly driven out of their souls, and they and a bare existence stand face to face, Reality will take a wolfish turn, and make an end of you.[76]

In his obsession with utilitarianism, critics have charged, Dickens failed to recognize not only the true nature of the social problem but also the only realistic, progressive force available to meliorate it, the trade unions.[77] In *Hard Times*, trade unionism itself becomes part of the problem. Slackbridge, the union organizer, is a fitting adversary for Bounderby, the employer; they are equally disagreeable and hypocritical, selfish and obdurate. Slackbridge's influence on the workers is thoroughly pernicious, his demagogy undermining their native good sense. The hero, Stephen Blackpool, refuses to join the union and is "sent to Coventry" by his coworkers. Unhappily, he is not so much a hero as a victim, doomed by circumstances beyond his control, saddled with a drunken wife, alienated from his fellow workers, fired by his employer for no good reason, and, finally, dying as a result of an accident—not in the factory but in the open fields (he falls down an abandoned mine shaft on a dark night).* As he lies there dying, he recalls the hundreds who have died in similar accidents and the vain appeals of the workers to the lawmakers "not to let their work be murder to 'em." "See how we die an' no need, one way an' another—in a muddle—every day!"[78] Stephen's death, like his life, as he keeps saying, is "aw a muddle"—hardly the stuff of heroism, still less the stuff of which working-class novels are normally made.

If Stephen's role is not simply that of the oppressed worker, neither is Bounderby's simply that of the exploiting industrialist. More often identified as a banker than as a factory owner, Bounderby is never seen in his factory, only in his home and bank. He is dishonest and hypocritical in representing himself as a "self-made man," but it is a kind of democratic hypocrisy, a spurious claim of social equality. The only respect in which he professes to be different from his workers is the money he has acquired by his own efforts. And money, as Dickens's novels repeatedly suggest, is the least immutable of all class distinctions, far less divisive than speech, manners, education, or breeding. When Stephen wants to consult Bounderby about his personal problems (this itself belies the stereotype of employer-employee relations), he goes not to the factory or bank but to his home, and at a time when he knows Bounderby will be at lunch. Without an appointment, he knocks at the door, is announced by the servant, and is immediately ushered

---

*In the original manuscript and in the corrected proofs, there is an account of a horrific accident in the factory in which the heroine's little sister has her arm torn off by a machine. Critics have been at a loss to understand why Dickens eliminated that passage from the serial parts as well as the published volume. Perhaps it was because that would have made the book a "social novel" in the familiar sense—a novel about industrialism per se rather than utilitarianism and materialism.

into the parlor where Bounderby is having his meal.* Whatever Bounderby's faults—he is a bad son, a bad husband, and a bad friend as well as a bad employer—they are the faults of character rather than class. He is obtuse, callous, willful, cruel, but he is not an "absentee" employer removed from his workers by an impassable barrier of class. On the contrary, it is precisely when he is most accessible to them, in his own parlor, discussing their personal problems, that his bad nature emerges most sharply.

At every point where the novel seems to falter in its purpose— the purpose later critics have assigned it, of being an "industrial" novel—it is in fact carrying out Dickens's purpose. Trade unionism is condemned on the same grounds as utilitarianism and laissez faire, because each of them threatens to undermine the already precarious personal relations that are the only basis for a decent society. Asked how he would set right the "muddle" of the strike, Stephen protests that it is not for him to say, but he does know that Bounderby's solution—to transport half a dozen union organizers to penal colonies—is no solution. So long as workers are treated "as so much Power, and reg'latin 'em as if they was figures in a soom [sum], or machines . . . wi'out souls to weary and souls to hope," so long as masters and workers are divided by a "black impassable world," the muddle will get worse.[79]

Poverty is only part of the muddle, and not the most important part. The "hard times" of the title go well beyond poverty. The workers of Coketown are poor but not acutely, intolerably poor. What is "hard" is the unrelieved, grinding, hopeless nature of their work and lives. "Look how we live, an' wheer we live, an' in what numbers, an' by what chances, and wi' what sameness; and look

---

*There is a similar scene in Elizabeth Gaskell's *Mary Barton*, where a worker goes to the house of his employer and is brought into the library while he is having his breakfast.

how the mills is awlus a going, and how they never works us no nigher to onny dis'ant object—ceptin awlus, Death."[80] For Dickens, the "social problem" (the "condition-of-England question," as it was known at the time) had to do less with material or physical deprivation than with moral and spiritual impoverishment, the emptiness and meaninglessness of a mechanical, impersonal, soulless existence. When Bounderby treats his workers as machines or figures in a sum, he is only following the model of Gradgrind addressing the pupils by number rather than name. And Slackbridge, the trade union leader, is equally culpable, seeing the workers en masse, as a power to be used in the struggle against the employers, quite like the "steam power" they are to the employers. Appealing to them to rally around as "one united power" in support of the union, the "United Aggregate Tribunal" (a name that might have been coined by Gradgrind himself, or by Bentham), he instructs the workers that "private feelings must yield to the common cause" and orders them to condemn Stephen to a "life of solitude."[81]

Gradgrind's daughter, on the other hand, finds salvation when she enters Stephen's house and meets for the first time an individual worker. Louisa had known the workers as "crowds passing to and from their nests, like ants or beetles," as "something to be worked so much and paid so much . . . by laws of supply and demand," as something rising and falling "en masse" like the sea. She could no more think of "separating them into units, than of separating the sea itself into its component drops."[82] It is the discovery of them as real persons, as individuals, that finally makes her aware of her own individuality and of her spiritual and emotional impoverishment. Like her, they are caught up in their domestic travails, their lives differentiated and complicated by personal relations, emotions, frustrations, and tragedies that have little to do with their work in the factory. They cannot be defined merely as workers, as she cannot be defined merely by her relation to her father.

At the same time *Hard Times* was being serialized in *Household Words*, Dickens wrote an article in the journal on a real strike that was the model for one in the novel. He recounted an argument he had with a gentleman to whom he gave the name of Mr. Snapper, who proudly announced himself a partisan of "Capital" against "Labour" and called on Dickens to declare his sympathies. Dickens replied that he rejected those labels as he rejected all the abstractions of the political economists. He was on the side of workers, he explained, but not of "Labour," and he was for trade unions but not as a panacea. The relations between employers and workers, like all other relations, had to have in them "something of feeling and sentiment; something of mutual explanation, forbearance, and consideration; something which is not to be found in Mr. McCulloch's [the political economist's] dictionary, and is not exactly stateable in figures; otherwise those relations are wrong and rotten at the core and will never bear sound fruit."[83]

Mr. Snapper, no doubt, was not convinced. Nor are critics today who find *Hard Times* "ambivalent" on the subject of the working classes. Contemporaries more often complained not that Dickens failed to make a good trade unionist out of Stephen Blackpool but that he made a "dramatic monster" out of Bounderby—a complaint shared by Ruskin, who was hardly well disposed to the Bounderbys of this world.[84] Macaulay charged Dickens with fostering a "sullen socialism," Bagehot with cultivating a "sentimental radicalism," and Harriet Martineau with being a "humanity monger" and "pseudophilanthropist."[85] Toward the end of the century, criticism took a different turn. George Gissing faulted Dickens for not knowing the "north of England," therefore knowing only "poor men," not real workers.[86] George Bernard Shaw, in his introduction to *Hard Times*, described Slackbridge as a "mere figment of the middleclass imagination," nothing like a real factory worker.[87] The criticism may have been justified, although it came oddly from Gissing and Shaw, who knew little enough of northern England or, for that matter, real factory workers (but both of whom did admire Dickens for other reasons). More recently the same point was made by George Orwell, who also knew little enough of northern England but who objected that Dickens was a "south of England man, and a cockney at that," out of touch with "the oppressed masses, the industrial and agricultural labourers." Dickens, he complained, had an "almost exclusively moral" conception of the problem and no constructive—that is, socialistic—suggestions for reform; his target was "human nature" rather than the "economic system."[88]

If Dickens had a deficient sense of class and an exacerbated sense of morality, if he was not a socialist and did not think in terms of economic "systems," he was all the more faithful to the reality of his own time as most of his contemporaries, including a good many radicals, perceived it. What emerges from his novels is a multitude of people of varied conditions and dispositions, who could not easily be accommodated in any class schema because they were not simply members of a class but rather highly individualized characters—inimitable and unforgettable "characters," in the idiomatic sense of that word.

In 1853 a Nonconformist minister told his flock: "There have been at work among us three great social agencies: the London City Mission; the novels of Mr. Dickens; the cholera."[89] It was a tribute Dickens would have appreciated, for it suggested that his novels had touched, even "bettered," the lives of the poor not by reforming or classifying them but by personalizing, individualizing, and dramatizing them. This was, perhaps, what Daniel Webster also had in mind when, during Dickens's visit to America in 1842, he said that Dickens had done more to "ameliorate the condition of the

English poor than all the statesmen Great Britain had sent into parliament."[90] What other reformers tried to do by legislation, he did
by a supreme act of moral imagination. He brought the poor into
the forefront of the culture, and thus into the forefront of the consciousness and the conscience of his own generation and of generations to come—not as an abstract class but as notable individuals.

Benjamin Disraeli

The Tory Imagination

~ More than a century after Disraeli's death, a conference on current British politics was diverted by an animated discussion about the rival claims of Margaret Thatcher, leader of the Conservative party, and Michael Foot, then leader of the Labour party, to the label "Disraelian." (Foot had something of an edge by virtue of his dog named "Dizzy.")[1] In the United States some years earlier, Daniel Patrick Moynihan, then counselor to the president, had urged President Nixon to assume the mantle of Disraeli by adopting the Family Assistance Plan. When the human rights issue was being debated in 1981, an article in the *Wall Street Journal* recalled the "Bulgarian Massacres" of 1876 and held up Disraeli's policy as a model for similar cases in our own day.[2] Most recently, Disraeli has been celebrated as "the inventor of modern conservatism."[3]

Historians are made uncomfortable by such latter-day invocations of Disraeli; they have difficulty enough with the real Disraeli in his own time and place. Yet the allusions tell us something important about the historical Disraeli, something many historians have yet to learn. However inconsistent or eccentric he may have been, however much of an opportunist or charlatan, as his critics claim, he did represent a distinctive political mode, a disposition and sensibility that did not quite qualify as a systematic philosophy but that were recognized as unique and significant in his own time and still have resonance today. He speaks to us as his great antagonist does not; it is a long time since anyone invoked the name of Gladstone to lend authority to a political figure or cause.

Biographies of Disraeli continue to be written, undaunted by the great Monypenny and Buckle *Life* published between 1910 and 1920, six fascinating volumes that give the lie to Carlyle's comment on that genre: "How delicate, decent, is English biography, bless its mealy mouth!"[4] Robert Blake's one-volume biography in 1966 was a major work of scholarship, although it did not pretend to compete with Monypenny and Buckle.[5] Nor did Blake's book deter a score of other biographers from making their contributions, nor Blake's publisher from reissuing his work as recently as 1998, nor other biographers since then; almost every year seems to produce yet another book or collection of essays. Nor have Disraeli's own works been slighted. His two most famous novels, *Coningsby* and *Sybil*, are still in print, as is a volume of his "sayings" and selected letters. More gratifying to the scholar is the publication, beginning in 1982 and still uncompleted, of the definitive edition of his letters; the seventh volume, covering the years of 1857–1859, appeared in 2004.[*] The true Disraeli enthusiast will also welcome so minor a work as *A Year at Hartlebury, or The Election*, a novel originally published anonymously in 1834 and only recently revealed to have been written by Disraeli and his sister Sarah (largely by Sarah, it is now supposed).

As with all the eminent Victorians, one is astonished by the sheer quantity of written matter—in Disraeli's case, not only

---

[*]It is a commentary on the present state of "little England" that this edition of Disraeli's letters, like the collected works of John Stuart Mill, should have been undertaken by Canadian scholars, subsidized by Canadian foundations, and published by a Canadian university press (Toronto).

speeches, letters, essays, political tracts (one running to three hundred pages), and a political biography (of Lord Bentinck, a colleague and benefactor), but also a dozen novels. (Churchill had an even more impressive bibliography, but only one unmemorable novel.) Disraeli was all of twenty-one when the first part of his first novel, *Vivian Grey*, was published, anonymously, in 1826 (the second part appeared the following year). A racy tale about high society, it achieved something of a *succès de scandale* because of speculation about the author as well as the identity of the characters. (It belonged to the popular genre called "silver-fork" novels, about high society or aspirants to high society.) Four other novels were published before 1834, when *A Year at Hartlebury* appeared. This novel, about a parliamentary election, drew upon Disraeli's own electoral experiences, for by then he had twice been defeated at the polls and on two other occasions had unsuccessfully sought nomination. (In the novel the hero is elected by one vote.)

It was at this time, fresh from these defeats, that Disraeli informed Lord Melbourne, then home secretary and shortly to become prime minister, that he himself intended one day to be prime minister, to which a startled Melbourne replied: "No chance of that in our time. It is all arranged and settled. Nobody can compete with Stanley [the future Earl of Derby]."[6] Disraeli was to lose two other elections and publish two more novels, two political works, and an epic poem before finally winning a seat in Parliament in 1837, at the age of thirty-two. His maiden speech was a disaster, partly because of its subject (questioning the validity of some Irish elections hardly went down well with other members of Parliament), and partly because of its inflated rhetoric. Hooted and hissed, he managed to get to the end, shouting, in order to be heard above the catcalls, "I will sit down now, but the time will come when you will hear me."[7] It was to be another thirty-one years before he succeeded Derby as prime minister. But long before that, in spite of a series of rebuffs and reverses, Disraeli had reason to be confirmed in his self-confidence and self-esteem.

Electioneering and writing were not Disraeli's only occupations in these early years. Indeed, they seem to have been minor distractions in an endless round of parties and travels (including a grand tour of the Middle East in 1830–1831), flirtations and amours, entrepreneurial schemes, financial speculations, and stratagems to pacify creditors and avoid bankruptcy and arrest. Had Disraeli gone to debtors' prison, as he very nearly did in the spring of 1837, his parliamentary career might well have been thwarted even before it began. His marriage the following year, to the widow of a fellow member of Parliament, was also inauspicious. Twelve years older than he, Mary Anne was a most unlikely mate, chattering, frivolous, impulsive, light-headed, famous for her oddities and social gaffes, hardly a proper wife for an ambitious politician. But she was also warmhearted, good-natured, generous—and very rich. It was said at the time that he married her for her money. Disraeli denied this, but even if it were so, the marriage of convenience soon became a marriage of love. His biographer, Blake, not given to sentimentality, judged it to be a great success, Disraeli behaving toward his wife "with a devotion and respect which was considered exemplary, even by Gladstone"—the severest of judges (especially in the case of Disraeli).[8] He was totally attentive to her in the final years of her illness and genuinely mourned her when she died in 1872. Deprived of her love, he soon fell madly in love with another woman (again, the wife of a member of Parliament). His love letters to her were written on the black-edged writing paper memorializing his wife.

Much else in Disraeli's mode of life was perilous, yet finally not disastrous. Writing novels—and such novels, *romans à clef* caricaturing politicians who were important to his career, novels mocking the rich and mighty and lauding the poor and oppressed, or fantasizing and eulogizing the Hebrew "race"—were hardly a prescription for political success. His father, in some ways more worldly than he, once asked him: "How will the Fictionist assort with the Politician?"[9] The problem was not so much the particular kinds of novels he wrote as the fact that he wrote them at all. This objection told against him in the social world as in the political; his inveterate "fictionizing" was one of the reasons he was blackballed from the prestigious Athenaeum Club. (He was elected thirty years later.)

So, too, his dandyism. After walking up crowded Regent Street arrayed in a blue frock coat, light blue trousers, black stockings with red stripes, and low shoes (most men wore boots), he reported to his friend, "The people quite made way for me as I passed. It was like the opening of the Red Sea which I now perfectly believe from experience." Upon which his friend commented in his diary, "I should think so!"[10] Dandyism, to be sure, was itself, in some circles, a convention, as was being in debt. Indeed the two went hand in hand—but not in the circle of aspiring prime ministers and not in the brazen spirit displayed by Disraeli.

There was something wanton about all this, a deliberate courting of danger. Disraeli flaunted his debts as he flaunted his attire. They were part of his romantic persona, the same image that emerged in his novels and in his relations with women. He not only called attention to himself by defying bourgeois conventions, taking on the airs and manners of a bohemian aristocrat, narcissistically preening and indulging himself. He was also, like any good romantic hero, making things hard for himself, stimulating himself to greater exertion, testing and proving himself, to himself as well as to others. In *Tancred* (the third novel in the trilogy that included *Coningsby* and *Sybil*), he said of one of his characters: "Fakredeen was fond of his debts; they were the source indeed of his only

real excitement, and he was grateful to them for their stirring powers." More revealing was Fakredeen's own confession: "I am actually so indolent, that if I did not remember in the morning that I
was ruined, I should never be able to distinguish myself."[11]

What made Disraeli's appearance and behavior even more egre-
gious was his Jewishness. He was not, in fact, Jewish in religion,
having been baptized, on the instructions of his father, at the age
of twelve, a few months before he would have qualified for the Bar
Mitzvah rite. But he prided himself on being of the Jewish "race"
(his word, not his enemies'). "All is race, not religion—remember
that," he told Lady Rothschild. In *Tancred* that dictum was
emended by the hero: "All is race; there is no other truth."[12] In his
biography of Lord Bentinck, he used the controversy over Jewish
emancipation to insert an entire chapter celebrating the history of
the Jews. And in his person he deliberately drew attention to his
Jewishness, exaggerating his racial features by having his black
hair set in elaborate ringlets (it was dyed in his later years by his
wife), and by an unconventional attire that made him seem even
more exotic and foreign. (The hero of *A Year at Hartlebury* was
hated by the local magnates because "he had not a snub nose, because he was suspiciously curious in his linen, because his coat was
not cut after their fashion.")[13] Even while he was assiduously
climbing the social ladder, he made not the least effort to dissociate himself from his Jewish friends and relations.

If Disraeli gave himself a more romantic and exalted ancestry
than he actually had, he also romanticized and exalted the Jewish
"race" as a whole.* Psychologists may explain all this as "compen-

---

*In a memoir prefacing the collected works of his father, Disraeli claimed de-
scent from a family that had been expelled from Spain in 1492 and had settled
in Venice, where they deliberately, he said, assumed the name Disraeli, a name
that had never been used before "in order that their race might be for ever

sation" or "overcompensation," testifying to his shame at having been a Jew and guilt at having ceased to be so. But on any straightforward reading of the evidence, there is not the slightest intimation of shame, guilt, or even unease. On the contrary, he seems genuinely to have believed in his superiority by virtue of his ancient and honorable lineage. There is a ring of authenticity in his comment: "Fancy calling a fellow an adventurer when his ancestors were probably on intimate terms with the Queen of Sheba."[15]

People did call him an adventurer, however, and worse. Anti-Semitism in Victorian England was not the virulent disease it has been at other times and places, but it was chronic and often enough exceedingly disagreeable. Until 1829 Jews, like Catholics and Dissenters, were excluded from public office and Parliament by the Test Acts. After the repeal of these acts and until the passage of the Jewish Disabilities Bill in 1858, Jews continued to be excluded if they refused to take the oath "on the true faith of a Christian." Religion, however, not "race," was the legal barrier, so that even before 1829, converted Jews (David Ricardo, most notably) sat in Parliament. And socially, in London literary circles, for example, the barrier was not as great as might be supposed. Disraeli's father was a Reform Jew who did not observe the dietary laws, but his children were circumcised and taught Hebrew, and he himself belonged to a synagogue. It was only when the synagogue required him, against his wishes, to serve as warden that he left the congregation and had his children, although not himself, baptized. Yet he

---

recognized." In fact, there is no evidence that the family had been Spanish, and the family name, "Israeli" before his father changed it to "D'Israeli," was a common Arabic name applied to Jews in Spain and the Levant. Even "Disraeli" was not unique. There was a Protestant family of that name in London during the eighteenth century; the last member, a Benjamin Disraeli, was a rich Dublin moneylender who had no connection with our Benjamin Disraeli.[14]

was a member of the Athenaeum and counted among his friends such literary lights as Byron, Robert Southey, Walter Scott, the editor John Lockhart, and the publisher John Murray.

Had Disraeli been content to be, like his father, "a quiet member of a tolerated minority," Blake says, he too could have enjoyed the amenities of the Athenaeum.[16] The fact is that he did not wish to be tolerated. He wanted to be accepted on his terms, as the most conspicuous member of the most "superior race," and not only for memberhip in the Athenaeum but as a candidate for the highest public office. When he appeared on the hustings in his customary attire, he brought upon himself the familiar gibes: "Shylock," "Old Clothes," "Judas," "Bring a bit of pork for the Jew."[17] Daniel O'Connell, the Irish Radical leader, responding to an attack by Disraeli, said that while there were "respectable Jews," Disraeli was not one of them: "He has just the qualities of the impenitent thief on the Cross"; this was his genealogy and this his "infamous distinction."[18] With less provocation, Carlyle railed against this "Pinchbeck-Hebrew, almost professedly a Son of Belial," a "cursed old Jew, not worth his weight in cold bacon."[19] Trollope disliked Disraeli for being a Tory as well as a Jew (and a novelist as well, who received larger advances for his novels than Trollope did for his). A moneylender in Trollope's *Barchester Towers* was called Sidonia (the name of the protagonist in Disraeli's trilogy), and an especially unprincipled Tory politician in his *The Prime Minister* and *Phineas Finn* was clearly patterned on Disraeli himself.

Historians and biographers are still debating the meaning and import of Disraeli's Jewishness. How authentic was his profession of pride in being of the Jewish "race," although of the Christian religion? Was he serious, in *Tancred*, in reconciling the two by declaring that Christianity was Judaism "completed," Judaism for the "multitude," and that Jews deserved to be venerated, not vilified, for making possible the Crucifixion and hence the salvation of humanity?[20] Did he really believe that his colleagues in Parliament, debating the Jewish emancipation bill that same year (1847), would accept his explanation that it was as a Christian that he supported the admission to Parliament of "those who are of the religion in the bosom of which my Lord and Saviour was born"?[21] And how did he, in spite of such eccentric views and impassioned rhetoric, to say nothing of the prevailing anti-Semitism, manage to climb that "greasy pole" toward success—in the Tory party, to boot, home of the landed aristocracy and country backwoodsmen?*

In his biography, Blake had been skeptical of the romantic, almost mystical nature of Disraeli's views about Judaism. Only after he himself, years later, visited Jerusalem for the first time and reread Disraeli's books and the letters written during his tour of the Near East in 1830–1831 did he begin to appreciate the profound effect that Jerusalem had had upon the young man and the lasting influence of that experience. A diary of Lord Stanley (son of the Earl of Derby, who was then leader of the Tories), published after his own book had appeared, confirmed Blake in his new estimate of Disraeli's beliefs and sentiments. Stanley recorded a conversation in 1851 in which Disraeli spoke movingly of the restoration of the Jews to their homeland and even worked out the means of financing it: the Rothschilds and other Jewish capitalists would provide

---

*A century later, another Tory prime minister, Harold Macmillan, recalled being told that shortly before Disraeli became the party leader, the sons of Lord Bentinck told their father that there was only one man who could lead the party, and he was a Jew. "But is he a country gentleman?" the duke asked. "No," they replied, "he is a fancy little Jew." "Only a country gentleman can lead the Tory Party," the duke said. "We'll make him one," the sons said, whereupon they bought the Hughenden estate for Disraeli. They did not, however, Macmillan observed, give it to him outright, retaining the ownership for eighteen years, at which time Lord Rothschild acquired the deeds and gave them to the Earl of Beaconsfield (as Disraeli then was).[22]

funds for the purchase of land, and the Turkish government, desperate for money, would agree to the sale. Such plans, Disraeli assured Stanley, were widespread among the Jews, and the man who
carried them out would be "the next Messiah, the true Saviour of his
people." Recalling this conversation, Stanley observed that Disraeli
seemed to be in utter earnestness and that this was the only time he
ever appeared to "show signs of any higher emotion." Reading that
passage, Blake had no doubt that Disraeli genuinely meant what he
said, that he did not follow up on that proposal only because nothing could realistically be done at that time, and that he would surely
have welcomed the Balfour Declaration, more than half a century
later, pledging support for a Jewish homeland in Palestine.[23]

If one may now take more seriously Disraeli's ideas about the "Hebrew race," perhaps it is also time to take more seriously his ideas
about society and politics. It is easy to mock the "Young England"
party with which Disraeli identified himself—which, indeed, he
invented. That "party" consisted of all of four young men, newly
elected to Parliament, whose alliance, such as it was, lasted for exactly two sessions in 1843 and 1844. But even as that abortive enterprise disintegrated, the ideas behind it were circulated and
popularized, largely by means of Disraeli's novels. (Contrary to his
father's advice, the "Fictionist," it would seem, assorted well with
the "Politician," indeed turned out to be an asset rather than a lia-
bility.) *Coningsby*, published in May 1844, may be the first English
political novel. It also had the distinction of being satirized by
Dickens almost as soon as it appeared. "The Chimes" features a
member of Parliament, a self-styled "Poor Man's Friend and Father," who preaches the "Dignity of Labour" and whose paternalistic exertions on behalf of the poor consist of playing skittles with
them and drinking their health on New Year's Day. His wife
teaches "pinking and eyelet-holding" to the men and boys of the
village and composes a ditty for them to sing while they work.

Oh let us love our occupations,
Bless the squire and his relations,
Live upon our daily rations,
And always know our proper stations.[24]

There was much in *Coningsby* for Dickens to parody (he was not, in any case, well disposed to Disraeli) but also much that even he must have found congenial. Taper and Tadpole, Disraeli's version of Tweedledum and Tweedledee, who resolved the affairs of state at dinner parties and settled the vexing question of the malt tax while sipping claret, could have come straight out of Dickens's own novels, together with the Poor Law commissioners' rules and sub-commissioners' reports epitomizing the utilitarianism that was as distasteful to Dickens as to Disraeli. He would also have appreciated the exchange between Taper and Tadpole:

> "Hush!" said Mr. Tadpole. "The time has gone by for Tory governments; what the country requires is a sound Conservative government."
>
> "A sound Conservative government," said Taper, musingly. "I understand: Tory men and Whig measures."[25]*

---

*This was not the first recorded usage of "Conservative" as a party label. As early as 1830 the Tory politician and writer J. Wilson Croker reported that "Conservative" was replacing the venerable term "Tory." Two years later the Irish leader Daniel O'Connell spoke of the Reform Bill as "Conservative"—"that is the fashionable term, the new fangled phrase now used in polite society to designate the Tory ascendancy." Macaulay, that same year, extended the term to the French revolutionary leader Mirabeau, who would have died, "to use the new cant word, a decided 'Conservative.'" By 1847, after Peel had succeeded in repealing the Corn Laws, his faction of the party—representing, Monypenny and Buckle observe, that contradiction in terms, a "middle-class Toryism"—was generally identified as Conservative. But Disraeli's definition of conservatism, "Tory men and Whig measures," is still the most memorable.[26]

Coningsby represented the political side of the Young England movement—Toryism, in contrast to Peelite conservatism. *Sybil*, published the following year, represented the social side. It was there that Disraeli elaborated upon the "condition-of-the-people-question," a phrase Carlyle had coined but that Disraeli took for his own and made the heart of his cause.[27] The phrase that Disraeli could take credit for popularizing (although not inventing) was "the two nations," which appears as the subtitle of *Sybil* and again in the much-quoted dialogue between Egremont, the good aristocrat (one is tempted to capitalize these identifications, as in a morality play) and the "stranger," Stephen Morley, an Owenite.

> "Say what you like [Egremont observes], our Queen reigns over the greatest nation that ever existed."
>
> "Which nation?" asked the younger stranger, "for she reigns over two."
>
> The stranger paused; Egremont was silent, but looked inquiringly.
>
> "Yes," resumed the younger stranger after a moment's interval. "Two nations; between whom there is no intercourse and no sympathy; who are as ignorant of each other's habits, thoughts, and feelings, as if they were dwellers in different zones, or inhabitants of different planets; who are formed by different breeding, are fed by different food, are ordered by different manners, and are not governed by the same laws."
>
> "You speak of—" said Egremont, hesitatingly.
>
> "THE RICH AND THE POOR."[28]*

*In his *Memoir on Pauperism*, in 1835, Tocqueville spoke of the poor law as breaking the link between "two rival nations," the rich and the poor. Half a dozen years later, William Channing, the American Unitarian minister, wrote (in an uncanny foretaste of Disraeli): "In most large cities there may be said to be two nations, understanding as little of one another, having as litle intercourse, as if they lived in different lands."[29]

In fact, that dichotomy, in that sharp, uncompromising form, is not borne out in the novel itself. It is Stephen Morley, the Chartist radical, speaking, not Disraeli, the Tory radical. And not Disraeli the novelist, for it is precisely the point of the novel that within both nations, and particularly within the nation of the poor, there are many subcategories: rural and industrial workers, hand-loom weavers, coal miners, ironmongers—each with its distinctive characteristics, manners, attitudes, speech. Moreover, each group takes a jaundiced view of the others. Morley may think of the poor as a nation united, but the poor themselves do not. The miners regard the ironmongers as "divils carnal," "no less than heathens," and warn Morley against venturing into their quarters, known as "Hell-house Yard."[30] Nor are these groups impoverished in the same degree or to the same effect. The novel is by no means a tract against factories or industrialism. On the contrary, the conditions of the rural poor are said to be far worse than those of the factory workers, and those of the handloom weavers far worse than those working in the cotton mills. And some factory workers (like Sybil's father) are fortunate enough to work in a model factory in a model town, where they are well paid and well housed, entertained and instructed, rather than in the country where, as one of them says, the laborers are "obliged to burn ricks to pass the time."[31]

Even the degenerate ironmongers are in that state not because of poverty; they are, in fact, skilled workers whose products, we are told, are sought after throughout England and even Europe. Yet they live in a state of nature, not so much human beings as "animals, unconscious, their minds a blank, and their worst actions only the impulse of a gross or savage instinct." They have no church or magistrate, no vestry or school, no public building or institution of any kind—not even a factory, for their work is carried on by master workmen in their own houses, each master having tyrannical and utterly brutal power over his apprentices.[32]

The dramatic account of this community, so degraded as to be "unconscious of their degradation," is followed by a chapter in which Sybil's father, Walter Gerard, an ardent Chartist, declaims upon "the degradation of the people":

> There are great bodies of the working classes of this country nearer the condition of brutes than they have been at any time since the Conquest. Indeed, I see nothing to distinguish them from brutes, except that their morals are inferior. Incest and infanticide are as common among them as among the lower animals.[33]

Gerard thinks he is speaking of the "working classes," but in the novel only the "queer set" of ironmongers is in that degrading condition. Gerard, it is evident, knows nothing about them, or, indeed, about most workers. He himself is employed in the model factory, where, his daughter is pleased to report, "he labours among the woods and waters" instead of being "cooped up in a hot factory in a smoky street."[34]

Sybil is surely a "social novel" but not a tract against industrialism, still less a tract for socialism.* What Sybil, the romantic idealist, learns by the end of the book is that "the characters were more var-

---

Coningsby, even more than *Sybil*, displays a highly romanticized view of industrialism. Both novels have cotton mills that are model factories in model towns. Visiting the mill in Manchester, Coningsby rhapsodizes about the miracle of the machine:

> A machine is a slave that neither brings nor bears degradation; it is a being endowed with the greatest degree of energy, and acting under the greatest degree of excitement, yet free at the same time from all passion and emotion. It is, therefore, not only a slave but a supernatural slave. And why should one say that the machine does not live? . . . Does not the spindle sing like a merry girl at her work, and the steam-engine roar in jolly chorus, like a strong artisan handling his lusty tools, and gaining a fair day's wages for a fair day's toil?[35]

ious, the motives more mixed, the classes more blended, the elements of each more subtle and diversified, than she had imagined."[36] And the hero, who is to be her husband, is not a worker, not even the model factory owner, but the model aristocrat—Mr. Egremont, as he is early in the novel, the Earl of Egremont toward the end when he comes into his estate (an estate, the gossiping ladies estimate, equaled by only three peers in the kingdom). It is he who carries the moral burden of the book, preaching the social gospel as affirmed by the author himself: "Power has only one duty—to secure the welfare of the PEOPLE."[37] Egremont finally disabuses Sybil of her often repeated conviction that the gulf between the nations is "impassable," and that the only solution is a transfer of political power to the people.[38] The people, he tells her, are not the natural repositories of power. A natural aristocracy is that, and a new generation of aristocrats is arising which has the mind and heart to assume that responsibility. "They are the natural leaders of the people, Sybil; believe me they are the only ones." And theirs is the true principle of equality: an equality to be achieved "not by levelling the Few, but by elevating the Many."[39]

In *Sybil*, the two-nations problem is resolved with the marriage of Sybil and Egremont, the Radical and the Tory mating and assuming the marital name of Tory Democrat. That fictional marriage was an almost literal rendition of the political marriage that Disraeli had sought from his earliest days in public life. In 1832, even before his first venture into electoral politics, he published (anonymously) a two-hundred-page pamphlet attacking the foreign policy of the Whigs as a form of "Gallomania," in the course of which he announced, "I am neither Whig nor Tory. My politics are described by one word, and that word is England."[40] The following year, in another pamphlet supporting his candidacy (the third of his failed attempts to get a seat), he hit upon another name for his party. In a passage that might have been part of a dialogue between Sybil and Egremont, Disraeli explained: "A Tory and a Radical, I understand; a Whig—a democratic aristocrat, I cannot comprehend." The true aristocratic principle could be restored only if the Tories saw it their duty to "coalesce with the Radicals, and permit both nicknames to merge in the common, the intelligible, and the dignified title of a National Party."[41]

Again and again, as Disraeli sought one seat or another, that ideal dominated his speeches and writings—his *Vindication of the English Constitution*, for example, in 1835, where he attacked the Whigs for violating the traditions and institutions of the English polity, and asserted the Tory party as the national and democratic party; or a pamphlet the same year supporting his candidacy in the name of the true Tory party.

> I still am of opinion that the Tory party is the real democratic party of this country. I hold one of the first principles of Toryism to be that Government is instituted for the welfare of the many. This is why the Tories maintain national institutions, the objects of which are the protection, the maintenance, the moral, civil, and religious education of the great mass of the English people: institutions which whether they assume the form of churches, or universities, or societies of men to protect the helpless and to support the needy, to execute justice and to maintain truth, alike originated, and alike flourish for the advantage and happiness of the multitude. I deny that the Tories have ever opposed the genuine democratic or national spirit of the country; on the contrary they have always headed it.[42]

It is often said that Disraeli's opposition to Robert Peel, as expressed in Parliament in 1843–1844 and, more dramatically, in *Coningsby* and *Sybil*, had its origin in his failure to receive a cabinet post in Peel's government in 1841.[43] In fact, the grounds of that opposition go back to his earliest ventures in public life before he was even seated in Parliament, let alone could aspire to a cabinet post. The "National Party," the true Tory party that he made so much of in those early years, was the very antithesis of the "Conservative government" (Peel's government, obviously) defined so pithily by Taper: "Tory men and Whig measures." In this sense, Disraeli remained a Tory, even after the party officially became the Conservative party.

It was also in those early years that Disraeli anticipated one of the most celebrated coups of his later career: "dishing the Whigs," when he sponsored the Reform Act of 1867 that enfranchised the urban working classes. In 1835 he had taken pride in the Tories' support of a £50 tenancy clause increasing the electorate—"*a most democratic measure*," he emphasized, "that has eminently tended to the salvation of the State." His Whig opponent, he noted, was very annoyed that a Tory should have pledged himself to promote the cause of Reform. "Why," Disraeli protested, "are the Whigs to have all the Reform to themselves!"[44]

Whether in 1835 or 1867, the tactic of preempting the cause of reform was not the Machiavellian maneuver it has been made out to be. Disraeli never thought of the Whigs (or, later, the Liberals) as the natural party of reform—of political reform, still less of social reform—because he regarded the Tory party, his kind of Tory party, as the "natural" leaders of the people. And because he never subscribed to the "do-nothing" doctrine of laissez-faire liberalism, he had no difficulty supporting whatever social reforms he believed to be in the interests of the people. Nor did he have any difficulty in giving the largest possible extension to the term "people"—a word, he said, that was vastly different from "constituency" or "electorate." The people were the whole of the nation, whether represented in Parliament or not, and it was their happiness that was the purpose of government. In 1839, at the height of the Chartist movement, he made a speech in Parliament anticipating Egremont's argument with Sybil. "I am not ashamed to say," he declared (to the consternation of most of his party), "however much I disapprove of the Charter, I sympathize with the Chartists." He disapproved, that is, of the idea that the remedy for the social problem (the condition-of-the-people problem) lay in political reform, but sympathized with the problem itself and the need for social reforms.[45] He was also one of the few in Parliament to oppose the severe punitive measures taken against the Chartists.

Later, when he "dished the Whigs" by passing the Reform Act of 1867, he did so not because he was converted to the cause of political equality but because he was neutral or indifferent on the subject of political representation. Secure in his faith in a "national party," he could contemplate with equanimity any change in the franchise requirement. (The borough franchise was based upon the annual value of the premises occupied by the householder.) While Gladstone was calculating the exact effect any proposed change would have on the size and nature of the electorate, Disraeli was cavalierly (or so it seemed to Gladstone) prepared to accept any measure of reform. Confronted with a multitude of schemes to fix the franchise at "£8, £7, £6, and all sorts of pounds," Disraeli decided that there was no "sound resting-place" other than household suffrage (enfranchising all tax-paying residents in the boroughs).[46]

Gladstone was furious and also uncomprehending. A "straightforward" bill from the Conservatives, he had confided to a colleague, would be "an £8 franchise without tricks," which he could then counter with the magnanimous offer of £7. But the "Ethiopian," he was afraid, would be as "tortuous" now as he always was, obliging Gladstone to be tortuous in return by proposing still more liberal measures.[47] This was in fact what happened, but Gladstone never understood quite why it happened. He was defeated not by the wily "Ethiopian" but by his own failure of imagination, compounded by a failure of nerve. He knew only how to play the game of pounds and pence, hoping to arrive at a figure that would represent a safe electorate (safe, that is, for the Liberals). At one point in the debate, his complicated calculations and repeated references to "the Rule of Three Sum" moved the House to laughter, upon which he feebly retorted that he was pleased his "studies in arithmetic prove so amusing."[48] Disraeli had no need for such arithmetic calculations because he was confident in the natural disposition of the working classes and in the national character of his own party. As a result, he could take credit for the most radical reform of the century: a doubling of the electorate resulting in the enfranchisement of most of the urban working classes. The *Times*, in its obituary many years later, captured this aspect of Disraeli in the famous metaphor: "In the inarticulate mass of the English populace, he discerned the Conservative working-man as the sculptor perceives the angel imprisoned in a block of marble."[49]

When a prominent radical praised Disraeli, in 1840, for coming to the defense of the Chartists, Disraeli replied that "a union between the Conservative party and the Radical masses offers the only means by which we can preserve the Empire. Their interests are identical; united they form the nation."[50] The nation and the empire—a united nation at home and a strong nation abroad—this too had been the theme of his earliest political addresses, as it also was of his ministries. Soon after the passage of the Reform Act of 1867, Disraeli attended a Conservative banquet in Edinburgh. His host, who had not met him before, was fascinated by the "potent wizard," with olive complexion and coal-black eyes, unlike any man he had ever seen. Although he did not look English, his host had no doubt of his Englishness. "England is the Israel of his imagination, and he will be the Imperial Minister before he dies—if he get the chance."[51] And he did get the chance—only briefly in 1868, succeeding Derby as prime minister for the few months before the election turned the Conservatives out of office, and again, for an eventful six years starting in 1874.[*]

Disraeli's biographers, Monypenny and Buckle, distinguish between Disraeli, the promoter of "Tory Democracy," and Lord Beaconsfield (as he later became), "the imperial and European statesman."[53] But the distinction, they quickly point out, was not quite so stark. Long before he was raised to the peerage (in August 1876), indeed, long before he was in Parliament, he had defended the "empire" as a natural appendage of the "nation." In 1833, in an early unsuccessful bid for a seat, he appealed for a Tory-Radical alliance under the name of the "National Party" that would undertake "to maintain the glory of the Empire and to secure the happiness of the People." The following year, in *A Year at Hartlebury*, the hero castigates the Whigs as an "anti-national" party and predicts that their victory will lead to the "dismemberment of the Empire."[54] Two decades later, when Palmerston proposed to turn over the Ionian Islands to Greece, Disraeli vigorously protested, rebuking those "professors and rhetoricians" who would always find reason for any action. "But you are not going, I hope," he told Parliament, "to leave the destinies of the British Empire to prigs and pedants. A country, and especially a maritime country, must get

---

[*]One is reminded yet again of the cardinal principle of politics: No good deed goes unpunished. Just as Churchill was turned out of office after his spectacular role in a victorious war, so Disraeli was turned out in 1868 after bringing the new electorate into power, and again in 1880, after enacting an ambitious policy of social reform. Another more trivial reminder of Churchill: a speech in Manchester in April 1876, when Disraeli, then sixty-eight years old and not in the best of health, spoke for three and a quarter hours, sustained, one of the organizers of the event recalled, by two bottles of white brandy (white, so as to blend with the water he took with it).[52]

possession of the strong places of the world if it wishes to contribute to its power."[55]

That theme emerged more sharply in his famous Crystal Palace speech in 1872, when he enunciated yet again what he took to be the three fundamental principles of the Tory party: maintaining English institutions, elevating the condition of the people, and upholding the empire. Under the first principle, he called attention to the respect due to the institution of the monarchy in general and to the person of the queen in particular. The second, on the condition of the people, evoked a defense of the social reforms he had proposed in Parliament—reforms involving housing, sanitation, factory conditions, food, and the water supply—which had been derided by the Liberals as a "policy of sewage." These measures, Disraeli objected, were for the people nothing less than a matter of life and death; indeed, more than life and death, for they all had "moral consequences" that were no less considerable than their physical consequences.[56]

It was the third point, however, that attracted most attention—the defense of the empire against the Liberals whose foreign policy, Disraeli said, was a subtle yet energetic and sustained effort to bring about "the disintegration of the Empire of England." Liberals had shown, "with mathematical demonstration," just how much money was lost on the colonies, how expensive India, that "jewel in the Crown of England," had been, and how desirable it would be to rid England of that "incubus." Their policy of self-government for the colonies was designed to attain that end. Not, Disraeli quickly added, that he himself objected to self-government. How else could distant colonies be administered save by self-government? But this should have been part of a larger policy of "imperial consolidation," defining the responsibilities as well as the securities of both the people of England and of the colonies. That larger perspective, however, was denied to leaders who looked upon the colonies, and upon India especially, as a burden, "viewing everything in a financial aspect, and totally passing by those moral and political considerations which make nations great, and by the influence of which alone men are distinguished from animals."[57]*

Disraeli's administration of 1874–1880 reflected the spirit of that speech. The social reforms the Liberals had characterized as "sewage" were passed; the queen was named (over bitter opposition) empress of India; the government purchased the shares giving England control of the Suez Canal; the island of Cyprus was peaceably acquired; and the much disputed "Eastern Question" was resolved to Disraeli's satisfaction. The last was a great personal as well as political coup for him. The issue flared up in 1876 when Gladstone published an enormously successful pamphlet—40,000 copies were sold within a week, and 200,000 by the end of the month—denouncing the massacre by the Turks of thousands of Bulgarians following the outbreak of a widespread revolt; the deaths were reported to range from 10,000 to 25,000. Religious as well as humanitarian passions were inflamed, and the affair became a major international event when Russia threatened to invade Turkey (and finally did so) under the pretext of a crusade on behalf of oppressed Balkan Christians. In England the "atrocitarians," who believed the worst of the Turks, were opposed by the "jingoists," who believed the worst of the Russians and were prepared to go to war against them if necessary. (The term "jingo" was popularized in a music-hall ditty at this time.)

Disraeli had no illusions about the Turks; during his grand tour almost half a century earlier, he had written home flippantly about

---

*It is interesting that contemporaries, on both sides of the issue, thought that the empire, and India in particular, was economically disadvantageous to England. Disraeli himself never tried to dispute this and rested his own case entirely on moral and political grounds.

dining with the bey in Albania, who was "daily decapitating half the province."[58] But he had still fewer illusions about Russia, either about her capacity for atrocities or her designs on Constantinople. While Gladstone whipped up a frenzy of anti-Turkish, pro-Russian sentiment (and anti-Semitic as well, accusing Disraeli of being indifferent to the sufferings of Christians because of his "crypto Judaism" and "race antipathy"),[59] Disraeli countered by insisting that however deplorable the atrocities, British policy must be based on British national interests. And those interests dictated that Russia be prevented at all costs from realizing her imperial dream of gaining control of the Dardanelles and the Mediterranean.

Disraeli had not only to convince the country of its national interests; he had to convince his own Foreign Office and cabinet. At the height of the crisis he wrote to the queen, who was his staunchest supporter: "This morning a torturing hour with Lord Derby [the foreign secretary] who was for doing nothing and this afternoon with Lord Salisbury [secretary of state for India] who evidently is thinking more of raising the Cross on the cupola of St. Sophia than of the power of England."[60] In fact, as Disraeli discovered, Derby was not quite for "doing nothing"; he was deliberately leaking cabinet secrets to the Russian ambassador in London. (Salisbury later proved to be a loyal and able foreign secretary.) But it was Disraeli who was the architect of foreign policy and, in 1878, at the age of seventy-three, the leading figure at the Congress of Berlin. By being bold and determined, threatening to break up the Congress and even declare war, he succeeded in depriving Russia of the crucial gains she had achieved after her victory over Turkey and in bringing about a settlement of the crisis that was more to the liking of the European powers than of either Turkey or Russia. He returned home from Berlin a conquering hero.

Historians may speculate about what might have happened had Gladstone presided over Britain at that particular moment and Russia been permitted to expand, possibly to Constantinople. They may also question the principles that guided Disraeli in this instance and in foreign and imperial affairs in general. About some matters, however, there is little doubt. His solicitude for the empire was not motivated by economic gain for England; he apparently believed the argument of the little Englanders (in any case, he never tried to rebut it) that the empire was a net cost to England rather than a gain. Nor did his idea of empire entail extensive or aggressive aggrandizement; indeed, he generally counseled against annexation. Nor did he give evidence of anything like the "white man's burden" ethic used later to justify imperialism. What did motivate him was a passionate concern for Britain's strength, prestige, and influence, and a determination to pursue a vigorous foreign policy to that end. Some historians have labeled him the "progenitor of the New Imperialism," an imperialism content to preside benignly over a "peculiar" dominion, as Disraeli put it, scattered around the world, inhabited by persons of different races, religions, laws, manners, and customs. It was this "peculiar" empire, respectful of the diversity of its separate parts, that lay behind Disraeli's proud assertion: "England has achieved the union of those two qualities for which a Roman Emperor was deified: '*Imperium et Libertas.*'"[61]

After the conclusion of the Congress of Berlin, Bismarck paid tribute to Disraeli: "*Der alte Jude, das ist der Mann.*"[62] It is a haunting observation. Historians are still fascinated by the image of *der alte Jude* climbing that "greasy pole" to power, and intrigued by the country and the party that enabled him to do so. No less interesting are the ideas he took with him as he reached that eminence, ideas that make him distinctive in British history. The last word may lie with Disraeli himself, a young Disraeli who noted in his diary in 1833: "The Utilitarians in Politics are like the Unitarians

in Religion. Both omit Imagination in their systems, and Imagination governs Mankind."[63]

Disraeli's political career, as much as his literary career (and
his personal life, for that matter), was a triumph of imagination.
It is a tribute to the boldness and complexity of that imagination
that, more than a century later, biographers still debate the meaning of his ideas and historians argue about his political bequest
and succession.

John Stuart Mill
The Other Mill

It may be useful to recall a time, not so long ago, when great philosophers were thought to be immune to the vagaries of biography and history, when their ideas were presumed to be of universal and eternal validity, sufficient unto themselves, independent of race, color, class, gender, nationality, or personality. It was also presumed that those ideas constituted a coherent, integral whole; if the reader or critic found them otherwise, it could only be because of insufficient study or understanding. Not all philosophers, to be sure, could fulfill those conditions as perfectly as Kant did. The story is told about Kant that the great event in his life was a nonevent. Upon the urging of friends, he agreed, toward the end of his life, to leave Koenigsberg for the first time and visit Berlin; he actually packed and set out in the coach, only to return after a few miles. That seems to epitomize the pure philosopher, whose personal life provides so little material for the biographer that the magisterial book about him, Ernst Cassirer's *Kant's Life and Thought*, might have been titled *Kant's Life* as *Thought*.

The eminent thinkers in Victorian England were of another breed. John Stuart Mill, Thomas Carlyle, Matthew Arnold, Cardinal Newman, Lord Acton, all went through searing personal experiences. And all of them took those experiences not only to heart, as the saying goes, but to mind, causing them to consider, and often reconsider, the largest questions of philosophy, society, politics, and religion. Like the *philosophes* in France a century before, they were eminent intellectuals rather than eminent philosophers. And as the *philosophes* put their indelible mark on the French Enlightenment, so these intellectuals gave Victorian England its unique character and vitality.

John Stuart Mill was the most eminent of these eminent intellectuals. The drama of his life—and of his mind—centers on two figures: his father and his wife. "I was born in London," his *Autobiography* opens (after a paragraph justifying the writing of an autobiography), "on the 20th of May, 1806, and was the eldest son of James Mill, the author of the *History of British India*."[1] This introduction is entirely fitting for an autobiography in which the father plays a major part and the mother is not so much as mentioned—a matter of some embarrassment to latter-day feminists, who claim Mill for one of their own. The few sentences in the original draft about his mother (which were later expurgated by his wife) are dismissive, almost contemptuous, describing her as a drudge who worked tirelessly for her family but was incapable of loving them or of being loved by them. And because she failed to provide an atmosphere of tenderness and affection, her son believed, her husband was also deprived of those qualities. But it was not only affection that was lacking in that "ill assorted marriage." It was intellect as well, for she brought to it none of "the inducements of kindred intellect, tastes, or pursuits" that would have made more agreeable her husband's life—or, presumably, her son's.[2]

If Mill's mother was incapable of providing those intellectual "inducements," his father more than made up for it. It was he who personally supervised the young Mill's awesome education: Greek at the age of three, Plato (in Greek, of course) at seven, Latin (belatedly) at eight, and so on; the list of books read by the youth comprises something like a bibliography of Western literature. But this was a classical education with a difference, for it was supplemented by an initiation into the most modern of modern philosophies, utilitarianism. It was this that provoked the "crisis in my mental history" recorded so dramatically by Mill—the profound depression that came upon him when he discovered that this rigorously analytic, rationalistic, utilitarian mode of thought was destructive of feeling, sentiment, and imagination, and that the course of life for which he was being prepared, as a thinker and reformer of the Benthamite school, was meaningless and heartless.

One of the most moving moments in the *Autobiography* is Mill's account of the "ray of light" that began to dispel his deep depression. He was reading a memoir by the French *philosophe* Jean-François Marmontel when he came upon a passage recounting the death of the father and the boy's realization that he would now take his father's place in the family. Suddenly Mill was moved to tears, and his "burden grew lighter." It is curious that, even in a pre-Freudian era, Mill could have related this episode with no apparent perception of what it signified about himself and his own father, pleased only with the realization that he could, after all, be moved to tears, that all feeling was not dead in him, that he was not "a stock [sic] or a stone."[3]

That epiphany was reinforced in the next few years by his reading of the romantic poets Wordsworth, Coleridge, and Shelley, and by such dissident spirits as Carlyle, Comte, and the Saint-Simonians. Together they provided a powerful antidote to utilitarianism, and their influence was reflected, in one fashion or another, in Mill's early essays. Published in the 1830s and '40s, they remain among the most memorable of his writings. And not only memorable in themselves, expressing ideas about culture and society, politics and history, that resonate today almost as powerfully as they did at the time, but also as a counterpoint to the best known of Mill's works, *On Liberty*.

As Mill's father monopolized his youth, so Harriet Taylor monopolized his mature life—personally, certainly, and to a remarkable extent intellectually as well.* Mill met her when he was not quite twenty-five (there is no intimation that he was ever interested in any other woman, before or afterward), and she was twenty-three, married and the mother of two sons (a daughter was to be born the following year). Their "affair," if it can be called that—and some of their friends did call it that—began almost immediately and went on for almost two decades while she remained married to John Taylor. They made no secret of their love for each other but insisted that it was of a nonsexual or nonsensual nature. To a German friend, Harriet described herself as a *Seelenfreundin*, and when Mill was writing his *Autobiography*, she advised him to describe their premarital relationship as one of "strong affection, intimacy of friendship, and no impropriety." It would provide an "edifying picture," she added, for "those poor wretches who cannot conceive friendship but in sex—nor believe that expediency and the consideration for feelings of others can conquer sensuality."[4] According to one biographer, they did "the honorable thing . . . at great personal sacrifice" by not sleeping with each other[5]—and at some sacrifice to Harriet's husband, one might add, because that "honorable thing" required that she not sleep with him either. John Taylor compliantly went to his club so that she and Mill could dine together, and he remained home while they weekended at her coun-

*Like most biographers of Mill, I sometimes first-name Harriet (while surnaming Mill), for reasons of convenience, not disrespect. Harriet was Harriet Taylor long before she was Harriet Mill, and it would be awkward to alternate between those surnames depending upon the period being discussed (or overlapping periods, when she was first Mrs. Taylor and then Mrs. Mill).

try home or traveled abroad, sometimes, but not always, chaper-
oned by her children. After he died in 1849, they waited almost
two years before marrying, out of respect for the proprieties.*

Whether they continued to be celibate after marriage is still an
open question. If they did so, they could summon up the loftiest
reasons in their favor. Late in life, provoked by a passage in a book
justifying prostitution, Mill wrote a letter to his friend Lord Amberley, explaining that a civilization dominated by men had had
the unfortunate effect of greatly exaggerating "the force of the natural passions." But that would soon change, he assured him—
indeed, was already beginning to change, thanks to women.

> I think it most probable that this particular passion will become
> with men, as it is already with a large number of women, com-
> pletely under the control of the reason. It has become so with
> women because its becoming so has been the condition upon
> which women hoped to obtain the strongest love and admiration
> of men. The gratification of this passion in its highest form,
> therefore, has been, with women, conditional upon their restrain-
> ing it in its lowest. . . . Men are by nature capable of as thorough
> a control over these passions as women are.[7]†

*Mill's sense of propriety was such that a year after their marriage, he wrote a
formal letter to his wife suggesting that they go though another ceremony, this
time in church, to dispel any question of its legality. He was worried that his
signature in the marriage register had "an unusual appearance" because he had
signed it in his usual manner with his initials and had then squeezed in his full
name. Another ceremony, he said, would ensure that there be no doubt, "either
to their own or to any other minds," of the legality of their marriage. (There is
no record of such an additional ceremony.)[6]

†In his *Autobiography*, Mill attributed the same opinion to his father, who anticipated, "as one of the beneficial effects of increased freedom, that the imagination would no longer dwell upon the physical relation and its adjuncts." Such
sensuality, the elder Mill believed, was "a perversion of the imagination and feelings . . . one of the deepest seated and most pervading evils in the human mind."[8]

Whether Mill and his wife (perhaps under her influence, as this passage would suggest) did exercise this kind of "control" is not known. What is known is that they chose to live if not an ascetic life, at least a thoroughly reclusive one, alienated from his family and deliberately separating themselves from their old friends. It was a brief marriage. Harriet died seven years later, in 1858, at Avignon, where they happened to be at the time. Mill bought a house overlooking the cemetery where she was buried, furnished it with the contents of the room in which she died, and spent part of every year there for the rest of his life. In London, however, he resumed an active personal and public life, reconciling himself with the surviving members of his family, rekindling old friendships, giving and attending dinner parties, writing and publishing voluminously, and serving briefly in Parliament. In 1851 he had refused the offer of a seat; in 1865 he accepted it and held it until the general election three years later, when he stood again but failed to be returned. His stepdaughter Helen presided over his household and became the executor of his estate, supervising and sometimes editing his posthumously published work.

Even the most sympathetic biographer may be embarrassed by Mill's many effusive tributes to Harriet in his *Autobiography* (drafts of which she read and, in effect, vetted) and in the dedications to his books. The extravagance of the dedication in *On Liberty* may be attributed to the fact that it was published early in 1859, only a few months after her death.

> To the beloved and deplored memory of her who was the inspirer, and in part the author, of all that is best in my writings—the friend and wife whose exalted sense of truth and right was my strongest incitement, and whose approbation was my chief reward—I dedicate this volume. Like all that I have written for many years, it belongs as much to her as to me; but the work as

it stands has had, in a very insufficient degree, the inestimable advantage of her revision; some of the most important portions having been reserved for a more careful reexamination, which they are now never destined to receive. Were I but capable of interpreting to the world one half the great thoughts and noble feelings which are buried in her grave, I should be the medium of a greater benefit to it, than is ever likely to arise from anything I can write, unprompted and unassisted by her all but unrivalled wisdom.[9]

This was more than the pious sentiments of a grieving husband, for it was repeated, even more vigorously, in a revision of his *Autobiography* written almost a decade later. "The 'Liberty' was more directly and literally our joint production than anything else which bears my name, for there was not a sentence of it that was not several times gone through by us together. . . . The whole mode of thinking of which the book was the expression, was emphatically hers."[10]*

The *Autobiography* was also remarkably prescient about the importance of *On Liberty* for later generations. "The 'Liberty'," Mill wrote, "is likely to survive longer than anything else that I have written (with the possible exception of the 'Logic'), because the conjunction of her mind with mine has rendered it a kind of philosophic text-book of a single truth . . .: the importance, to man and society, of a large variety in types of character, and of giving full freedom to human nature to expand itself in innumerable and con-

---

*Mill's assertion of Harriet Taylor's influence on *On Liberty* gains credibility from one of the few specimens of her writings that have survived. A short unpublished essay by her (about two thousand words), probably written in 1832, strikingly anticipates some of the main themes of *On Liberty:* conformity and society as enemies to individuality, eccentricity as a valuable expression of individuality, the absolute importance of truth and at the same time the relativity of truth.[11]

flicting directions."[12] *On Liberty* has indeed survived longer than Mill's other writings (not excepting the *Logic*)—has survived longer, in fact, than any other work by any other eminent Victorian, apart from Darwin's *Origin of Species* (published, as it happened, the same year).

The introductory chapter of the book sets the scene for that "single truth." In all previous periods, we are told, the struggle between liberty and authority was a struggle between subjects and tyrannical rulers, the people and an oppressive government. The modern problem of liberty emerges when the people are the government, when the majority exercises its tyranny not only over a minority but over all individuals, and does so even more compellingly in society than in government. "Society is itself the tyrant—society collectively over the separate individuals who compose it." That "social tyranny" is more formidable than political oppression because "it leaves fewer means of escape, penetrating much more deeply into the details of life, and enslaving the soul itself."[13]

It is this uniquely modern situation that calls for the "one very simple principle" of liberty.

> The object of this essay is to assert one very simple principle, as entitled to govern absolutely the dealings of society with the individual in the way of compulsion and control, whether the means used be physical force in the form of legal penalties or the moral coercion of public opinion. That principle is that the sole end for which mankind are warranted, individually or collectively, in interfering with the liberty of action of any of their number is self-protection.[14]

The rest of the passage reaffirms the absoluteness and singleness of this principle (the recurrent words are "absolute," "only," "own"), concluding with the message: "Over himself, over his own body and mind, the individual is sovereign."[15] This principle is applied in the following chapters on the freedom of thought and discussion, the primary importance of individuality, and the limits on society's authority over individuals.

This is the Mill of *On Liberty*—the historic Mill, so to speak, the Mill who has come down to us as the great exponent of the principle of liberty. But there is another Mill, less familiar today, a liberal Mill who had a more subtle and complicated view of liberty. For this Mill, the freedom of thought and discussion is neither an end in itself nor the sole means to the higher end of truth; individuality is neither a good in itself nor the means to achieve the higher goods of human beings; and society is not the natural enemy of the individual.

The Other Mill antedated and postdated the Mill of *On Liberty*. Thirty years earlier the young Mill (he was all of twenty-three) wrote a letter that reads today as if it were an anticipation and refutation in advance of the main assumptions and postulates of *On Liberty*. To a French friend who was much taken with the positivist philosophy of Auguste Comte, Mill argued that that philosophy, professing to make a science of politics, was fundamentally flawed because it treated politics as if it were an exercise in mathematics, a set of propositions that were true or false in the same way that mathematical propositions were true or false. The most common errors in politics, however, came not from premises that were untrue but rather from ignoring other truths that limited or qualified those premises. The fallacy was in "insisting upon only seeing one thing when there are many, or seeing a thing only on one side, only in one point of view when there are many others equally essential to a just estimate of it." Government did not exist for the purpose of promoting "some one end." Nor was society directed to "one single end." "Men do not come into the world to fulfil one single end, and there is no single end which if fulfilled even in the most complete manner would make them happy."[16]

If this repeated, almost obsessive, assault upon the idea of a single end, or single truth, struck at the heart of the thesis he was to propound in *On Liberty*, a series of articles less than two years later, "The Spirit of the Age," delivered the fatal blows. Here another basic tenet of *On Liberty* was at issue—nothing less than the value of free discussion. Mill now described his own age as in a "transitional" state, a time of "intellectual anarchy," when old institutions and doctrines had fallen into disrepute and new ones lacked the authority to replace them. Such an age is marked by the diffusion of superficial knowledge rather than the acquisition of sound knowledge. Men reason more, but not better; they have more opinions but less confidence in those opinions. Discussion flourishes, but the "increase of discussion" is not accompanied by any "increase of wisdom." At best, discussion is an effective means of exposing error, because a single fact might disprove a doctrine, but the truth of a doctrine depends upon analysis rather than discussion, upon the examination of a vast number and variety of facts. Indeed, the mood generated by discussion might actually hinder the discovery of truth, for men eager to discuss tend to be impatient and ill equipped for the slow and careful reasoning by which truth is established; thus they are all too ready to settle for less than the truth.[17]

The proclivity for discussion also has the unfortunate effect of attaching too much value to "the exercise of private judgment," even asserting a "right" of private judgment. "Every dabbler," Mill observes, "thinks his opinion as good as another's." Men assume that truth is under "a peremptory obligation of being intelligible to them, whether they take the right means of understanding or no." But the "right means of understanding" are not accessible to all men. Only those who have had the opportunities of study and experience, who have devoted themselves to the pursuit of "physical, moral, and social truths" and have made that their "peculiar calling," have a natural claim to "authority." For such men the disregard of authority is a virtue; for others it is "both an absurdity and a vice."[18]

> If you once persuade an ignorant or a half-instructed person that he ought to assert his liberty of thought, discard all authority, and—I do not say use his own judgment, for that he can never do too much—but trust solely to his own judgment . . ., the merest trifle will suffice to unsettle and perplex their minds. . . . It is right that every man should attempt to understand his interest and his duty. It is right that he should follow his reason as far as his reason will carry him, and cultivate the faculty as highly as possible. But reason itself will teach most men that they must, in the last resort, fall back upon the authority of still more cultivated minds, as the ultimate sanction of the convictions of their reason itself.[19]

Lest it be thought that these reflections about discussion and the liberty of thought are pertinent only to a "transitional" stage of society, Mill went on to apply the same principles to the "natural" stage that would follow. For it is precisely in this stage that "the opinions and feelings of the people are, with their voluntary acquiescence, formed *for* them, by the most cultivated minds, which the intelligence and morality of the times call into existence."[20] Once the present possessors of world power are divested of their monopoly of power, a true moral and intellectual authority will reassert itself. "The most virtuous and best-instructed of the nation will acquire that ascendancy over the opinions of the rest, by which alone England can emerge from this crisis of transition and enter once again into a natural state of society."[21]

This series of articles was published anonymously (as was the custom) in the Radical journal the *Examiner*. A second series by

Mill the following year lost the journal some two hundred readers because of such provocative statements as: "The test of what is right in politics is not the *will* of the people, but the *good* of the people, and our object is not to compel, but to persuade the people to impose, for the sake of their own good, some restraint on the immediate and unlimited exercise of their own will."[22] To Carlyle, Mill wrote shortly afterward: "I have not any great notion of the advantage of what the 'free discussion' men call the 'collision of opinions,' it being my creed that Truth is *sown* and germinates in the mind itself, and is not to be struck *out* suddenly like fire from a flint by knocking another hard body against it."[23] Truth as emerging from a "collision of opinions"—Mill was anticipating the very wording of *On Liberty*, where truth was indeed seen as "produced by its collision with error." [24*]

These themes reappear in 1836 in the essay "Civilization," which foreshadows *On Liberty*—although in reverse. As in *On Liberty*, Mill deplores the increased power of the masses and a corresponding decline in the power of individuals. But he now attributes the declining influence of individuals, and of superior individuals especially, to the vast increase of literature and the large number of competing ideas in circulation. He quotes a passage from one of his earlier reviews on the inverse relationship between the quantity and quality of intellectual activity.

> The world reads too much and too quickly to read well. . . . When almost every person who can spell, can and will write, what is to be done? . . . The world, in consequence, gorges itself with intellectual food, and in order to swallow the more, *bolts* it. . . . The

*It also suggests that Mill was not quite the voice in the wilderness that he sometimes appears to be in *On Liberty*. There had been, evidently, for a quarter of a century or more, a coterie of "free discussion" men propounding just that creed.

public is in the predicament of an indolent man, who cannot bring himself to apply his mind vigorously to his own affairs, and over whom, therefore, not he who speaks most wisely, but he who speaks most frequently, obtains the influence.[25]

Unlike *On Liberty*, where the competition of ideas is encouraged even to the point of deliberately stimulating false ideas, "the system of individual competition" is now said to be obsolete, to have "worked itself out." What is now needed is not more competiton but "a greater and more perfect combination among individuals," an "organized cooperation among the leading intellects of the age," even something like a "collective guild" of authors. The purpose of such a guild would be to permit works of merit, of any source or point of view, to appear "with the stamp on them, from the first, of the approval of those whose name would carry authority."[26]

This was not a passing whim on Mill's part. In his essay on Coleridge, four years later, he endorsed Coleridge's idea of an official "clerisy," an "endowed establishment" to be supported and maintained by the state for the purpose of cultivating and transmitting not religion but the national culture. Within that clerisy there would be something of a hierarchy. Its more distinguished members, representing the "fountain heads of the humanities," would be charged with preserving and enlarging the stock of knowledge as well as instructing their lesser colleagues. The latter, in turn, the ordinary professionals, would serve as the "resident guide, guardian, and instructor" in each locality. Thus knowledge—not mere opinion—would be diffused throughout the country.[27]

The same principle applied to political society, for here too unlimited discussion was not a virtue but a vice.

In all political societies which have had a durable existence, there has been some fixed point; something which men agreed in holding sacred; which it might or might not be lawful to contest in theory, but which no one could either fear or hope to see shaken in practice; which, in short (except perhaps during some temporary crisis), was in the common estimation placed *above* discussion. . . . But when the questioning of these fundamental principles is (not an occasional disease, but) the habitual condition of the body politic; and when all the violent animosities are called forth, which spring naturally from such a situation, the state is virtually in a position of civil war; and can never long remain free from it in act and fact.[28]*

This mode of reasoning was obviously antithetical to the utilitarianism that his father was totally committed to and that prevailed in the Radical circle in which the young Mill still traveled. Shortly after Bentham's death in 1832, Mill had written a critique of him that was published the following year (against his wishes, he said) as an anonymous appendix to Bulwer-Lytton's *England and the English*. "It is not," he wrote anxiously to a friend, "and must not be, known to be mine."[30] In 1838, liberated by his father's death two years earlier, he published another longer essay on Bentham that was a near total repudiation of utilitarianism. (Even his few feeble attempts to find merit in aspects of the philosophy, relating to the law, for example, were subject to reservations and qualifications.) Mill's critique was directed not only against the calculus of interest (of pleasure and pain) that was at the heart of that philosophy, but also, more tellingly, against the conceptions of human beings and society implicit in that calculus. By reducing human nature to the level of interests and passions, Bentham

---

*Mill thought so well of this passage that he reproduced it three years later in his *System of Logic,* slightly revising it for the third edition in 1851. (To the parenthetical clause "not an occasional disease," for example, he added the phrase "or salutary medicine.")[29]

had done so at the expense of conscience, character, and a sense of morality. And by making the individual the only reality, he had denied the legitimacy of both society and history, which were the carriers of morality. "Even the originality which dares think for itself," Mill protested, "is not a more necessary part of the philosophical character than reverence for previous thinkers, and for the collective mind of the human race."[31] The lack of respect for tradition, for the collective mind of the past, reflected badly on the individual's character and on the "national character" as well—the collective spirit that enables human beings to exist together as a society, that causes one nation to be great and another to decay, "one nation to understand and aspire to elevated things, another to grovel in mean ones."[32] Bentham's philosophy, in short, might be appropriate for the "business" part of life but was totally inadequate for the moral and spiritual side.

A twin essay on Coleridge, two years later, made these points more powerfully—and, from the point of view of his father, even more heretically. For Mill was now criticizing not only Bentham but the French *philosophes* as well, who, like Bentham, took a totally negative stance toward society. Instead of attacking the old regime for "sapping the necessary foundations of society," the *philosophes* exulted in the fact that those foundations were being undermined.

> In the weakening of all government they saw only the weakening of bad government; and thought they could not better employ themselves than in finishing the task so well begun—in expelling out of every mind the last vestige of belief in that creed on which all the restraining discipline recognized in the education of European countries still rested, and with which in the general mind it was inseparably associated; in unsettling everything which was still considered settled, making men doubtful of the few things of which they still felt certain; and in uprooting what little remained

in the people's minds of reverence for anything above them, or respect to [sic] any of the limits which custom and prescription had set to the indulgence of each man's fancies or inclinations, or of attachment to any of the things which belonged to them as a nation, and which made them feel their unity as such.[33]

As against this subversive philosophy, Mill posited three essential conditions for a "permanent political society": education, allegiance, and nationality. The latter two are obvious. "Allegiance," or loyalty, requires that there be in any durable government, whatever its form, "*something* which is settled, something permanent, and not to be called in question," something "*above* discussion."[34] "Nationality"—not, Mill hastened to say, an antipathy to foreigners or a cherishing of "absurd peculiarities" merely because they were one's own—is the sense of sympathy and common interest uniting those sharing the same government, the same natural or historical boundaries, and having the same stake in their common lot.[35] "Education," the first of these conditions, is more novel and provocative, bearing little resemblance to the meaning of that word.

Education, as Mill presents it here, is moral education, and a special kind of moral education at that, its "main and incessant ingredient" being a "*restraining discipline*" (italicized). This discipline, from infancy and throughout life, is designed to instill in every citizen the habit "of subordinating his personal impulses and aims to what were considered the ends of society; of adhering, against all temptation, to the course of conduct which those ends prescribed; of controlling in himself all the feelings which were liable to militate against those ends, and encouraging all such as tended towards them." It is this that differentiates the citizen from the slave. Indeed, the relaxation of this discipline would have catastrophic effects upon society, the nation, and the state, for it would result in a reversion to the anarchy that is the "natural tendency of mankind." The state would become disorganized from within, the struggle for selfish ends would neutralize the energies required to keep at bay the "natural causes of evil," and after a period of progressive decline the nation would become prey either to a despot or to a foreign invader.[36]

From the perspective of *On Liberty*, the rhetoric of this essay is itself notable. All the pejorative terms here, all those inimical to a durable society—"personal impulses," "feelings," "desires," "inclinations"—are favorable terms in *On Liberty*; they are the "raw material" of human nature, the basic ingredients of the individuality, eccentricity, and variety that are the touchstones of liberty. Conversely, all the positive terms here which make for a viable society—"restraining," "controlling," "subordinating," "disciplining"—are negative terms in *On Liberty*, the very antithesis of liberty. In *On Liberty* it is the individual who must be protected from society, not society from the individual. It is almost as if in deliberate recantation of his earlier views that Mill wrote in *On Liberty*: "Society has now fairly got the better of individuality, and the danger which threatens human nature is not the excess, but the deficiency, of personal impulses and preferences."[37]

That the conditions for a durable society laid down in this essay were not casual or passing reflections inspired by Coleridge is suggested, first, by the fact that Coleridge is not quoted or even mentioned in the whole of this discussion, and then, by Mill's reprinting it in its entirety (some fifteen hundred words) in his *System of Logic* in 1843. (The *Logic* was reissued in seven other editions in the course of Mill's lifetime, each time with small changes of wording in this extract, showing that he reread it with care.) In the final section of the *Logic*, on the "Moral Sciences," Mill spoke of the need for a "political ethology" to explain the character of a people, and a "science of social statics" to determine "the requisites of stable political union."[38] He then quoted "from myself," as he said, these pages from the Coleridge essay (not identifying it under that name), illustrating the kinds of "theorems" such a science might arrive at. Lest the reader miss the point, Mill repeated the message: "Social existence is only possible by a disciplining of those more powerful [selfish] propensities, which consists in subordinating them to a common system of opinions. The degree of this subordination is the measure of the completeness of the social union."[39]*

The major work that occupied Mill after the *Logic* was the *Principles of Political Economy*, which was completed in December 1847 and published the following April. Mill was sufficiently pleased with the final product to want to dedicate it to Harriet Taylor, and was persuaded not to do so because of her husband's objections. He did, however (with her permission and against her husband's wishes), dedicate it to her in a private edition distributed as gift copies. (She apparently did not object to his description of her as "the most eminently qualified of all persons known to the author either to originate or to appreciate speculations on social improvement.")[42] An important part of the book was a strong critique of socialism (or communism—Mill used the words interchangeably) as being neither economically feasible nor socially and politically

---

*The *Logic* also anticipated—and refuted—another crucial part of the argument of *On Liberty*: the distinction between "self-regarding" acts, where liberty was deemed absolute (not subject to either social or political regulation), and "other-regarding" acts, where liberty might legitimately be limited. There were those, Mill admitted in *On Liberty*, who refused to admit that distinction.[40] In the *Logic,* Mill was one of those. The great difficulty, he then argued, in discovering moral and social laws is the fact that all the phenomena of society are inextricably interrelated. "Whatever affects, in an appreciable degree, any one element of the social state, affects through it all the other elements. . . . There is no social phenomenon which is not more or less influenced by every other part of the condition of the same society."[41]

desirable. A second revised edition, appearing a year later, was more conciliatory toward socialism; and the third, the most extensively revised edition in 1852, was almost favorable to socialism.[43]

Intervening between the first and the second editions was the French Revolution of 1848, which seized Harriet's imagination and which she interpreted as an invitation to socialism—and an invitation to revise the *Political Economy* accordingly. Her intervention is documented in Mill's letters, as she raised and he acquiesced in one after another of her objections. When she protested "strongly and totally" to a sentence in the first edition critical of the claim that socialism would bring about "freedom from anxiety," he reminded her that it had been originally included "on your proposition and very nearly in your own words," that it was "the strongest part of the argument" against socialism, and that to alter it would be to abandon his position entirely. But he would think about it, he assured her, for "by thinking sufficiently I should probably come to think the same [as you]—as is almost always the case, I believe always, when we think long enough." "Long enough" in this case was two or three weeks, by which time he rewrote the sentence, making freedom from anxiety a great gain for "human happiness," and thus an argument for socialism.[44] Responding to another passage she wished to delete, he replied that without it his entire argument collapsed and nothing could be said against communism at all. "One would only have to turn round and advocate it," which could be better done in a separate book rather than a new edition. Yet he did delete that passage. And when finally nothing remained of the case against communism except a caveat about the present applicability of Fourier's version of it, he offered to remove that as well, if she liked, "even if there were no other reason than the certainty I feel that I never should long continue of an opinion different from yours on a subject which you have fully considered." Thus the exchange went on, concluding with Mill's assurance that he had "followed to the letter every recommendation."[45]

If these letters, and the successive editions of the *Political Economy*, provide dramatic evidence of the influence of Harriet Taylor in this period of Mill's life, his return to the subject toward the end of his life testifies to the reemergence of the Other Mill, the Mill of the early essays and of the first edition of the *Political Economy*. The book on socialism he began writing in 1868 was never finished, but five chapters (about fifty pages) were published in the *Fortnightly Review* in 1879 under the title "Chapters on Socialism." In submitting them, Helen Taylor reminded readers that these were "rough drafts" and that it had been Mill's habit to rewrite and reorganize his writings.[46] It would have taken a great deal of rewriting to mitigate the seriousness of the critique of socialism (and/or communism) presented here. Disposing of the socialists' objections to the current system, Mill pointed out that wages, so far from declining, were in fact increasing; and personal interest, private property, and competition, for all their faults (which could be corrected within the existing system), were the only natural and effective stimuli for economic activity. Moreover, the alternative offered by the socialists was worse. The idea of trying to conduct the economy from a single center was "chimerical," and the attempt to do so would be most unfortunate, for society would acquire even more control over the opinions of individuals, and private life would be brought "in a most unexampled degree within the dominion of public authority."[47]

Utilitarianism, Mill's first major work after *On Liberty*, is in a sense a bridge between the two Mills. Originating as essays begun in 1854, about the same time as the first draft of *On Liberty*, it was published serially, in a much revised form, in *Fraser's Magazine* in 1861 (two years after *On Liberty*), and as a volume in 1863. In the course of refining and qualifying the doctrine of utilitarianism, Mill confronted the problem of deducing a principle of social morality from the principle of utility. As a utilitarian (even a qualified one), he had to reject any idea of an innate or intuitive moral sense. Instead he found in man "a powerful natural sentiment" deriving from his very nature, which provided the foundation for social morality.

> This firm foundation is that of the social feelings of mankind; the desire to be in unity with our fellow creatures, which is already a powerful principle in human nature, and happily one of those which tend to become stronger, even without express inculcation, from the influences of advancing civilization. The social state is at once so natural, so necessary, and so habitual to man, that, except in some unusual circumstances or by an effort of voluntary abstraction, he never conceives of himself otherwise than as a member of a body; and this association is riveted more and more, as mankind are further removed from the state of savage independence.[48]

This "social state," the feeling of "unity," was natural, to be sure, but it could also be "inculcated," "taught as a religion." There are echoes here of the idea of "education" described in the Coleridge essay, for Mill was now proposing to bring "the whole force of education, of institutions, and of opinion, directed, as it once was in the case of religion, to make every person grow up from infancy surrounded on all sides both by the profession and by the practice of it."[49] This, of course, was not religion in any conventional sense, any more than it was education in any conventional sense. It was rather something very like the Comtean Religion of Humanity that had always intrigued Mill, a secular religion in which man was deified—not the individual man but a collective "humanity," endowed with a collective will, interest, and moral purpose.

Utilitarianism came a long way from the utilitarianism of Bentham or his father—and a long way as well from *On Liberty*, where not "social feelings" but "personal feelings" were prized, and where the highest civilized state was not "unity with our fellow creatures" but the highest degree of individuality, even to the point of "eccentricity" and "experiments in living." Certainly the individual in *On Liberty*, even the entirely "self-regarding" individual, could not be denigrated, as he was in *Utilitarianism*, as "a selfish egotist, devoid of every feeling or care but those which centre in his own miserable individuality."[50] And the education *cum* religion Mill was now proposing, designed to foster those social feelings and sense of unity, was far from the religion depicted in *On Liberty*.

"Religion," in *On Liberty*, was simply Christianity. A good part of the first chapter, on "Thought and Discussion," was a criticism of Christianity as the archetypical promoter of persecution and repression, in the present as well as the past. After dwelling at some length upon the familiar historic examples of persecution in the name of Christianity, Mill cited three current examples of "legal persecution." Although these, he admitted, were but "the rags and remnants of persecution," there was no security that such persecution of heretical opinions would not continue, so long as religion continued, for "the revival of religion" was always, "in narrow and uncultivated minds, at least as much the revival of bigotry."[51]

It is interesting that one of the last of Mill's works, written (like his "Chapters on Socialism") a few years before his death and published posthumously, was on the subject of religion. "Theism" is a long essay (a short book, really—sixty dense pages in one published version) consisting of a careful analysis of the familiar theological arguments about the evidence for the existence of God: the first cause, design in nature, the attributes of God (omnipotence, omniscience, benevolence), immortality, revelation, and miracles.

The tone is consistently respectful, Mill presenting himself as neither a believer nor an atheist but as a mere skeptic. He went beyond skepticism, however, in assigning some "probability," if only a "lower degree of probability," to the idea of God—an Intelligent Mind who did not create the universe but did preside over the "present order" of it[52]—and, more important, in assigning a high value to belief itself.

Belief, Mill explained, is something other than truth. Truth falls within the "province of reason" and is attainable only by the rational faculty. But it is precisely when reason is strong that "the imagination may safely follow its own end," doing its best to "make life pleasant and lovely inside the castle," secure in the fortifications erected by reason outside. This combination of reason and imagination gives rise to an "indulgence of hope" with regard both to the existence of God and the immortality of man—a hope that is "legitimate and philosophically defensible" as well as of considerable human benefit.

> It makes life and human nature a far greater thing to the feelings, and gives greater strength as well as greater solemnity to all the sentiments which are awakened in us by our fellow-creatures and by mankind at large. It allays the sense of that irony of Nature which is so painfully felt when we see the exertions and sacrifices of a life culminating in the formation of a wise and noble mind, only to disappear from the world when the time has just arrived at which the world seems about to begin reaping the benefit of it.[53]

It is not only the idea of immortality that has this humanizing and elevating effect; it is the idea of God as well, the imaginative conception of a "morally perfect Being" who has "his eyes on us and cares for our good," and who provides human beings with the standard of excellence by which they regulate their characters and lives.

Moreover, it is not only God that serves this purpose but the "Divine Person" of Christ.

> For it is Christ, rather than God, whom Christianity has held up to believers as the pattern of perfection for humanity. It is the God incarnate, more than the God of the Jews or of Nature, who being idealized has taken so great and salutary a hold on the modern mind. . . . About the life and sayings of Jesus there is a stamp of personal originality combined with profundity of insight, which if we abandon the idle expectation of finding scientific precision where something very different was aimed at, must place the Prophet of Nazareth, even in the estimation of those who have no belief in his inspiration, in the very first rank of the men of sublime genius of whom our species can boast.[54]

These reflections, Mill makes it clear, are those of a "rational sceptic," who realizes that after all that rational criticism can do by way of disputing the "evidences" of religion (revelation, miracles, the supernatural), what remains is the undoubted evidence of the fortunate effect of religion on character and morality. Conventional religion can thus supplement that "purely human religion" called the Religion of Humanity, fortifying it with those "supernatural hopes" that are allowed even to a rational skeptic like himself.[55]

By orthodox religious standards, this "indulgence of hope" is an attenuated religion, perhaps no more than a will to believe. But it is so movingly and eloquently expressed as to have almost the force and status of genuine belief. Certainly in tone and substance, "Theism" stands in dramatic contrast to the view of religion presented in *On Liberty*, which was not so much skeptical as hostile. It also stands in contrast to a much earlier essay, "Utility of Religion," which was written (although not published) in 1854, shortly before *On Liberty* was written. In that much briefer essay, Mill argued

that religion might have been useful in an early stage of civilization, as the support of social morality, but in an advanced stage it
more often serves to protect from discussion and criticism erro-
neous practices and beliefs. Only the Religion of Humanity, Mill
then claimed, "stands wholly clear both of intellectual contradiction and of moral obliquity"; only it satisfies the needs of the individual as well as society without being hobbled by the "moral
difficulties and perversions" of Christianity. Even the idea of immortality is more a burden than a comfort for the "common order
of mankind," let alone for "philosophers."[56]

After Mill's death, this early essay, as well as another, "Nature,"
dating from the same period, were published together with "Theism" under the title *Three Essays on Religion.* An introductory note
by Helen Taylor explained that the essays had been written at considerable intervals of time, were not meant to appear together, and
should not be regarded as a "connected body of thought." "On the
other hand," she went on, "it is certain that the Author considered
the opinions expressed in these different Essays, as fundamentally
consistent," as evidence of which she cited Mill's intention, after
concluding "Theism," to publish "Nature" with only slight revisions. (She made no mention of any intention on his part to publish "Utility of Religion," which suggests that, unlike "Nature," he
did not plan to publish it.) Whatever "discrepancies" there might
appear to be in these essays she attributed largely to the fact that
the last had not undergone the revisions to which Mill customarily
subjected his work.[57] (In fact, by her own account, "Theism" was
written between 1868 and 1870, so that Mill did have ample time,
in those two years and the three years that followed before his
death, to make such revisions.)

Some of Mill's friends took a more serious view of those "discrepancies," regarding "Theism" as a radical departure from the
secularism they associated with Mill. John Morley disclaimed it in

an article in the *Fortnightly*, Fitzjames Stephen in the *Pall Mall Gazette* called it "a diet of anaesthetic," and Alexander Bain, his biographer, while praising Mill's courage in admitting his change of mind, could only assume that he had been seeking an anodyne for the loss of his wife.[58] They might have been even more disturbed by a letter Mill wrote to another friend, while he was writing the essay, suggesting that the effect of prayer could not be proved to be an entirely natural phenomenon and that he could not exclude the possibility of some "supernatural influence."[59]

"Theism" may be read as the final testament of the Other Mill—a Mill liberated from the influence of both his father and his wife. It may be thought unseemly to place such emphasis on personal factors in the thinking of a serious philosopher and intellectual. Yet Mill himself did just that, so that it is on his authority, not the willful speculations of a biographer or commentator, that one must credit (shorn, perhaps, of the effusions of an uxorious husband) his assertions of the influence of Harriet Taylor. He may have exaggerated that influence, but that it was considerable is abundantly testified to by the evidence of his letters as well as the *Autobiography* and dedications.

The drama of Mill's intellectual history is obscured by those who think it demeaning to him, almost *lèse-majesté*, to dwell on such matters. The unwitting effect of this denial, however, is to diminish Mill's true status as an intellectual, perhaps the most interesting intellectual of his time. To try to impose a unity and consistency upon his ideas is not only to homogenize and blunt them, to dull their edge. It also minimizes the true import of *On Liberty*—the radical implications of that "simple principle" of liberty. More important, it deprives us of the Other Mill, who is at least as worthy of our regard.

For almost a century and a half, *On Liberty*, for liberals and conservatives alike, has been a major text in intellectual history and a source of inspiration in practical affairs. But there is the Other Mill, who wrote essays that were bold and novel in his time and that remain remarkably prescient and pertinent today. The idea of liberty, Mill explained in the opening paragraph of *On Liberty*, had special meaning "in the stage of progress into which the more civilised portions of the species have now entered." It may be that the ideas of the Other Mill are even more meaningful in the "stage of progress" we are now entering. We have learned much from the familiar Mill. We have now, as liberal society becomes more self-critical, to learn to live with the Other Mill as well.

Toward the end of his essay on Coleridge, Mill made the celebrated statement that he took to be Coleridge's claim to fame: "We may have done something to show that a Tory philosopher cannot be wholly a Tory, but must often be a better Liberal than Liberals themselves; while he is the natural means of rescuing from oblivion truths which Tories have forgotten, and which the prevailing schools of Liberalism never knew."[60] So we may now say of the Other Mill: He has shown us that a Liberal cannot be wholly a Liberal, but must often be a better Tory than Tories themselves; while he is the natural means of rescuing from oblivion truths which Liberals have forgotten, and which the prevailing schools of Toryism never knew.

Walter Bagehot
"A Divided Nature"

The current intellectual fashions put a premium on simplicity and activism. The subtleties, complications, and ambiguities that until recently have been the mark of serious thought are now taken to signify a failure of nerve, a compromise with evil, an evasion of judgment and "commitment." It is as if the "once-born" (to use the terms invented by Francis Newman and immortalized by William James) were reasserting themselves over the "twice-born": the once-born, simple and "healthy-minded," having faith in a beneficent God and a perfectible universe; the twice-born in awe of His mystery, impressed by the recalcitrance of men and the anomalies of social action.

In Walter Bagehot one may see a reconciliation of the two types. He was a political commentator who stopped just short of being a political philosopher, a social critic who empathized with and at the same time transcended his subjects, an editor of the *Economist* who wrote with as much facility and perception about Shelley or Coleridge as about the rate of interest or currency reform. (His writing was so pithy and epigrammatic that any commentary on him is a series of quotations.) He once described himself as "between sizes in politics."[1] In fact he was between sizes in everything. He was that rare species of the twice-born who could give proper due to the rights and merits of the once-born. And he did so not by a denial of his own nature but by virtue of the very subtleties, complications, and ambiguities that informed his nature. He was, as he said of Saint Paul, a "divided nature."[2]

The "dark realities" of life he often alluded to had an obvious personal reference. His mother, to whom he was deeply attached, had recurrent fits of insanity, and his half-brother was feeble-minded; both predeceased him by only a few years, so that his entire life was passed in their shadow. "Every trouble in life is a joke compared to madness," he once remarked.[3] Elsewhere he wrote: "We see but one aspect of our neighbor, as we see but one side of the moon: in either case there is also a dark half which is unknown to us. We all come down to dinner, but each has a room to himself."[4]

Yet there was nothing tragedy-ridden about Bagehot, either in his person or in his ideas. The point about the twice-born, and pre-eminently about Bagehot, is that the "dark realities" are only one-half of reality—we all have rooms to ourselves but we do also come down to dinner. His biographer and the editor of his collected works, Norman St. John-Stevas, distinguished between Bagehot the "mystic" and Bagehot the "man of the world," the one revealing himself in his private life, the other in his writings.[5] But this is to deny the peculiar quality of the man and the genius of his work. For the characteristic of both was the ability to combine the disparate, to keep in focus at the same time both sides of the moon, to be, as he said of himself, "cheerful but not sanguine."[6] Bagehot was as much a man of the world as one could want; a man, indeed, of many worlds—banking, journalism, literature, and politics. And it was his practical experience of these worlds, filtered through a subtle and sensitive mind, that gave him his remarkable intellectual power.

If his writings abound in irony and paradox, it is because his sense of reality was multifaceted, shaped by the simple and the complex, the commonplace and the recondite. "Taken as a whole," he declared, "the universe is absurd," in evidence of which he attested the disparity between "the human mind and its employments": "How can a soul be a merchant? What relation to an immortal being have the price of linseed, the fall of butter, the tare on tallow, or the brokerage on hemp? Can an undying creature debit 'petty expenses' and charge for 'carriage paid'?" To which his answer was: "The soul ties its shoes; the mind washes its hands in a basin. All is incongruous."[7]

This sense of incongruity and absurdity permeated Bagehot's writings on history, politics, society, and literature. It also permitted him to see private vices in the guise of public virtues: to appreciate the irony of the fact that "much stupidity" might be "the most essential mental quality for a free people";[8] to understand why it was that the statesman who carried the first Reform Act might have done so precisely because he was so bad a speaker and so slow of mind in an assembly that prized facile speech and quick wit;[9] or to rebuke a philosopher for having contempt for the "formidable community of fools" who made up the world—the world being often wiser than such a philosopher.[10] By the same token he saw private virtues functioning as public vices. The intellectual lucidity and sobriety that were the great distinctions of one Liberal politician were serious political defects, since the absence of passion in himself caused him to mistake the passion in others: "Such extreme calmness of mind is not favorable to a statesman; it is good to be without vices, but it is not good to be without temptations."[11]

In the same spirit, Bagehot rebuked the poets and writers who failed to draw upon the common experience and wisdom of the world. Shelley was a notable example of that defect; he was too fanciful, ethereal, "unconditioned" by reality. "Before a man can imagine what will seem to be realities, he must be familiar with what are realities."[12] Shelley lacked that familiarity. "We fancy his mind placed in the light of thought, with pure subtle fancies playing to and fro. On a sudden an impulse arises; it is alone, and has nothing to contend with; . . . it bolts forward into action."[13] He was like a child who thought that anyone who was bad was very bad indeed, that anyone who did evil wished to do so and had a special impulse to do so, as the child himself felt such an impulse. Like the child, Shelley could not conceive of the mature adult with a "struggling kind of character," who gave way to good or bad or a combination of both only after a conflict within his own double nature.[14] This single-minded, overriding impulse was exhibited in his self-styled "passion for reforming mankind":

> No society, however organized, would have been too strong for him to attack. He would not have paused. The impulse was upon him. He would have been ready to preach that mankind were to be "free, equal, pure, and wise"—in favour of "justice, and truth, and time, and the world's natural sphere"—in the Ottoman Empire, or to the Czar, or to George III. Such truths were independent of time and place and circumstance; some time or other, something, or somebody (his faith was a little vague), would most certainly intervene to establish them.[15]

That Bagehot was not simply attacking Shelley for being a radical is evident from the similar charge he brought against the Tory Southey. Where Shelley's lack of common wisdom made him prone to intellectual impulsiveness, the same failing on Southey's part led to academicism and mechanical professionalism. Southey was like the German professor who could apply himself to any subject because he did not feel the need to know more of that subject than other writers had told him. The reason so few good books were written, Bagehot complained, was because "so few people that can write know anything." The professional thought it enough to read and write; he did not feel it his job to think or feel or know with any intimacy and depth. "He [the professional] wrote poetry (as if anybody could) before breakfast; he read during breakfast. He wrote history until dinner; he corrected proof sheets between dinner and tea; he wrote an essay for the *Quarterly* afterwards."[16]

What Bagehot said of the professional writer in criticism—that he wrote poetry before breakfast, history until dinner . . .—another Victorian might have said in praise. Leslie Stephen, for example, an eminently professional (and enormously prolific) writer, prided himself on his ability to apply common sense to any subject.* For Bagehot, this was an exercise not in common sense but in philistinism, the same kind of philistinism he found in the early *Edinburgh Review*. It was no accident, he said, that writers of this mode should have created a genre of popular literature so well suited to the railway age, so that a traveler could pick up a magazine at a railway stall, peruse it en route, and dispose of it at the end of the line. "People take their literature in morsels, as they take sandwiches in a journey."[18] Like the box lunch, the essays in the journal were meant to be tasty, digestible, and agreeable to all palates, the assumption being that all literate men had the will and capacity to absorb the same fare, and that all ideas could be dished up in the same manner. Both the writer and the reader profited from this tidy arrangement: the writer because it permitted him to write an

---

*Leslie Stephen, for his part, criticized Bagehot for precisely the opposite reasons. While praising Bagehot for being able to enliven so dry a subject as the British constitution, Stephen faulted him for being excessively theoretical and cynical, rather than simple, straightforward, and "manly."[17]

article on anything or everything, as was his boast; and the reader because such an article was bound to be written in a form he could most readily assimilate.[19]*

Bagehot conceded that the virtues of the *Edinburgh Review* were considerable, especially in its early years. Against the Tory's "stupid adherence to the status quo," it brought to bear a cool, collected, quiet, practical, "improving" Whiggism.[20] But this cool intelligence spawned its own variety of philistinism. Its "firm and placid manliness"[21] rejected zeal, eccentricity, and novelty, whether in the service of poetry, philosophy, religion, or politics. "This will never do"—the famous opening words of Lord Jeffrey's review of Wordsworth's "Excursion"—might have been used (were in fact used) on other occasions to condemn similarly uncongenial effusions. "So in all time," Bagehot commented, "will the lovers of polished Liberalism speak, concerning the intense and lonely prophet."[22]

Bagehot would not have had the audacity to speak of himself as a "lonely prophet." But he did value and even identify with that prophet. "A clear, precise, discriminating intellect shrinks at once from the symbolic, the unbounded, the indefinite. The misfortune is that mysticism is true."[23] Thus Bagehot distinguished himself from both the radical rationalism of a Shelley and the liberal rationalism of a Sydney Smith. Shelley lacked not only the common sense that would have made him appreciate the complexities of

---

*It is a measure of the distance our culture has traveled from the Victorian age that the ephemera of that time (as Bagehot described the *Edinburgh Review*) should appear to us today to be of the most exemplary solidity. Those "morsels" to be consumed casually in the course of a railway journey consisted of 20,000- to 35,000-word articles, and the magazine itself was the equivalent of a good-sized volume. Nor can we fail to be impressed by the elegant style with which those tidbits were dispensed, or the number of people who consumed them. (The *Review* had a circulation of over 10,000, in a literate population of perhaps 100,000.)

human nature but also the intuition that turned men from the world without to the contemplation of a world within, "from the things which are seen to the realities which are not seen." He could so easily dismiss the idea of God because he was himself deficient in the "haunting, abiding, oppressive moral feeling" that was part of the reality of most men's inner lives and that made them receptive to the idea of God.[24]

So, too, Sydney Smith, Bagehot judged, was too good a liberal (in tone and temper rather than party affiliation) to be much of a divine. "Somebody has defined Liberalism as the spirit of the world. It represents its genial enjoyment, its wise sense, its steady judgment, its preference of the near to the far, of the seen to the unseen; it represents, too, its shrinking from difficult dogma, from stern statement, from imperious superstition."[25] The only kind of religion congenial to this type of liberal is a "natural religion," a "plain religion." Awe, dread, mystery are not for him. "You cannot imagine a classical Isaiah; you cannot fancy a Whig St. Dominic; there is no such thing as a Liberal Augustine."[26]

The motif running through each of Bagehot's literary essays was the two sides of the moon, the double nature of man, the dual aspect of reality. One writer was rebuked for not sharing the common experiences of man, another for not probing deeply enough into his own soul. But both came to the same thing, because no one could truly know himself without knowing others or others without knowing himself. Similarly, reality and unreality were symbiotically joined, uniting the things seen with those unseen. Shakespeare was a master of reality, as that word is commonly understood; but he was also, and by the same token, a master of "Such shaping fantasies as apprehend / More than cool reason ever comprehends." It was the immaturity of Shelley that made him look on the material world as a "preposterous imposture";[27] and it was the wisdom of Cowper to see that "the ludicrous is in some sort the imagination of common life."[28] The tragedy of Arthur Clough (Matthew Arnold's poet friend) was that he was unable to come to terms with the preposterous and ludicrous, with the normal human condition of making the best of both worlds, so that "we know that we see as in a glass darkly, but still we look on the glass."[29]

Judging by the sheer quantity of Bagehot's writings and the variety of subjects to which he addressed himself, one might be tempted to suspect him of the same superficial fluency that he found in the *Edinburgh Review*. What redeemed him, however, was his point of view—or rather, his double point of view. This duality was not an intellectual strategy, the strategy of the disarming admission, of the lulling counterpoint of "on the one hand" and "on the other." It was a coherent, compelling vision that inevitably brought with it a complexity, subtlety, and depth that he found lacking in much of the discourse of the time.

In Bagehot's political writings the terms of this duality were the common and the uncommon, the people and the statesmen, public opinion and political wisdom. What is remarkable is not only that the two were inseparable, but also that he should have made so much of the first. More than any other political commentator or social critic, Bagehot persistently invoked such concepts as "popular opinion," "public opinion," "the public mind," "popular sentiment," "popular imagination," the "sense of the country." And this not only in respect to the England of his own time, when it might be said that the common people were finally coming into their own as a power so that their opinions were becoming of some moment, but in respect to every other period and subject. Macaulay has been justly esteemed for his famous third chapter on the "State of England in 1685." But where Macaulay confined the "people" to this one chapter and rarely permitted them to intrude into the rest of his narrative, Bagehot gave them free range over the whole of history, bringing them into the limelight in the most unexpected times and places. This constant invocation of the people is even more striking in view of the fact that his most memorable political writings (apart from *The English Constitution* and *Physics and Politics*) were essays on individual statesmen.

The theme of each of these essays was the relation of its hero to the public, of political wisdom to common sense. Thus Bolingbroke did not share the prejudice against the House of Hanover felt by the "unthinking people of the common sort," but he made himself the organ of that prejudice; he was important in Parliament because he was "the eloquent spokesman of many inaudible persons."[30] Pitt's great gift was the ability to express "in a more than ordinary manner the true feelings and sentiments of ordinary men; not their superficial notions, nor their coarser sentiments, for with these any inferior man may deal, but their most intimate nature, that which in their highest moments is most truly themselves."[31] Burke, on the other hand, far more brilliant than Pitt, had the defect of his genius: in his mind "great ideas were a supernatural burden, a superincumbent inspiration; he saw a great truth, and he saw nothing else."[32] Adam Smith popularized political science "in the only sense in which it can be popularized without being spoiled; that is, he has put certain broad conclusions into the minds of hard-headed men, which are all which they need know, and all which they for the most part will ever care for."[33] Palmerston "was not a common man, but a common man might have been cut out of him"; and he had the good sense to know that he would succeed only so long as he kept faith with the "common part of his mind."[34] Disraeli's misfortune was that he was a political romantic: he preferred to deal with "ideal measures" and "ideal heroes" when he should have been trying to get at "the heart of a deep national conviction."[35]

If it was incumbent on the statesman to respect the wisdom of the common people, the political thinker could do no less. Yet

Bagehot himself has often been charged with just this failing. St. John-Stevas, himself a Conservative member of Parliament, has said that Bagehot had "no sympathy with the masses of men, and his conservatism sprang in part from lack of compassion."[36] *The English Constitution* in particular has often been read in this light. The main thesis of that book—the distinction between the "dignified" and the "efficient" parts of the constitution, the one necessary for the gratification of the common people, the other for the working of the government—is assumed to be condescending and demeaning. But the condescension may be on the part of those who make this assumption, who think that the populace is demeaned by that distinction.

Indeed, Bagehot may be said to have been more respectful of the populace than his critics, for he credited the common people with a peculiarly intellectual, one might say, reverence for ideas. The people were interested more in the theatricalities than in the mundane workings of government because they saw the theatricalities as the "embodiments of the greatest human ideas." They refused to become "absorbed in the useful" because they did not like "anything so poor." They could not be appealed to on the basis of material wants, unless those wants were thought to be the result of tyranny. They were willing, in fact, to sacrifice their material goods, their very persons, "for what is called an idea—for some attraction which seems to transcend reality, which aspires to elevate men by an interest higher, deeper, wider than that of ordinary life." It was the upper classes, by implication, who were so poor in mind and soul as to be contented with the useful, the material, the efficient.[37]

Bagehot minced no words. The common people were "stupid." But their stupidity was their virtue—and their wisdom as well. For not only did it spare them the futile turmoil and suicidal excesses of a more nimble-minded people like the French; it also meant that they were never taken in by the typically French fallacy of supposing that political problems could be solved rationally, by the criteria of consistency, simplicity, or logical coherence. The wise English statesman had enough in common with the people to feel the force and the good sense of their stupidity. Bagehot was not saying that the good statesman was one who knew best how to exploit or manipulate the masses in the interests of good government. He was saying that the masses themselves had an instinct for good government, which the statesman was bound to respect.

The statesman had not merely to respect the people; he had also to respect himself—the "uncommon" as well as the "common" part of his mind. "An English statesman in the present day lives by following public opinion; he may profess to guide it a little; he may hope to modify it in detail; he may help to exaggerate and to develop it; but he hardly hopes for more."[38] For this reason, because public opinion was so compelling and common sense so urgent, the statesman had to know when to assert himself against the public and pit his own good sense against the common sense. This was all the more difficult for the "constitutional statesman" (democratic statesman, we would say today), so much of whose mind and time were necessarily given over to the function of persuasion, the oratorical attempt to modify and convert public opinion.

In the role of orator, the essential ambivalence of the statesman revealed itself. By means of oratory the statesman tried to mediate not only between the public and himself but also between the two parts of his own mind. In doing so, the statesman/orator exposed his great weakness. "We know that the popular instinct suspects the judgment of great orators; we know that it does not give them credit for patient equanimity; and the popular instinct is right."[39] The popular instinct correctly suspected that the orator was too subservient to popular opinion. Here again the people displayed their peculiar wisdom and virtue: their wisdom in being suspicious of the orator, and their virtue in finding cause for suspicion not so much in the orator's attempt to impose upon them his own opinions as in his excessive solicitude for theirs.

The oratorical process, Bagehot concluded, was a necessary but profoundly disorganizing one, tempting the statesman to shift and trim in obedience to a fluctuating opinion, to advocate what he might privately dislike, to oppose at one time what he might defend at another, to defend or oppose without sufficient reflection, to lose sight of the larger design. It was particularly disorganizing in a statesman like Gladstone, whose mind was naturally "impressible, impetuous, and unfixed," "defective in the tenacity of first principle," inclined to an "elastic heroism."[40] And it was particularly dangerous at a time like Gladstone's, when what was wanted were deliberative, constructive, far-ranging policies, an adherence to settled principle rather than an accommodation to transient popular moods.

Bagehot's essay on Peel is a brilliant commentary on this theme. No Marxist or sociologist could hope to improve upon this account of the Lancashire businessman *qua* statesman—the son of a baronet, educated at Harrow and Christ Church, a Tory MP at the age of twenty-one. Personally dissociated from the source of his fortune, Peel nevertheless showed, in the manner, language, and substance of his politics, the ineradicable "grain of the middle class," the stamp of the "transacting and trading multitude."[41] It was from this class that he derived the characteristic traits of the constitutional statesman. A "man of common opinions and uncommon abilities," having "the powers of a first-rate man and the creed of a second-rate man," he managed never to be in advance of his time but always in step with it.[42] He was a great administrator, with the energy, appetite for detail, patience, tact, and adaptability of the businessman, and happily lacking those "fixed opinions" that might inhibit these talents.[43] Moreover, he had the mode of oratory appropriate to his class. He could not rival the elegance, fluency, wit, or classical embellishments of an older generation of parliamentary orator, but he was a master of "middle-class eloquence," the rhetoric of exposition and arithmetic detail.[44] His oratory reflected his ideas, which were not so much his own ideas as the "quiet leavings" of other men's ideas.[45] And because his intelligence was practical rather than speculative, his rhetoric was "specious," giving the impression of plausibility rather than of truth.[46]

In other times—in Gladstone's, for example—these qualities would have been inadequate, even fatal. Peel lived at a more fortunate time, when his mind and manner were fitting to his tasks. Most of the necessary legislation involved problems of administration and regulation; and most of the necessary reforms were destructive rather than constructive, requiring the repeal of outmoded laws (Corn Laws, anti-Catholic laws, criminal statutes). In Peel, England found the precise virtues and vices that suited it at that time and place:

> A nature at once active and facile, easily acquiring its opinions from without, not easily devising them from within, a large placid adaptive intellect, devoid of irritable intense originality, prone to forget the ideas of yesterday, inclined to the ideas of today. . . . So long as constitutional statesmanship is what it is now, so long as its function consists in recording the views of a confused nation, so long as success in it is confined to minds plastic, changeful, administrative—we must hope for no better man. You have excluded the profound thinker; you must be content with what you can obtain—the business gentleman.[47]

Lancashire, Bagehot observed on another occasion, was sometimes called "America-and-water"; but he suspected that it was "America and very little water."[48] Lancashire today is not what it was; still less is America today the Lancashire of yesteryear. But Bagehot's reflections on statesmancraft—on the relation of populace and politician, of public opinion and political imagination, of common sense and wisdom—are as pertinent to the America of today as they were to the England of his time.

Lord Acton

The Historian as Moralist

~~ Sixty years ago, introducing my biography of Lord Acton, I
wrote: "He is of this age, more than of his. He is, indeed, one of
our great contemporaries."[1] A decade and a half later, in an essay
on Acton, I described him as being "totally out of sorts with his
times"—but I no longer ventured to claim him for our times.[2] Today, more than a century after his death, he seems to me once again
to speak to our age, if only to remind us of the ideals we still share
and the perils to which we are subject. His governing passions, liberty and morality, religion and history, are of no less concern today
and are perhaps still more in dispute.

The barest account of Acton's life helps explain one of the most
curious facts about him: that this eminent Victorian (his life was
almost coterminous with the reign of Queen Victoria) was, in many
respects, so un-Victorian. By birth, education, and disposition, he
was thoroughly cosmopolitan. The Actons were descended from an
old English family of squires and baronets, the estate at Aldenham
in Shropshire dating back to the early fourteenth century. In the
eighteenth century, the head of the family, Sir Richard, converted
to Catholicism, and other members of the family, also converts,
sought their fortunes abroad. With the death of Sir Richard, the title and estate reverted to a John Acton who was then the prime

minister of Naples. John's eldest son, Richard, married Marie, the only daughter of the Duke of Dalberg. (The Dalbergs, resident in the Rhineland, held the premier dukedom in the Holy Roman Empire; the Duke's wife came of an ancient Genoan family.) Some of the Dalbergs, like the Actons, left their ancestral home, one of them becoming a nationalized French citizen during the Napoleonic Wars and a peer of France after the Restoration. It was into this multinational, multilingual family that the son of Richard and Marie, John Edward Emerich Dalberg Acton, was born in Naples in 1834.

Acton's father died when the boy was three, and his mother's remarriage brought the family into another, very different social milieu. Lord Leveson, later the second Earl Granville, met Marie Acton in Paris when he was Under-Secretary for Foreign Affairs in the Whig government and his father was the English ambassador to France. (The Dalbergs, who were part of Talleyrand's entourage, and the Actons, who maintained a house in the faubourg St. Honoré, spent the "season" in Paris.) If Acton proved to be an untypical Victorian, his stepfather was the quintessential Victorian aristocrat, a member of one of the grand Whig—and, of course, Anglican—families. The marriage was not without its tensions; Acton's mother was a devout Catholic, and her son resisted the social life and political career that his stepfather thought natural and proper.

At every point, Acton's life reflected the complexities and anomalies of his heritage. Refused admission to three Cambridge colleges because he was Catholic, he pursued a decidedly un-English course of studies at Munich under the tutelage of the eminent Catholic theologian, Johann Ignaz von Döllinger. Forty years later he received an honorary degree from Cambridge, and later still was appointed Regius Professor of Modern History. His first position was as editor of the *Rambler*, a small Catholic journal; his last as editor of the monumental *Cambridge Modern History.* As a young man, on the urging of his stepfather, he served for one undistinguished term as a Liberal Member of Parliament for an Irish constituency; failing to be renominated, he was elected for an English borough, only to be unseated on a recount prompted by charges of bribery (on the part of his agent, not himself). His elevation to the peerage in 1869 put an end to any thought of a parliamentary career, but as the friend and adviser of Prime Minister Gladstone, he entertained hopes of an ambassadorship or even a position in the cabinet. Instead, in 1892, Gladstone, in his last Prime Ministership, made him Lord-in-Waiting to the Queen, the most onerous of Acton's duties being dining with the royal family. He was relieved of this task by his appointment three years later (not by Gladstone but by his successor, Lord Rosebery) to the Regius Professorship, whereupon he delivered an inaugural lecture so allusive and abstruse that reviewers complained that they could not understand it.

These are only the more superficial paradoxes and ironies of Acton's life. Others are more serious, even tragic. A pious Catholic, for whom communion with the Church was, as he said, "dearer than life itself,"[3] he found himself passionately engaged in one of the most contentious Catholic events in modern times, the controversy over the doctrine of papal infallibility; he was spared excommunication only because of his influential political connections. A liberal, who was as zealously devoted to liberty as he was to religion, he had as little in common with the laissez-faire, utilitarian mode of liberalism prevalent in his day as with the welfare-state liberalism of our own. And a historian, who was perhaps the most learned and intellectually ambitious of his generation, he is best known today as the coiner of the aphorism (generally misquoted), "Power tends to corrupt and absolute power corrupts absolutely," and as the author, so to speak, of the most famous book that was never written, "The History of Liberty." Long before the end of his

life, he began to speak privately of this work as his "Madonna of
the Future," a reference to Henry James's story of an artist who de-
votes his life to the creation of a single masterpiece which after his
death is exposed as a blank canvas.[4]

The most dramatic event in Acton's life was his battle against
the doctrine of papal infallibility. He was well prepared for that by
his theological studies in Munich under Döllinger, and then, after
his return to England, by his conflicts with the English Catholic
hierarchy over his editorship of two liberal Catholic journals, the
Rambler and the *Home and Foreign Review*. He was in Rome in 1870
when the Vatican Council met, his relationship with Gladstone
and Granville giving him a quasi-diplomatic standing, and his theological and historical knowledge making him the most influential
Catholic layman—and the most effective opponent of the new
dogma. He not only formulated and publicized the case against infallibility—in Catholic circles and to the outside world—he also
played an important part in coordinating the activities of the minority of bishops who opposed the doctrine. Papal infallibility, he
argued, was a perversion of both history and religion, denying the
spirit of Christianity, falsifying the history of the church, and subverting the legitimate relationship of pope and church. He delivered this uncompromising message to Catholics and non-Catholics
alike. "The passage from the Catholicism of the Fathers to that of
the modern Popes," he wrote in an English journal, "was accom-
plished by willful falsehood; and the whole structure of traditions,
laws, and doctrines that supports the theory of infallibility, and the
practical despotism of the Popes, stands on a basis of fraud."[5]

Acton never deviated from that position. After the promulgation of the doctrine he formally professed obedience to the church,
being careful, however, not to profess belief in the doctrine of infallibility itself. He bitterly reproached those Catholics, like John

Henry Newman, who had also opposed the doctrine and had then, all too easily, in Acton's opinion, submitted to the church. More serious, and far more painful, was his disillusionment with Döllinger, who refused to submit and was excommunicated. Yet even he did not appreciate the enormity of the doctrine itself, Acton insisted, for by objecting to it on theological rather than historical grounds, he implicitly sanctioned all the evils in the church before the promulgation of the doctrine.

The shadow of infallibility hovered over Acton the rest of his life, the moral issues raised by it informing his thinking about philosophy, politics, and history, as well as religion and the church. Before the Vatican Council he had eulogized Edmund Burke as "the law and the prophets," the "teacher of mankind," the exponent of a "purely Catholic view of political principles and of history."[6] One can also hear the echo of Burke in Acton's defense of the South at the time of the American Civil War and in his criticism of the abolitionists for exhibiting an "abstract, ideal absolutism, which is equally hostile with the Catholic and with the English spirit"—very different from the Church, which sought to "reform mankind by assimilating realities with ideals, and accommodating herself to times and circumstances."[7]

After the Vatican Council, as Acton's judgments of Döllinger and Newman became harsher, so did his judgment of Burke. The pragmatic, accommodating "Catholic" Burke was now rebuked for encouraging men to "evade the arbitration of principle," to think of politics "experimentally," as an exercise in "what is likely to do good or harm, not what is right or wrong, innocent or sinful." Burke became the quintessential, opportunistic Whig rather than the principled liberal. In his notes and letters, Acton dwelt upon this contrast between Whiggism and liberalism. Where the Whig revered "legality, authority, possession, tradition, custom, opinion," the liberal respected only "what ought to be, irrespective of what is." The Whig believed in the "repression of the ideal," the liberal in its affirmation. "The Whig governed by compromise; the Liberal begins the reign of idea." "To a Liberal, all the stages between Burke and Nero are little more than the phases of forgotten moons."[8]

The unwritten History of Liberty was meant to trace the development of liberalism as well as the idea of liberty. Parts of this history survive: in two substantial lectures, "The History of Freedom in Antiquity" and "The History of Freedom in Christianity," delivered in 1877 to a local historical society and published in their journal; in a score of essays and reviews on a variety of subjects reprinted in various volumes; and in his lectures on the French Revolution in Cambridge in the late 1890s, published posthumously. These writings are full of brilliant analyses and observations, recondite facts and sources, provocative assertions and allusive references, such as "the greatest man born of a Jewish mother since Titus" (identified elsewhere as the German statesman and philosopher Friedrich Julius Stahl), or "the most prodigal imagination ever possessed by man" (the Renaissance poet, Ariosto).[9] An industrious young historian could make a career annotating and amplifying Acton's essays, a task made even more challenging because of the vast amount of manuscript notes, reflecting the breadth and depth of his scholarship as well as the boldness and passion of his ideas.

Early in his lecture on antiquity, Acton cited, seemingly approvingly, the "famous saying of the most famous authoress on the Continent" (Mme. De Staël) that "liberty is ancient, and it is despotism that is new."[10] He went on, however, in this and the succeeding lecture on Christianity, to qualify that assertion so abundantly that little was left of it. The great contribution of the Greeks, he said, was the principle of representation, government by consent, but by failing to limit the power of the sovereign people or to provide for any law superior to the lawgiver, the principle of democracy undermined the principle of liberty. "The vice of the classic State" (he apologized for the anachronism) "was that it was both Church and State in one. . . . In religion, morality, and politics there was only one legislator and one authority."[11] That fatal flaw was corrected by Christianity, whose dictum, Render unto Caesar, laid the ground for the inauguration of freedom by giving to the civil power "a sacredness it had never enjoyed" and at the same time "bounds it had never acknowledged."[12] Civil liberty was the result of the ensuing conflict between church and state, each aspiring to absolute authority and each limited by the other. The Middle Ages furthered the cause of freedom by extending representative government, abolishing slavery, recognizing the right of insurrection, and acknowledging duties superior to those imposed by man. The church, however, before the Reformation and still more afterward, undermined freedom when it became the instrument of the ruling monarchs. The kings of Spain appropriated the tribunal of the Inquisition, and the absolute monarchy of France was established by "twelve political cardinals."[13] "In the ages of which I have spoken," Acton sadly observed toward the end of his lecture on Christianity, "the history of freedom was the history of the thing that was not."[14]

Although the first tentative overtures toward freedom came in ancient and medieval times, only in modernity, Acton claimed, did it emerge in its true nature. English Protestant sects in the seventeenth-century discovered that "religious liberty is the generating principle of civil, and that civil liberty is the necessary condition of religious." But not until the American Revolution had "men sought liberty knowing what they sought."[15] Unlike earlier experiments in liberty, which had been tainted by expediency, compromise, and interest, the Americans demanded liberty simply and purely as a right. The three-pence tax that provoked the revolution was three-pence worth of pure principle. "I will freely spend nineteen shillings in the pound," Acton quoted Benjamin Franklin, "to defend my right of giving or refusing one other shilling." Acton himself went further. The true liberal, like the American revolutionist, "stakes his life, his fortune, the existence of his family, not to resist the intolerable reality of oppression, but the remote possibility of wrong, of diminished freedom."[16] The American Constitution was unique in being both democratic and liberal. "It was democracy in its highest perfection, armed and vigilant, less against aristocracy and monarchy than against its own weakness and excess. . . . It resembled no other known democracy, for it respected freedom, authority, and law."[17]

The French, unhappily, did not follow the example of the Americans. In his *Lectures on the French Revolution*, Acton traced in great detail the course of events and the logic of ideas by which the revolution, starting with the promise of liberty, ended in tyranny and terror.* Decades earlier, in his lectures on freedom, he had anticipated that theme when he contrasted the two revolutions, declaring the fatal flaw in the French to be the commitment to the ideal of equality and unqualified democracy. "The passion for equality made vain the hope of freedom."[18] Unlike the Americans, who wisely complemented their declaration of rights with a mixed constitution, the French permitted nothing to stand in the way of equality. In a passage reminiscent of Tocqueville, Acton explained the potential for tyranny in such a democracy: "It is bad to be oppressed by a minority, but it is worse to be oppressed by a majority. For there is a reserve of latent power in the masses which, if it

---

*Those who deplore Acton's failure to fulfill his potentialities as a historian sometimes overlook this substantial, scholarly volume. It is all the more remarkable because it is the work of a historian for whom the French Revolution was only one of his many interests, and by no means the major one.

is called into play, the minority can seldom resist. But from the absolute will of an entire people there is no appeal, no redemption, no refuge but treason."[19]

It is not only Acton's view of liberty that made the History of Liberty so formidable a task. It is also his view of history—the writing, as well as the actuality, of history. The audience at his inaugural lecture in Cambridge on "The Study of History" may have found much of it obscure, but there is no mistaking the moral fervor that inspired it and the moral burden it laid upon the historian. The historian, for Acton, is nothing less than a "hanging judge."

> The weight of opinion is against me when I exhort you never to debase the moral currency or to lower the standard of rectitude, but to try others by the final maxim that governs your own lives, and to suffer no man and no cause to escape the undying penalty which history has the power to inflict on wrong. . . . Opinions alter, manners change, creeds rise and fall, but the moral law is written on the tablets of eternity.[20]

The idea of a moral law that is absolute and immutable—a law that governs history as much as religion and society—is a recurrent, almost obsessive theme in Acton's notes and correspondence. "The inflexible integrity of the moral code is, to me, the secret of the authority, the dignity, the utility in history." If that code is debased, "history ceases to be a science."[21]

History as "science"—Acton did not at all mean by this what latter-day positivists do, for this "science," so far from being morally neutral ("value-free," we now say), was predicated on a moral absolute. His instructions to the contributors to the *Cambridge Modern History* were uncompromising. Nothing, he insisted, should reveal their country, religion, or party: "Contributors will understand that we are established, not under the Meridian of

Greenwich, but in Long. 30° W.; that our Waterloo must be one
that satisfies French and English, Germans and Dutch alike; that
nobody can tell, without examining the list of authors, where the
Bishop of Oxford laid down the pen, and whether Fairbairn or Gasquet, Liebermann or Harrison took it up."[22]*

The idea of a "scientific" history written by scholars so objective as to be virtually anonymous is quixotic in itself, and it is even
more so when conjoined to the idea of a universal history— history,
moreover, which was to be not so much a history of nations as a history of ideas, an "illumination of the soul."[24] To Acton there was
nothing utopian in this proposal, for it derived from a morality
that was fixed and absolute, in history as in life. This idea of morality also inspired his much quoted, and misquoted, maxim about
power. It is not all power that corrupts, but power that tends to
corrupt, and absolute power that corrupts absolutely. Although
Acton was careful to make that qualification, it is overshadowed by
the passion with which he brought to the idea.

> Great men are almost always bad men, even when they exercise
> influence and not authority: still more when you superadd the
> tendency or the certainty of corruption by authority. . . .[25]

> The experience of history teaches that the uncounted majority
> of those who get a place in its pages are bad. . . . The Men of
> the Time are, in most cases, unprincipled, and act from motives
> of interest, of passion, of prejudice cherished and unchecked, of
> selfish hope or unworthy fear. . . .[26]

---

*Acton made the same point in his Inaugural Lecture: "If men were truly sin-
cere, and delivered judgment by no canons but those of evident morality, then
Julian would be described in the same terms by Christian and pagan, Luther by
Catholic and Protestant, Washington by Whig and Tory, Napoleon by patriotic
Frenchman and patriotic German."[23]

History is not a web woven with innocent hands. Among all the causes which degrade and demoralize men, power is the most constant and the most active.[27]

This view of history is hardly conducive either to the actual pursuit of liberty or to the writing of a History of Liberty. One can account for Acton's failure to write that history by saying of him what he said of Döllinger, that "he knew too much to write."[28] Or one can cite Acton's lament when he discovered that even Döllinger did not share his moral views (Döllinger having criticized the church for its "errors" rather than "crimes"). "I am absolutely alone in my essential ethical position, and therefore useless. . . . The probability of doing good by writings so isolated and repulsive, of obtaining influence for views, etc., is so small that I have no right to sacrifice to it my own tranquility and my duty of educating my children."[29] The problem is more fundamental still, for it lies in a liberalism so morally rigorous and absolute that it could not be implemented, still less sustained, without critical, even fatal consequences.

Again and again Acton returned to the theme: Liberalism is the beginning of the "reign of ideas," and the reign of ideas is that which "we call the Revolution."

> The affirmative response [of the American revolutionists] is the Revolution, or as we say, Liberalism.
>
> The story of the revolted colonies impresses us first and most distinctly as the supreme manifestation of the law of resistance, as the abstract revolution in its purest and most perfect shape.
>
> The principle of the higher law signifies Revolution.
>
> Liberalism essentially revolutionary. Facts must yield to ideas.
>
> Peaceably and patiently if possible. Violently if not.

One note goes further still. The liberal theory of history requires that "what ought to be" take precedence over "what is"; it requires, that is, nothing less than a "revolution in permanence."[30]

"Revolution in permanence"—shades of Trotsky's "permanent revolution"! And shades of the French Revolution, whose degeneration from a "Republic of Virtue" into a "Reign of Terror" Acton so graphically described. But even as he was lauding this idea of liberty, his notes show him to have been acutely aware of the perils of any idea so absolute.

> Government by Idea tends to take in everything, to make the whole of society obedient to the idea. Spaces not so governed are unconquered, beyond the border, unconverted, unconvinced, a future danger. . . .
>
> Government that is natural, habitual, works more easily. It remains in the hands of average men, that is of men who do not live by ideas. Therefore there is less strain by making government adapt itself to custom. An ideal government, much better, perhaps, would have to be maintained by effort, and imposed by force.[31]

It might have been Burke who wrote these trenchant criticisms of "government by idea." But it was not Burke who was trying to write a History of Liberty. That book was not written because the very ideas of history and liberty, as Acton understood them, were problematic. If the Italian philosopher Benedetto Croce could write a *History as the Story of Liberty*, it was because he had all the confidence of a philosophical idealist whose ideals were immanent in history, whereas Acton had the *angst* of a moral historian whose ideals were always being violated by history. Yet it was Acton who wrote so powerfully and poignantly (although with ambiguous effect) about the subjects that occupied him throughout his life—liberty and morality, religion and history. This is his legacy to later generations who may marvel at his prescience in alerting us to the false prophets of our time: revolutionists, like the Bolsheviks, who start with the promise of liberty and equality and end in tyranny and violence; or religious fundamentalists who exemplify the despotic consequences of "government by idea"; or political leaders who all too often "tend" to be corrupt (and absolute leaders who are so absolutely); or historians who pride themselves on being "value-free," only to ignore the historic realities of vice and evil; or post-modernists who denigrate history itself by denying the very ideas of objectivity and truth.

In his autobiography written after World War II, the historian G. M. Trevelyan confessed that he found Acton "always interesting, but sometimes strange": "I remember, for instance, his saying to me that states based on the unity of a single race, like modern Italy and Germany, would prove a danger to liberty; I did not see what he meant at the time, but I do now!"[32] That conversation took place well before those countries fell victim to fascism, Nazism, and racism. So, too, Catholics, once discomfited by his criticisms not only of the dogma of infallibility but of the other "crimes" committed by the Church, now find him at least partially vindicated by Pope John Paul II, whose first major address in the new millennium was a plea for forgiveness for "the past and present sins" of the Church.[33]

Acton was obviously a more complicated and more tragic figure than his admirers may think—"out of sorts" with his contemporaries (as he often complained), and to some extent with himself. "Have you not discovered," he once wrote to Mary Gladstone, "what a narrow doctrinaire I am. . . . Politics come nearer religion with me, a party is more like a church, error more like heresy, prejudice more like sin, than I find it to be with better men."[34] Yet Acton's ideas, even at his most "doctrinaire," may be a useful antidote to the prevailing ideas of our own time. If we cannot share his moral absolutism, we can see the perils of an absolutistic relativism that is all too common today, in the culture at large as well as among historians, philosophers, and intellectuals. Acton recalls us to first principles and challenges us to reconsider how those principles may be carried out without falling victim to the absolutism that is itself subversive of those principles.

Alfred Marshall

"The Economics of Chivalry"

❦ In 1876, the Political Economy Club commemorated the centenary of *The Wealth of Nations*. "The great work has been done," Robert Lowe, former Chancellor of the Exchequer, announced. Unless sociology (he apologized for the barbarous neologism) took a sudden leap forward, he anticipated no significant development in political economy. Gladstone agreed; perhaps the currency might be reformed, but little else was required by way of theoretical or legislative innovation. Some members looked forward to some small reduction in the role of the government, others to some small expansion. William Stanley Jevons went so far as to suggest that the deviations from laissez faire—in matters of housing, sanitation, and public facilities (promenades, libraries, museums, a meteorological office)—might constitute a new branch of economics.[1]

The spokesmen on that occasion were pleased that political economy had come to so happy a fruition. Others, especially those of a more rigorously laissez-faire disposition, took a gloomier view of the state of the discipline. One year after that dinner, George Goschen, a prominent Liberal, gave the House of Commons the unhappy tidings that "Political Economy has been dethroned in that House and Philanthropy had been allowed to take its place."[2] Lord Milner later recalled that when he went up to Oxford in

1872, laissez faire held the field, but within ten years the few men who continued to adhere to that doctrine with any rigidity were regarded as "curiosities."[3]

The appointment in 1885 of Alfred Marshall to the coveted chair of Political Economy at Cambridge confirmed him as England's preeminent economist. Joseph Schumpeter dated this event as the beginning of the "Marshallian Age."[4] Yet Marshall's major work, *Principles of Economics*, was not to appear for another five years. At this time his only published book was *Economics of Industry*, written in collaboration with his wife and intended for use in university extension courses. (He was later so displeased with it that he tried to have it withdrawn from circulation.) His reputation was based on essays, lectures, courses, and the acclaim of students and colleagues. Within three years of his accession to the chair at Cambridge, one of his colleagues (a former student) observed that "half the economic chairs in the United Kingdom are occupied by his pupils, and the share taken by them in general economic instruction in England is even larger than this."[5] His influence outside of academia was even more impressive. He invited working-class and trade-union leaders to Cambridge to address the undergraduate Discussion Society, and he had close relations with the men and women who made up the world of philanthropy, social work, and social research (Charles Booth, for example, author of the magisterial inquiry, *Life and Labor of the People of London*). After the publication of the *Principles*, the head of Ruskin College (a working-class college established at the end of the century) reported that "work-people studying the *Principles of Economics* recognized in the author a sympathetic friend"—a tribute not only to Marshall but to the workers who were studying and appreciating that weighty tome.[6]

Marshall's distinctive contribution to economics reflects the curious intellectual route by which he came to that discipline. As an undergraduate at St. John's College, Cambridge, he read mathematics, and when he was elected a fellow of the college in 1865 he supplemented his stipend by coaching students in mathematics. He planned to become a molecular physicist, but his interest soon shifted from physics and mathematics to theology and then to metaphysics and philosophy. Coming under the spell of Kant— "my guide, the only man I ever worshipped"—went to Germany to learn the language properly.[7]* He was well on his way to becoming a philosopher in the German mode when his English heritage asserted itself. The important issues, he decided, were not metaphysical but psychological: the possibility of "the higher and more rapid development of human faculties." This, in turn, raised the ethical problem of the social order: whether the living conditions of the working classes "suffice for fullness of life." Older and wiser friends assured him that if he knew anything about political economy he would not ask that question, the resources of production being insufficient to give the great body of the English people the opportunity to enjoy that "fullness of life."[9] It was at this point, in 1868, that Marshall, who had just been appointed a lecturer in Moral Science at Cambridge, took up the study of economics. (One is reminded of Smith's initiation as Moral Philosopher before acquiring the chair of Political Economy).

This intellectual saga took all of three years, and every phase of it (except perhaps his initial interest in physics) is reflected in Marshall's subsequent work. He is generally credited with introducing the mathematical mode of analysis into economics. And so he did. Yet he deliberately relegated most of the mathematical

*During a later visit to Germany, at the time of the Franco-Prussian War, Marshall read and was much impressed by Hegel, especially his *Philosophy of History*. Benjamin Jowett, the great eminence at Oxford, wrote Marshall that he saw "a considerable element of Hegelianism" in the *Principles*. There are many references to Hegel in the *Principles* as well as in Marshall's other works.[8]

analysis in the *Principles* to an appendix, insisting that economics could be perfectly understood, indeed better understood, without it. Because every fact, he explained, was intimately related as cause and effect to many other facts which were not quantifiable, mathematical analysis was either useless or misleading, and the world would have been better off "if the work had never been done at all"—this in a letter to an economic statistician who was a former student.[10] He sent the same message to the readers of the *Principles*, warning them that economics was not a "simple science." The economist had "less need of elaborate scientific methods, than of a shrewd mother-wit, of a sound sense of proportion, and of a large experience of life."[11]

When Marshall's interests shifted from metaphysics to ethics, it was because he thought of ethics as a form of applied or practical metaphysics—Practical Reason rather than Pure Reason, as his favorite philosopher put it. And when he made the final move to economics, it was because he came to believe that economics was the practical application of ethics in the mundane workaday world. A few years earlier Henry Sidgwick, in his *Principles of Political Economy*, had repeated the familiar definition of political economy as an "inquiry concerned with the Production, Distribution, and Exchange of Wealth in a society."[12] Marshall opened his *Principles of Economics* with a different definition:

> Political Economy or Economics is a study of mankind in the ordinary business of life; it examines that part of individual and social action which is most closely connected with the attainment and with the use of the material requisites of well-being.
>
> Thus it is on the one side a study of wealth; and on the other, and more important side, a part of the study of man.[13]

Much is made of the fact that it was Marshall who introduced the term "economics" into popular discourse, thus replacing "political economy." The opening words of the book make it clear that he generally used these terms interchangeably; his "economics"was essentially the same as Smith's "political economy."* Just as Smith's "moral philosophy" infused *The Wealth of Nations*, so Marshall's "moral sciences" infused the *Principles*. Keynes pointed out that it was Marshall's rejection of an amoral ("value-free") utilitarianism that distinguished him from most of his predecessors. For Marshall the solution of economic problems involved "not an application of the hedonistic calculus, but a prior condition of the exercise of man's higher faculties, irrespective, almost, of what we mean by 'higher'."[15] This is not to say that Marshall denigrated or ignored the "lower" aspects of man's nature—self-interest and material wants. The job of the economist was concerned largely with such matters, if only because they were translatable into monetary units and therefore measurable. Because men were not and would never be "perfectly virtuous," interest and material gratification, would remain the guiding principles of economic activity.[16] There were, however, non-material factors which economists were beginning to appreciate: the growing importance of public opinion, for example, and "the desire of men for the approval of their own conscience and for the esteem of others."[17]

Schumpeter, hostile to any intimation of morality in economics, criticized Marshall for "the preaching of mid-Victorian morality, seasoned by Benthamism . . . a schema of middle-class values that knows no glamour and no passion."[18] In the *Principles*, Marshall repudiated just that Benthamite idea of morality. He preferred "satisfaction" to "pleasure," he explained, because the latter had a hedonistic or utilitarian connotation, whereas the former (he

---

*In passing (in the fourth chapter), Marshall suggested that the discipline was "better described by the broad term 'Economics' than by the narrower term 'Political Economy'"—"narrower" because it focused on the "exigencies" of party organization and political policies. It is a curious explanation, applying only to the mercantilists who were concerned with politics in that "narrow" sense, but not to Smith and his disciples who interpreted "political' as "social" or "moral."[14]

quoted T. H. Green to this effect) implied "the satisfaction of the permanent self." To pass from individualistic hedonism to a proper ethical creed, it was necessary to introduce another idea: the Kantian "categorical imperative," or, more simply, the "self-respect" implicit in any attempt to live so as to promote "the progress of the human race."[19] Earlier Marshall had identified that idea as "duty"—not duty in the Tory sense in which the upper class has a duty to care for the lower, but in the Kantian sense of a moral instinct inherent in each person by virtue of his reason, an instinct that bids each of us to "do unto others what you would that they should do unto you."[20]

Unlike moralists and economists of an earlier generation, Marshall had an evolutionary conception of moral character. This was another of his objections to conventional political economy; it had not only too low a view of human nature, it had too static a view. In Marshall's schema, the struggle for existence among human beings led to the survival not so much of individuals as of those races where "the individual was most willing to sacrifice himself for the benefit of those around him."[21] The growth of wealth, since at least the seventeenth century, had been accompanied by the strengthening and diffusion of such virtues as prudence, self-control, and farsightedness. Modern man, far more than his ancestors, was capable of sacrificing his present ease to his future satisfaction and his private interests to the public good. Economists had to take into account this social evolution, which ensured the moral as well as the physical progress of mankind. At the same time, they must heed the lesson of actual life: "that ordinary men are seldom capable of pure ideal altruism for any considerable time together." Thus competition, not cooperation, must continue to be the dominant form of the economy. It would be the height of irresponsibility to ignore the "imperfections which still cling to human nature," to decry competition in principle or to depreciate it in practice. Given the current state of human nature, the pertinent question in any particular situation was whether "the restraint of competition would not be more anti-social in its working than the competition itself."[22]

Ethics led Marshall to economics, and economics to the study of poverty. "I have devoted myself for the last twenty-five years," he informed the Royal Commission on the Aged Poor in 1893, "to the problem of poverty, and very little of my work has been devoted to any inquiry which does not bear upon that."[23] The remark seems suspiciously tailored to the occasion. Yet similar statements appear throughout his work. Early in his career, before he finally settled upon economics, he took to roaming the streets of the poorest quarters of whatever city he happened to be in, "looking at the faces of the poorest people."[24] It was then that he resolved to dedicate himself to the study of economics. That study led him to the two great questions:

> The first is, Is it necessary that, while there is so much wealth, there should be so much want? The second is, Is there not a great fund of conscientiousness and unselfishness latent in the breasts of men, both rich and poor, which could be called out if the problems of life were set before them in the right way, and which would cause misery and poverty rapidly to diminish?"[25]

Marshall's was the only economic treatise (not excepting Marx's *Capital*) to open with the subject of poverty. After identifying economics as principally concerned with the "material requisites of wellbeing," Marshall went on to define extreme poverty—the poverty of the "residuum"—as a state of "physical, mental, and moral ill-health." Ill-health, he explained, was no doubt due to other causes than poverty; but this was the chief cause. Thus "the study of the causes of poverty is the study of the causes of the degradation of a large part of mankind."[26] In an earlier essay Marshall had elaborated on the problem of the residuum—those suffering from "a poor physique and a feeble will, with no enterprise, no courage, no hope, and scarcely any self-respect." They may have come to that dire condition through a "hereditary taint," but it was exacerbated by the corrupting atmosphere of the large towns where they worked and lived. To remove them from that environment and break that hereditary pattern, Marshall proposed the establishment of a colony where they could be adequately housed and gainfully employed. The poor might resist this move, shrinking from the unfamiliar sunshine and greenery of the country. But with gentle persuasion and in the company of neighbors and friends, they could be prevailed upon to settle in the colony and create new lives for themselves and their children. This plan would benefit not only the residuum but also the "industrious poor" who would remain in London. Indeed the latter would be the main beneficiaries, for they would be relieved of the pressure of a class that depressed their wages, drove up their rents, took up jobs and space that they could better occupy, and had a deleterious effect upon the "average physique and the average morality of the coming English generation."[27]*

The residuum, however, Marshall insisted, was no longer the main problem; nor was pauperism. The problem was poverty. In his statement to the Royal Commission in 1893, he explained how far England had come from the time when the old poor law

---

*Parts of Marshall's account, particularly the term "residuum," may recall Charles Booth's *Life and Labor of the People in London*, the first volume of which was published the year before the *Principles*. But the writing of the *Principles* was well under way by 1885, when Booth started his research, and Marshall's essay, "Where to House the London Poor," was published in 1884, two years before Booth's first paper on the subject.

had aggravated the condition of pauperism by depressing wages, encouraging the growth of population, promoting political instability and administrative folly, and in general contributing to the "degradation of the laborers." The New Poor Law of 1834 corrected some of these faults by instituting the important principle of "less-eligibility," which required that the recipient of relief be no better off than the independent laborer and that relief be given only to the destitute, the test of destitution being the willingness to enter the workhouse. By 1893, when the purchasing power of the ordinary laborer had increased three- to five-fold, that kind of destitution no longer existed even among the very poor. It was now possible to give relief to those in distress rather than actual destitution. The new times required not only a more sympathetic attitude toward poverty, but also a more democratic one, a willingness to involve the working classes themselves in the administration of relief. In 1834 there had not been a "working class intelligence" capable of administering its own affairs. Since then, partly as a result of the Education Act of 1870, the working classes had acquired a knowledge and capacity that made the old oligarchic administration obsolete. They also had the incentive for more active participation because it was in their interest to promote a discriminating system of relief, which would help the deserving poor while applying "all needful discipline to the undeserving, the reckless and the profligate."[28]

In the course of his testimony before the Royal Commission, Marshall uttered one sentence that would have been banal had it come from a socialist but was remarkable for an economist. Explaining his reservations about some proposals for pensions, he said that he was afraid they would perpetuate themselves after the need for them passed. "I should regard all this problem of poverty as a mere passing evil in the progress of man upwards; and I should not like any institution started which did not contain in itself the causes which would make it shrivel up, as the causes of poverty itself shrivelled up."[29] This was not the only occasion when Marshall entertained the prospect of the elimination of poverty. In the opening pages of the *Principles*, he went so far as to question whether there need be any "so called 'lower classes' . . . whether there need be large numbers of people doomed from their birth to hard work in order to provide for others the requisites of a refined and cultured life; while they themselves are prevented by their poverty and toil from having any share or part in that life." As history had led to a diminution of pauperism, so it would lead to a diminution and eventual elimination of poverty. The rise of wages, the spread of education, the use of the steam engine instead of brute human labor, the increase of skilled work in proportion to unskilled, the advance of communication by means of railways and the printing press—all of this had already altered the nature and relation of the classes. Indeed, a great part of the artisan class no longer belonged to the "lower classes" as that term was originally understood; some had attained a more "refined and noble" life than had been the privilege of the majority of the upper classes only a century ago. This progress in the condition of the working classes, accompanied by the growing "earnestness of the age" ("social consciousness," we would now say), made it possible to contemplate a future in which poverty and ignorance would be extinguished and the lower classes would cease to exist.[30]

The extinction of poverty, for Marshall, did not imply that everyone would be in a state of equality. He had no expectation of that or even inclination for it. What he did look forward to was the end of the kind of work that was inherently degrading—hard corporeal work that made "producing machines" of workers, leaving them "with bodies exhausted and with minds dull and sluggish." Equally degrading was the supposedly light work of needlewomen, who toiled endless hours without respite until their hearts and minds were as benumbed as their hands. The elimination of such demeaning and debilitating labor would mean the elimination of poverty and thus of the "lower classes."[31]

This image of the degraded, dehumanized worker recalls the famous "alienation" or "immiseration" passage in Smith's *Wealth of Nations*.[32] Marshall's scene, however, provides an interesting contrast to Smith's. Smith's worker was dehumanized by the simple, mindless, effortless work in a factory; Marshall's by long hours of physically arduous labor. For Smith the only remedy was education, which would restore the intelligence and humanity that was being destroyed by the division of labor; for Marshall the remedy was the machinery itself, which made possible the division of labor and relieved the worker of those long hours of backbreaking, mind-numbing labor. Machinery also had the advantage of increasing the proportion of skilled to unskilled labor and of mental to manual work, thus reducing both the expenditure of physical energy and the time spent on monotonous tasks. The modern weaver, managing several looms simultaneously, was engaged in more skilled, less monotonous work than the old-fashioned weaver plying his single loom. Moreover, the social life around the factory was stimulating, so that even those workers who seemed to be engaged in the most monotonous operations displayed "considerable intelligence and mental resource."[33]*

In an early essay Marshall put the case more boldly. It was not only the "lower classes" that would be eliminated. It was the "working classes" as well. "The Future of the Working Classes"

---

*The earlier editions of the *Principles* were more pointedly, if implicitly, directed against Smith, in Marshall's assertion, for example, that the factory worker was more intelligent and resourceful than the agricultural laborer in spite of the fact that the latter's work was more varied. This argument was removed in the major revision of the fifth edition in 1907.

concluded: "In so far as the working classes are men who have such excessive work to do, in so far will the working classes have been abolished."[34] This did not mean that men would cease to be workers; work itself, proper work, was "the healthy energetic exercise of faculties." In this sense, everyone would be a worker. But they would become workers who had the opportunity and the motive to stimulate their "higher energies." This, in turn, would lead to a momentous change in the relationship of the classes. "The question is not whether all men will ultimately be equal—that they certainly will not—but whether progress may not go on steadily if slowly, till the official distinction between working man and gentleman has passed away; till, by occupation at least, every man is a gentleman."[35] What distinguished the worker from the gentleman was not the fact that he worked with his hands; the sculptor did that. Nor that he was paid for his labor and had to obey his superiors; the army officer did that. Nor that he was paid to perform disagreeable duties; the surgeon did that. Nor even that he worked hard for little pay; the governess did that. The distinctive fact was the effect of his work upon him.

> If a man's daily task tends to give culture and refinement to his character, do we not, however coarse the individual man may happen to be, say that his occupation is that of a gentleman? if a man's daily task tends to keep his character rude and coarse, do we not, however truly refined the individual man may happen to be, say that he belongs to the working classes?"[36]

If "gentleman" was an unfamiliar word in the lexicon of economists, "chivalry" was positively bizarre. The readers of the *Economic Journal*, in 1907, must have been taken aback by an essay, "The Social Possibilities of Economic Chivalry," written by the most eminent economist of the generation. This was not a playful metaphor on Marshall's part; he meant it in all seriousness. Just as feudal chivalry had mitigated the horrors of warfare, so economic chivalry would mitigate the evils of commercial competition. As medieval chivalry had elicited an unselfish loyalty to prince or country, so economic chivalry would cultivate a spirit of public service. And as knightly chivalry put a man's courage and endurance to the test, so economic chivalry would delight in "doing noble and difficult things because they are noble and difficult." Indeed, there was already much "latent chivalry" in business; this was one of the symptoms of economic progress. Unfortunately there was also much economic activity that was not chivalrous. Economists studying the behavior of businessmen could distinguish the chivalrous and noble from the selfish and ignoble and impart that knowledge to the public. Public opinion would then act as an informal Court of Honor, paying homage to the high-minded, public-spirited businessman and discrediting the vulgar, self-serving one. Wealth acquired by chicanery would no longer be a warrant for social success, and a business enterprise, even if it did not produce great wealth, would be esteemed so long as it was honorable in its aims and methods.[37]

Toward the end of the *Principles*, Marshall referred the reader to that essay, repeating his conviction that the application of the idea of economic chivalry—"a devotion to public well-being on the part of the rich"—might help mitigate the all too common "anti-social strategy" of wealth acquired by speculation and manipulation rather than by constructive work.[38] In the course of the book, he offered proposals for the implementation of that idea: maximum hours of work, especially for manual workers; minimum wages (one level for men, another for women, adjusted to the family income); higher taxes on unearned income (such as land) than on earned income; expenditures by the government to improve the environment and reduce pollution; old age pensions (for the working classes alone); and profit-sharing and cooperative plans. He was less well disposed to trade unions, suspecting some of them of operating against the public interest. Above all, he looked to an expanded system of education, providing not only compulsory education but nonutilitarian, nonvocational education. The children of the working classes, as much as those of the middle classes, had need of a "truly liberal general education" that would develop their intellectual faculties, character, and "higher nature."[39]

At the same time, Marshall cautioned against expecting too hasty a remedy by legislation, which might itself prove to be either futile or mischievous. Legislation could be useful in improving the organization of joint-stock companies, railways, canals, and the like. It might also be helpful in ameliorating the conditions of the working classes by reducing the hours of labor. But learning to use those leisure hours well and forgo the "sordid and gross pleasures" developed over centuries was not so easily achieved. The penultimate page of the *Principles* issued the final warning:

> Now, as always, noble and eager schemes for the reorganization of society have painted beautiful pictures of life, as it might be under institutions which their imagination constructs easily. But it is an irresponsible imagination, in that it proceeds on the suppressed assumption that human nature will, under the new institutions, quickly undergo changes such as cannot reasonably be expected in the course of a century, even under favorable conditions. If human nature could be thus ideally transformed, economic chivalry would dominate life even under the existing institutions of private property.[40]*

---

*Marshall's metaphor was in some respects inapt. Surely it was not the medieval ethic but the Puritan ethic that believed that the inheritance of great wealth was bad for the character and that a noble spirit was seldom formed without the "pains of some self-compulsion and some self-repression."[41] But "chivalry" did dramatically express his revulsion against the utilitarianism that he saw exemplified in orthodox economics as well as in socialism.

The "economics of chivalry" was not only a criticism of capitalism as it was currently practiced. It was far more a criticism of socialism. Marshall recalled that in his early years, after reading Mill's essays on socialism, he had taken a more favorable view of socialism, but he later thought it "more important to dwell on the truths in Mill's *On Liberty* than those in his *Essays on Socialism*."[42] By the lax definition of socialism prevalent at the time, he observed, he might still be regarded as a socialist. "We are told sometimes that everyone who strenuously endeavors to promote the social amelioration of the people is a Socialist—at all events, if he believes that much of this work can be better performed by the State than by individual effort." In that sense of the word, he conceded that he, like, nearly every economist of his generation, was a socialist.[43] In any more rigorous sense, however, he was never a socialist, even in his early years, still less later.

The *Principles* took a dire view of socialism (or "collectivism"— he used the terms interchangeably). It was likely to "deaden the energies of mankind, and arrest economic progress," to "destroy much that is most beautiful and joyful in the private and domestic relations of life," and to give rise to all the dangers inherent in any "sudden and violent reorganization of the economic, social and political conditions of life."[44] In essays written at the same time or shortly afterwards, he repudiated socialism together with orthodox laissez faire, the latter because of "the cruelty and waste of irresponsible competition and the licentious use of wealth," the former because of "the tyranny and the spiritual death of an ironbound socialism."[45] The chief dangers of socialism came not from the desire for a more equal distribution of income—"for I can see no harm in that"—but from "the sterilizing influences on those mental activities which have gradually raised the world from barbarism."[46] Socialism was "a movement for taking the responsibility for a man s life and work, as far as possible, off his shoulders and putting it on to the State."[47] Socialism, in short, would be as fatal to a chivalric economy as to an unremittingly competitive one.

> The pressure of bureaucratic methods would impair not only the springs of material wealth, but also many of those higher qualities of human nature, the strengthening of which should be the chief aim of social endeavor.[48]
>
> The world under free enterprise will fall far short of the finest ideals until economic chivalry is developed. But until it is developed, every great step in the direction of collectivism is a grave menace to the maintenance even of our present moderate rate of progress.[49]

In one respect Marshall retained a lingering sympathy with socialism—not with its theories or policies but with its vision of human nature. And not with its idea of human perfectibility; he continued to believe that there was no warrant for that. But buried among the "wild rhapsodies" of the socialists was an appreciation of the "hidden springs of human nature." It was this that "business-like economists" lacked and that they could profitably learn from the socialists.[50]

Like Smith's *Wealth of Nations*, Marshall's *Principles of Economics* was immediately hailed as a major intellectual event. The two books had a similar history. Each was long in the making and long awaited by impatient admirers. And each, in spite of its formidable subject matter and length, became an instant classic of interest to laymen as much as to professionals. Marshall, the reviewers agreed, gave a new direction to economics. The old "dismal science" was now humanized. The *Manchester Guardian*, recalling Coleridge's warning that political economy would "dig up the charcoal foundations of the temple of Ephesus to burn as fuel for a steam engine," was relieved to find that the new political economy would do no such thing.[51] The *Athenaeum* praised Marshall for retaining his "mathematical precision" while "sharing to the full the most enthusiastic reformers' sympathy with distress."[52] The *Times* reminded readers not to be so overcome by Marshall's masterly treatment of human behavior in economic affairs as to forget that economics was still an essentially scientific discipline: "The 'Laws of Economics' are statements of tendencies expressed in the indicative mood, and not ethical precepts in the imperative."[53] Even the *Pall Mall Gazette*, despising the old political economy (which had begun to "stink in the nostrils of so many earnest men"), warned its readers that there was "a strict limit to the extent to which these trespassing 'ethical forces' are to be allowed on scientific preserves." The reviewer told the story, perhaps apocryphal, of Marshall being asked what he thought of the proposal to construct "a Christian Science of Economics," to which he replied: "I have no objection, if they will first construct a Christian chemistry, a moral Euclid, or an altruistic algebra."[54]

Marshall is reported to have said of his own work: "It's all in Adam Smith."[55] Not all, perhaps, but much of it. This was Marshall's historic contribution: to restore to economics the moral dimension that Smith had imparted to it, which Malthus, Ricardo, and their successors had so ruthlessly suppressed. Marshall, to be sure, went beyond Smith in allowing for a larger presence of the state in economic affairs. Where Smith had relied upon the invisible hand to bring about the public good, Marshall called upon the government to supplement—not supersede—the invisible hand. It was a minimum of intervention that Marshall sought; the hand of government was to be as light and unobtrusive as possible. But his minimum was greater than that anticipated by Smith. "Let the State be up and doing," Marshall counseled—and at the same time, "Let everyone work with all his might."[56] The double message was clear: individuals should do all they could do, and the government should do what it alone could do efficiently. Moreover, Smith's economic man did not have to be told to be moral.

He was that naturally, unwittingly; in acting in his own interests he promoted an end he had not intended. Marshall's economic man had to be reminded to be moral, to pursue the good of others by acting in accord with his "higher nature." And Marshall had a more elevated view of that "higher nature." All that was expected or required of Smith's economic man was "sympathy." Marshall's economic man was called upon to exercise the more arduous virtues of duty and chivalry.

One is reminded that Marshall came from a family of clerics. His father, although not a clergyman himself, was an ardent Evangelical who dearly wanted his son to become an Evangelical minister. Instead the son became an agnostic in religion and something of an evangelical (a lower-case evangelical) in economics.

John Buchan

An Untimely Appreciation

꩜ John Buchan—novelist, biographer, historian, member of Parliament, governor-general of Canada, and, in his final years, Lord Tweedsmuir of Elsfield—died in 1940, one of the last articulate representatives of the old England. He is the paradigm (the parody, some would have it) of a species of English gentleman now very nearly extinct. The manners and morals celebrated in his books, the social prejudices unwittingly disclosed in them, the attitudes and philosophy implicit in them have already acquired the faded tint of a period piece. Before they vanish altogether, it may be interesting to take pause, to inquire into an ethos that for some is an embarrassing memory, for others a remembrance of lost grandeur.

There is indeed matter for embarrassment in Buchan's novels. There is the clean, good life which comes with early rising, cold baths, and long immersion in fog and damp, in contrast to the red-eyed, liverish, sluggish, dissolute town dweller. There is the casual bravery, classically understated, of his heroes. ("There's nothing much wrong with me. . . . A shell dropped beside me and damaged my foot. They say they'll have to cut it off.")[1] There is the blithe provincialism and amateurishness of the spy-adventurer who complains that the natives in a Kurdish bazaar do not understand any

"civilised tongue," or the member of Parliament who cannot pro-
nounce "Boche" names and confuses Poincaré with Mussolini, or the
cabinet minister who will not be bothered to read the newspapers
while on vacation.[2] There is the penchant for sports that requires
every hero (and every respectable villain) to be a first-class shot, and
looks upon politics, espionage, and war alike as an opportunity to
practice good English sportsmanship. Richard Hannay, the hero of
several of Buchan's novels, is much distressed at not "playing the
game" when he abuses the hospitality of a particularly heinous villain; elsewhere he permits a German agent, plotting to spread anthrax germs through the British army, to escape rather than ignobly
shoot him in the back. Another hero, Sandy Arbuthnot, during a
tremendous cavalry attack involving Cossack, Turkish, German,
and British troops, can be heard crying, "Oh, well done our side!"[3]

Even more reminiscent of the English public school boy is the
curious blurring of sexual lines. All Buchan's heroes turn out to
have "something girlish" about them. A husky mountain guide has
hair "as flaxen as a girl's"; Peter Pienaar, the uncouth Boer adventurer, has a face "as gentle as a girl's," as does a general in the same
novel; Sandy Arbuthnot has "a pair of brown eyes like a pretty
girl's"; and a six-and-a-half-foot Negro chieftain has hands "more
like a high-bred woman's than a man's."[4] Even some of his historical heroes have the same ambiguous sexuality, Augustus, for example, having "features so delicately modelled as to be almost
girlish."[5] Conversely, his heroines have more than a little of the boy
in them: boyish hips, boyish stride, wholesome boyish manners
and interests. Even this reassuring boyishness, however, cannot entirely allay the unease of the hero. When Hannay, then well in his
forties, meets the bewitching Hilda von Einem, he is thrown into
panic at the thought of sitting beside her: "I had never been in a
motor-car with a lady before, I felt like a fish on a dry sandbank."[6]
His friend, Archie Roylance, had also been "as shy as a woodcock"

of those "mysterious and unintelligible" female creatures. "Fresh and unstaled by disillusion," he finally falls in love with Janet, but he succumbs, the author proudly reports, not to the vulgar charms of "swelling bosoms and pouting lips and soft curves and languishing eyes." The fresh and unstaled phrases that come to his lips are "jolly," "clean-run," "a regular sportswoman," and, as an afterthought, "amazingly good-looking."[7]

Occasionally Buchan might be found poking fun at this priggishness. Of Walter Scott he said: "For women he had an old-fashioned reverence, and . . . regarded them very much as a toast to be drunk after King and Constitution." But he respected Scott's diffidence: "I do not suggest the severe doctrine that no man can write intimately of sex without forfeiting his title to gentility, but I do say that for Scott's type of gentleman to do so would have been impossible without a dereliction of standards."[8]

So far the Buchan ethos amuses more than it offends. It becomes displeasing when private foibles begin to impinge upon public morality. The most serious item in one critic's indictment of Buchan is his preoccupation with success, his top-of-the-form ethic.[9] A dinner party in a Buchan novel assembles a typical assortment of guests: Bonson Jane "had been a noted sportsman and was still a fine polo player; his name was a household word in Europe for his work in international finance, . . . it was rumoured that in the same week he had been offered the Secretaryship of State, the Presidency of an ancient University, and the control of a great industrial corporation." Simon Ravelstone is president of "one of the chief banking houses in the world"; his son is "making a big name for himself in lung surgery." And another guest is "about our foremost pundit, . . . there were few men alive who were his equals in classical scholarship."[10] So closed is the universe inhabited by these Calvinist-minded characters that they can agree on the rank and order of their success. Sandy Arbuthnot is "one of the two or three most intelligent people in the world," Julius Victor is the "richest man in the world," Medina is the "best shot in England after His Majesty," Castor is the "greatest agent-provocateur in history," and there is one of whom it is said, with a fine conjunction of precision and vagueness, that "there aren't five men in the United States whose repute stands higher."[11]

Yet closer attention to the novels suggests that these marks of success are not the ends toward which Buchan's heroes—or villains—strive. They are the preconditions of their being heroes or villains at all, much as the characters in fairy tales are always the most beautiful, the most exalted, the most wicked of their kind. They are the starting points for romance, not the termination. Indeed, the theme of the more interesting of the novels is the ennui, the *taedium vitae* afflicting precisely those who have attained the highest state, and precisely because they have attained that state. In *John Macnab*, three of the most eminent men in England, dispirited by a surfeit of success, deliberately engage in an adventure in illegality in order to court exposure and disgrace. In *Mountain Meadow*, a famous American financier and an equally famous English barrister leave their comfortable establishments to suffer pain and death in the far north. All Buchan's heroes are periodically beset by fatigue and lassitude, a "death-wish" that is overcome by divesting themselves of their urban identities— success being an urban condition—and donning the shabby, anonymous clothes of the countryman. Only when the perils of nature and of the chase have roughened up the smooth patina of success, leaving the body scarred and the mind tormented, can they resume their normal lives and identities.

If Buchan's heroes are not as single-minded in the pursuit of success as a casual reading might suggest, neither are they as simpleminded or philistine. Revisiting Oxford in 1938, Sandy complains that the youth have become "a bit too much introverted—isn't that the filthy word?"[12] (Too much introverted: if Sandy is obliged to use the filthy word, he at least takes care to use the right syntax.) Yet Sandy himself is far from being an extrovert. He is given to spells of moodiness and despair, to a never-ending quest for an unattainable grail and a new identity (hence his predilection for exotic disguises).

Indeed, the introvert-intellectual is the hero of several of Buchan's works. One of these, Launcelot Wake in *Mr. Standfast*, is so far gone in introversion and intellectualism as to be a pacifist. He is represented in the opening of the book as the stock intellectual, sallow of complexion and red of eye, partial to modern poetry and modern art. Yet by the end of the book, as a result of one of those typical reversals that Buchan, like other romancers, is fond of (his critics seem not to realize that the ostensible truths of the prologue have turned into the half-truths of the epilogue), Wake has emerged as the hero. He has abandoned neither his intellectualism nor his pacifism and is still incapable of the easy sentiments of patriotism and duty:

> I see more than other people see, and I feel more. That's the curse on me. You're a happy man and you get things done, because you only see one side of a case, one thing at a time. How would you like it if a thousand strings were always tugging at you, if you saw that every course meant the sacrifice of lovely and desirable things, or even the shattering of what you know to be unreplaceable? . . . For me to fight would be worse than for another man to run away.

When he dies, after a gallant exploit, Hannay delivers his eulogy: "If the best were to be taken, he would be chosen first, for he was a big man, before whom I uncovered my head."[13]

Buchan's portraits of historical (not fictional) characters are similarly tributes to the complicated man torn by conflicting ideas and emotions, who barely manages to maintain a precarious balance: Lord Montrose, starting as a Covenanter in rebellion against the king and ending as the "noblest Cavalier" while still a Presbyterian; or Oliver Cromwell, the "practical mystic," the revolutionist with a passion for law and order, the commander given to spells of withdrawal and self-doubt.[14] In history as in fiction, his heroes are by no means the simple, clean-cut men of action who shoulder their way to victory. They are sensitive souls, fated to noble failures and Pyrrhic victories.

By modernist standards, to be sure, the literary standards of his own time as well as ours, Buchan may be judged a philistine. His description of the "advanced" community of Biggleswick in *Mr. Standfast* is a parody of such a community: the pretentious, arty folk with their gimcrack houses and "demented modish" paintings, who are determined "never to admire anything that was obviously beautiful, like a sunset or a pretty woman, but to find surprising loveliness in things which I thought hideous."[15] In his autobiography, Buchan spoke of his efforts to "get on terms with my contemporaries"—this in the 1920s—but could only record a series of failures. Their verse (he was apparently referring to T. S. Eliot) seemed to him "unmelodious journalism, . . . a pastiche of Donne." He disliked the "hothouse world" of Proust though he granted his literary skills, and he deplored the "tortuous arabesques" of the later Henry James. With the exception of *War and Peace* and a story or two by Turgenev, he found nothing of merit in the Russians and resolved never to try to read them again. Some contemporaries pleased him: Sinclair Lewis and Booth Tarkington had the narrative gift of the good novelist, and some of H. G. Wells's novels he believed to be of enduring value. But for the "rebels and experimentalists" he confessed a "radical defect of sympathy." They had their merits, he conceded, but he found the world they represented "ineffably dismal."[16]

Yet, alien as he was from the literature of modernity, his mind had a range and seriousness that belie the charge of philistinism. It was not only Scott, Tennyson, and Macaulay whom he (and the heartier characters in his novels) fondly quoted, but also such varied writers as Shakespeare, Hakluyt, Thomas Browne, Bunyan, Hazlitt, Walton, Thoreau, Whitman, Johnson, Chateaubriand, Calvin, and Augustine. Impatient with experiments in the arts as in politics, fearful of attempts to probe the unconscious in novels as in life, he was obviously limited in his aesthetic responses. Yet it can hardly be judged philistine or "anti-intellectual," as is sometimes said of him, to prefer Homer in the Greek to T. S. Eliot in English, or to admire Tolstoy more than Dostoevsky, or to write serious works of historical scholarship that are also refreshingly literate.

To understand Buchan is to enter a cultural tradition with distinctive social and literary manners. The English intellectual of Buchan's generation was loath to parade his intelligence; his Double First at the university had to be acquired without visible swotting or cramming. (Buchan's characters never admitted to memorizing anything; they had "fly-paper memories" to which long passages of poetry or facts adhered effortlessly.) His own writing was of this character, suggesting not the anguish of creation but the casualness of civilized conversation. In this relaxed manner he was able to produce fifty-seven books in the interstices of his other more absorbing occupations: the law, interrupted by a short period of service with Milner in South Africa, then business, Parliament, and finally the governor-generalship of Canada.

Such productivity could only be attained if one wrote not merely *as* one spoke but also *what* one spoke. This is the real clue to Buchan's (as to other Victorians') prodigious output. There are many writers today who are as rich in intellectual resources; there are few who feel as free to draw upon their capital. Buchan had confidence not only in his knowledge but also in his opinions, attitudes, intuitions, and prejudices. What he wrote for the public was what he felt in private; he did not labor for a subtlety or profundity that did not come spontaneously. Nor did he censor his spontaneous thoughts before committing them to paper. He had none of the scruples that are so inhibiting today, no temptation to adhere to the canons of political correctness. He was candid about race, nation, religion, and class because it did not occur to him that anything he was capable of feeling or thinking could be reprehensible. His creative strength was the strength of character.

It was authenticity as well as productivity that was enhanced by this self-confidence and self-reliance. His familiarity with the Scottish countryside does more than provide the background of many of his stories. The hunting and fishing scenes in *John Macnab*, described in great detail, are not appendages to the plot; they *are* the plot. The homely details of the domestic life of a retired Glasgow merchant in *Huntingtower*, interspersed with comments about Freudianism, communism, and international politics, lend verisimilitude to the fairy-tale character of the Russian princess and the wild improbabilities of the plot of that novel. Verisimilitude, not verity—for his novels remain unashamed romances. Because he believed that fantasy and reality naturally feed upon and nurture each other, he did not trouble himself overmuch with plot, relying on coincidence, hunch, luck, the stock character and situation, to an extent that no popular writer today would dare to do. And because he did not trouble himself unduly with niceties of style, he was unembarrassed by the cliché, the occasional longueur or discursive aside. The very laxity of plot and style served his purpose, not only to advance the tale with a minimum of effort but also to provide the commonplace background against which the romantic adventure is best played out. In an essay on Scott, Buchan argued the case for a *punctum indifferens*, a calm center around which rages the storm of romance: "The kernel of romance is contrast, beauty and valour flowering in unlikely places, the heavenly rubbing shoulders with the earthly. The true romantic is not the Byronic hero; he is the British soldier whose idea of a beau geste is to dribble a football into the enemy's trenches."[17]

A more serious charge than philistinism brought against Buchan is racism. At least one American publisher considered and then abandoned the idea of reissuing *Prester John* because it would offend liberal sensibilities. Published in 1910, *Prester John* is the story of a native African uprising led by a Western-educated Negro ("black" would be an anachronism) who seeks to harness the primitive religion and nationalism of the savages to set himself up as the demigod of a native republic. If the plot is provocative enough, the language is still more so: the hero, a white boy, speaks of the "niggers" with their "preposterous negro lineaments."[18] For Buchan, the fact of racial inferiority, as he thought it, was the rationale not for exploitation but for compassionate humanitarianism. To the modern reader this only exacerbates the offense. Laputa, the native leader, is represented as a noble figure and a worthy antagonist. When he is defeated in honorable battle, the classical note of the White Man's Burden is sounded:

> I knew then the meaning of the white man's duty. He has to take all risks, recking nothing of his life or his fortunes and well content to find his reward in the fulfilment of his task. That is the difference between white and black, the gift of responsibility, the power of being in a little way a king; and so long as we know this and practice it, we will rule not in Africa alone but wherever there are dark men who live only for the day and for their own bellies.

Moreover, the work made me pitiful and kindly. I learned much of the untold grievances of the natives and saw something of their strange, twisted reasoning.[19]

Prester John was one of Buchan's earliest books, a book meant for boys, which is perhaps why the message was so shrill. In his other work, the racist language and overtones were more casual than ideological. "A nigger band," he observed, "almost looking like monkeys in uniform, pounded out some kind of barbarous jingle."[20] This is the kind of language all too familiar in the literature of the day, even on the part of a writer of such distinction as Joseph Conrad, who had no qualms about speaking of the "repulsive mask of a nigger's soul," the "black mist," the "subtle and dismal influence" emanating from him.[21] By way of extenuation—perhaps feeble extenuation—it should be said that such sentiments, commonplace at the time, were meant to be descriptive rather than prescriptive, not an incitement to social or political action but an attempt to express differences of culture and color in terms that had been unquestioned for generations.

The same observation may be made of Buchan's anti-Semitism. There were, in fact, Jewish rag dealers and pawnbrokers, Jewish Communists and financiers, in England at the time, an England that was far more ethnically homogeneous than it is today. Yet it is disconcerting to find that the plot of one of his most successful novels, *Thirty-Nine Steps* (1915), centers upon an international conspiracy devised by Jewish anarchists and Jewish financiers led by a "little white-faced Jew in a bath-chair with an eye like a rattlesnake" who is avenging himself for centuries of persecution.[22] But if Buchan's Jewish villains are to be kept account of, the ledger ought also to include the Jewish heroes in *Three Hostages* (1924): the "richest man in the world," who is an entirely honorable and sympathetic figure and who is made the victim of another conspiracy precisely because his mission was to secure peace in the world; or his beautiful daughter, the fiancée of the Marquis de la Tour du Pin, one of Hannay's oldest and noblest friends.[23] And even the Jewish villain is not necessarily the nastiest of villains; in *Mr. Standfast* (1919) he is the most decent of the lot.

This is not to suggest that Buchan's novels can be acquitted of the charge of anti-Semitism. They were anti-Semitic in the same sense that they were racist. As one of Buchan's American heroes said of one of his Jewish heroes (vulgar Americans could be relied on to voice what polite Englishmen only thought), he simply "didn't like his race."[24] This kind of anti-Semitism, indulged in at that time and place, was too common and too passive to be scandalous. Men were normally anti-Semitic, unless by some quirk of temperament or ideology they happened to be philo-Semitic. So long as the world itself was normal, this was of no great consequence. It was only later, when social impediments became fatal disabilities, when anti-Semitism ceased to be the prerogative of English gentlemen and became the business of politicians and demagogues, that sensitive men were shamed into silence. It was Hitler who put an end to the casual anti-Semitism of the clubman. And it was then, when the conspiracies of the English adventure tale became the realities of German politics, that Buchan and others had the grace to realize that what was permissible under civilized conditions was not permissible with civilization *in extremis*. His last book, *Mountain Meadow*, composed on the eve of World War II and in the shadow of his own death, was a tract exalting "brotherhood." Among the many financiers appearing in its pages, there is not a single Jew.

Early in 1934, long before most Englishmen had become aware of Nazism, Buchan publicly denounced Hitler's anti-Semitism and espoused the cause of Zionism. It is tempting to remark upon the irony of the fact that the fictional perpetrator of Jewish-capitalist-communist conspiracies should have had his name inscribed, in solemn ceremony, in the Golden Book of the Jewish National Fund. Buchan himself would have found nothing ironic about this. His speech acknowledging the honor paid him took as its theme the racial similarities of Scotsmen and Jews, with particular reference to their high regard for learning. A participant in the ceremony, sharing the platform with Buchan, observed him, during the address following his, leaning forward and watching, with unconcealed delight and fascination, the ample gestures and bodily movements of the Yiddish-speaking rabbi.[25]

In the clubman syndrome, acute class consciousness was second only to race consciousness. It is sometimes suggested that for Buchan this class consciousness was both aggravated and made more reprehensible by its having been acquired rather than being indigenous. A Scotsman, the son of a Presbyterian minister, attending village schools, a grammar school, and finally the University of Glasgow, he was far removed from the upper-class English characters he described so lovingly. He did not even like school games, and although he did enjoy such country sports as hunting and fishing, it was without the ritual that a wealthy Englishman brought to them. Only when he entered Oxford in 1895, at the age of twenty, did he get a glimpse of upper-class life. And for some time it was just a glimpse. Older than most freshmen, much poorer and more puritanical, he associated at first only with other scholarship students. Not until his third year, when prizes and literary work had made him relatively affluent, did his circle expand to include rowing and rugby stars as well as poets, writers, and school orators. His social initiation was completed in London where he read law, and then in South Africa in 1901, when he was on the administrative staff of Lord Milner.

What redeems Buchan from the double charge of either not knowing the clubman society he purported to describe, or if he did know it, of having gained entree into it only by such an effort as to suggest social climbing and snobbery, is the fact of his Scottishness. The Scot is neither an outsider nor an interloper in the sense in which a Cockney or provincial might be. Like the American, he is alien enough to be assimilated without prejudice, and socially mobile enough to expect to be assimilated. His culture is not a despised subculture but a culture in its own right. His accent and schooling are a token of national peculiarity, not of class inferiority. This is not to say that there was no social climbing. Men accustomed to social mobility are accustomed to climbing. But it is not the same demeaning process to the foreigner that it would be to the native, for it does not involve the same repudiation of his past or alienation from himself.

It was his Scottishness, too, that made Buchan a Tory with a difference. (A Tory, not a Conservative—a distinction Disraeli understood.) The Scottish Tory, as he himself recognized, was a special breed. "A youth in Scotland who called himself a Tory was almost certain to be thinking about politics, and not merely cherishing a family loyalty."[26] Buchan was a Tory by choice and principle rather than economic or class interests. He thought the existing class structure both inevitable and desirable. Like William Morris, he could say that he respected the working class too much to want to turn it into a middle class. And like Disraeli, he wanted to cultivate the alliance between aristocracy and working class. "Democracy and aristocracy," Buchan said, "can co-exist, for oligarchy is their common enemy."[27] The word "oligarchy" was used advisedly, for what Buchan deplored was the tendency to make of class an exclusively economic category and to use social position as an economic instrument. He had no liking for the "genuine reactionaries" of his own party who "woke to life only in the budget season."[28] Not committed to the principles of laissez-faire, he had no prejudice against social reforms, public authorities, or welfare economics.

Class was malleable; history and character could alter what birth and money had established. It was the possibility, indeed, the actuality, of such alteration that attracted Buchan to the study of the English Civil War. And it was a fine political judgment that made him choose as his heroes Lord Montrose and Oliver Cromwell: Montrose for recognizing that there were occasions when revolution was warranted, Cromwell for recognizing that there came a time in a revolution when authority had to be reasserted. Cromwell, Buchan said, was no Leveller or egalitarian. "The world could not do without its masters, but why reverence a brocaded puppet larded by a priest with oil, when there were men who needed no robes or sacring to make them kingly?"[29] Authority remained, even as authorities were overthrown, and some men were the natural repositories of authority. "It is a melancholy fact which exponents of democracy must face that, while all men may be on a level in the eyes of the State, they will continue in fact to be preposterously unequal."[30]

This last quotation might have appeared in Buchan's biography of Cromwell; in fact it appeared in his novel *John Macnab*. The theme of this novel is not only the natural and rightful authority exercised by some men by virtue of their breeding, experience, and character but also the natural and rightful impulse to rebel against that authority. John Macnab's gallant wager, to kill and remove against great odds a stag and salmon from his neighbor's property, is not simply a paean to adventure—sheer, gratuitous, gentlemanly adventure, *le sport* for its own sake. It is rather a parable about authority and property, and the perpetual challenge to which both are subject. The ancient families, cherishing the tokens of their glorious antiquity and trying to remain unsullied by modern enterprise, are doomed to extinction, and justly so. The heroine describes her sister: "She's a sentimentalist and she'll marry Junius and go to America, where everybody is sentimental, and be the sweetest thing in the Western hemisphere." The will to fight has succumbed to the wish to survive, as a result of which Lancashire cotton spinners are succeeding to the ancient houses. And the Lancashire manufacturers are advised to pay heed too, for the right of property "is no right at all." Neither property, nor rank, nor power has a right in perpetuity. Everything is held under sufferance; every privilege must be defended and legitimized anew.[31]

Misled by the romantic cast of Buchan's novels, critics have assumed that his Toryism was of the romantic variety that loves a lord, venerates the past, and despises the clerks and entrepreneurs of the middle class. In fact, his Toryism was radical rather than romantic, and he respected enterprise as he respected labor. While agreeing with Samuel Johnson that "life is barren enough surely with all her trappings; let us be therefore cautious of how we strip her,"[32] he had no fondness for trappings that interfered with the business of living, and no regrets for the regime that died in World War I: "The radicalism which is part of the Tory creed was coming uppermost, and I looked forward to a clearing out of much rubbish."[33]

Buchan's attitudes to nation and empire were as complicated as his attitudes toward race and class. "For King and Country," the homily of generations of housemasters, is taken to be the archaic and fatuous message of his work. He himself described, in retrospect, the imperial vision of his youth: "I dreamed of a worldwide brotherhood with the background of a common race and creed, consecrated to the service of peace; Britain enriching the rest out of her culture and traditions, and the spirit of the Dominions like a strong wind freshening the stuffiness of the old lands."[34] Toward the end of his life, recalling his part in "Milner's kindergarden," Buchan acknowledged that "the white man's burden" had by then become an almost meaningless phrase. But at the time, he insisted, it signified a new political philosophy and ethical standard that were "serious and surely not ignoble."[35] In his biography of Cromwell, that message was conveyed in the words of the Commonwealthman, James Harrington: "You cannot plant an oak in a flower-pot; she must have earth for her roots, and heaven for her branches."[36] If the imperialists may be charged with an excessive romanticism or sentimentality, the anti-imperialists sometimes displayed an unseemly cynicism and pessimism. His old Oxford friend, Raymond Asquith, defended little-Englandism to Buchan with the lofty disdain of the aristocrat:

> The day of the clever cad is at hand. I always felt it would come to this if we once let ourselves in for an Empire. If only Englishmen had known their Aeschylus a little better they wouldn't have bustled about the world appropriating things. A gentleman may make a large fortune, but only a cad can look after it. It would have been so much pleasanter to live in a small community who knew Greek and played games and washed themselves.[37]

The dilemma of the imperial ideal was also the dilemma of the national ideal. Here too Buchan's views were more nuanced than might be supposed. He could not finally decide between the creeds of Cromwell and Montrose—Cromwell seeking to create a "spiritualized and dedicated" nation; Montrose satisfied with a modest, judicious government of checks and balances.[38] Buchan saw the glory of the first, but he realized that men might become satiated with high communal, as with high spiritual, ideals, and might prefer to devote themselves to their private concerns. The first path, he knew, was not without its dangers, the second not without its virtues.

There was a romantic streak in Buchan's politics, but it was not the sentimental romanticism with which the conservative is often associated, a mindless attachment to tradition, rank, and pomp. His was rather a Gothic, almost apocalyptic vision of the dark, destructive forces contained in human beings and society. The typical Victorian or Edwardian villain was a bounder and cad, a seducer of innocent girls, an extortionist of money, sometimes a trafficker in national secrets. The Buchan villain deals in a different order of villainy. He is not a fallen gentleman but a fallen man, the personification of evil. He dabbles in black magic rather than sex, seeks not money but power, and trades in the secrets of the soul as much as those of the nation. Compared with him, even the sadist of the present-day thriller is frivolous, for instead of private sexual perversions, Buchan's villains are satisfied with nothing less than the subversion of society and civilization.

Long before the H-bomb, A-bomb, and even ordinary old-fashioned aerial bombing, before the threat of fascism and in the infancy of communism, Buchan felt what later events seemed to confirm—that "civilization anywhere is a very thin crust."[39] That dictum, in a novel in 1922, was echoed in his autobiography in 1940. The danger in revolution, he then wrote, was not that it would overthrow any particular political or social institutions but rather that it would undermine all government and society. Bolshevism itself was less menacing than the nihilism it would release:

> A civilisation bemused by an opulent materialism has been met by a rude challenge. The free peoples have been challenged by the serfs. The gutters have exuded a poison which bids fair to infect the world. The beggar-on-horseback rides more roughshod over the helpless than the cavalier. A combination of multitudes who have lost their nerve and a junta of arrogant demagogues

has shattered the comity of nations. The European tradition has
been confronted with an Asiatic revolt, with its historic accom-
paniment of janissaries and assassins. There is in it all, too, an
ugly pathological savour, as if a mature society were being as-
sailed by diseased and vicious children.[40]

Unfortunately the poison now infecting the world had always
lain dormant in it; the diseased and vicious children are, after all,
our own progeny. What terrifies Buchan's hero, Richard Hannay,
is the fact that the villains are high in the Establishment, that
they might be found next to one at a shoot in Suffolk or a dinner
party in St. James'. Even when the villain in one of the spy stories is a German, it is neither the espionage as such nor his nationality that convicts him of villainy (Buchan was neither a
Germanophobe nor a Russophobe) but rather a moral depravity
bordering on diabolism.

This is hardly the housemaster's credo of King and Country.
Again, what distinguished Buchan was his Scottish Calvinism, a
sense of the unquiet depths that lie beneath the human surface.
Once the subconscious, lawless instincts of men were liberated and
broke through the barrier erected by civilization, "there will be a
weakening of the power of reasoning, which after all is the thing
that brings men nearest to the Almighty; and there will be a failure of nerve."[41] It was not the reason of state, even of a hostile state,
that alarmed him but the force of unreason itself. Shortly after
World War I he foresaw the development of a new kind of propa-
ganda, compared with which the old-fashioned Prussian militarist
variety was relatively innocuous. "We are only beginning to realize
the strange crannies of the human soul," Sandy Arbuthnot reminds
Hannay. "The real magician, if he turned up to-day, wouldn't
bother about drugs and dopes. He would dabble in far more deadly

methods, the compulsion of a fiery nature over the limp things that men call their minds."[42] Buchan's villains do not simply bribe, blackmail, or torture their victims; they operate by means of hypnotism, hysteria, fanaticism, and a quasi-religious mysticism. Hannay comforts himself with the fact that he is not susceptible to hypnotism, but he is liable to his "one special funk," the mob. "I hated the thought of it—the mess, the blind struggle, the sense of unleashed passions different from those of any single blackguard. It was a dark world to me, and I don't like darkness."[43]

Some of his characters may appear to be naive, may even be naive, but their creator is not. When Buchan pits the "jolly party of clean, hard, decent fellows" against the "abominable hinterland of mystery and crime,"[44] he seems to be subscribing to the decent-fellow ethic that belongs to the caricature of the phlegmatic, obtuse Englishman. But that ethic, for Buchan, has acquired the urgency of a desperate countermeasure; it is inseparable from the evil that called it into being. In good Calvinist fashion, Buchan is hard, realistic, unsentimental, apprehensive. In 1934, not in a novel but in his biography of Cromwell, he wrote words that turned out to be all too percipient: "It was a dogma of the elder liberalism that violence can never achieve anything, and that persecution, so far from killing a thing, must inevitably nourish it. For such optimism there is no warrant in history; time and again violence has wholly achieved its purpose, when it has been carried to its logical conclusion."[45]

What makes Buchan, and the ethos with which he is identified, so unfashionable today is not only the vision of a good life consisting of cold baths, rousing games, and indifferent sex; or the apparent philistinism that was so dismissive of modernist art and literature; or the stereotypically disagreeable images of race and religion; or an unseemly glorification of nation and empire. Beyond all of these is a temperament and mentality inimical to what Lionel Trilling called the "liberal imagination"—an imagination that celebrates the malleable and benevolent character of human beings rather than the recalcitrant and malevolent, that regards evil as a negative quality, a temporary aberration, unreal both in its impulse and in its effect, that is impatient with complication, difficulty, ambiguity, adversity.

Buchan—Calvinist in religion, Tory in politics, romantic in sensibility—is obviously the antithesis of the liberal. It is no accident that he was addicted to a genre, a tale of adventure and suspense, that was not the classic detective story set in the drawing room or village square but a "thriller" played out in the wilds of nature, in which good was pitted against evil on an almost cosmic scale.

Buchan died in 1940, before the revelations of the full extent of the horrors of Nazism and communism. In a sense, his fiction anticipated the reality. Hitler and Stalin might have been characters in his novels, as unbelievable as some of his other villains. Unfortunately they were not.

POSTSCRIPT[46]

Alistair Buchan, responding to the original publication of this essay in 1960, took issue with my characterization of his father as antithetical to the "liberal imagination." He found it ironic that I should use this phrase in view of the fact that his father, shortly before he died, had spoken of Lionel Trilling as "one of the best living literary critics." There is, however, nothing ironic about this. John Buchan would have admired Trilling's work precisely for the reason that I alluded to it. Trilling was not, after all, celebrating the liberal imagination in the famous work of that title. He was rather pointing to its limitations, to the fact that the political virtues of liberalism almost inevitably entailed a constriction of the imagination and of the social reality. All of Buchan's work is a confirmation of Trilling's thesis.*

*Trilling's *The Liberal Imagination* was published in 1950, well after Buchan's death. The book by Trilling that Buchan read and admired was *Matthew Arnold,* which appeared in 1939.

The Knoxes

A God-Haunted Family

~ Half a century ago, Noel Annan published a celebrated essay, "The Intellectual Aristocracy," tracing the interlocking genealogies that tie together, by birth and marriage, the great names of nineteenth- and twentieth-century English culture: Macaulay, Trevelyan, Arnold, Huxley, Darwin, Wedgwood, Galton, Stephen, Wilberforce, Dicey, Thackeray, Russell, Webb, Keynes, Strachey, Toynbee. . . .[1] Tucked into my copy of the book containing that essay is a yellowed clipping of a review written a dozen years later of *The Amberley Papers*, the journals and letters of Bertrand Russell's parents. The reviewer, Philip Toynbee, does not mention Annan, but he too speculates about the "mysteries of heredity" that connect the twentieth-century philosopher and radical activist Bertrand Russell with the Victorian Whig aristocracy. Lord Amberley was the son of the prime minister Lord Russell and, "as if by inheritance," a friend or acquaintance of such other eminent Victorians as Mill, Carlyle, Grote, Darwin, and Huxley. But the best confirmation of that "intellectual aristocracy" comes in a casual aside by the reviewer: "It happens that Kate Amberley's younger sister was my own great-grandmother"—that "montrous old tyrant," as Philip Toynbee remembers her.[2] (Philip did not bother to mention that he was the son of the eminent historian Arnold

206

Joseph Toynbee, and great-nephew of another Arnold Toynbee, the Victorian historian.)

Annan might have included another genealogical table in this pantheon of intellectual aristocrats: Knox. In 1977 that omission was repaired with the publication of *The Knox Brothers* by Penelope Fitzgerald, née Penelope Knox, the daughter of the oldest of the brothers, better known in her own right as a distinguished novelist, and displaying here all the wit and wisdom evident in her fiction.[3]

The Knox family story starts, as it ends, with a medley of religions. Ardent Presbyterians settled in northern Ireland, some of its members "lived to be hanged," as the patriarch of the family put it, when they were implicated in the uprising against the English in the late eighteenth century. One of the twenty-six children sought his fortune in the West Indies, married a sickly heiress, and returned to London as a merchant, only to discover that her estate had passed on to a cousin. His son, George (the grandfather of the Knox brothers memorialized by Fitzgerald), adopted the Anglicanism of his mother, took orders, and became a chaplain in the service of the East India Company in Madras. It was there that he met his wife, a Quaker, who was equally impoverished and had been sent off to India rather than going into service as a governess. Spared that ignominious fate, she married the chaplain—the kind of Irishman, Fitzgerald tells us, who, like Samuel Beckett's Watt, "had never smiled, but thought he knew how it was done." They returned to England in 1855 with their seven children (another was born later), and after serving in one curacy after another, George finally settled in a village near Croydon as the secretary of the Church Missionary Society. A cross between "Ulster thrift and Quaker sobriety," Fitzgerald puts it, the family was spiritually as well as economically impoverished. Books were restricted, novels forbidden, and floggings administered by a father who turned out to be as tyrannical as his own father had been. (And as eccentric; he never looked at a train schedule "but simply went down to the station and complained to the station-master if one was not ready for him.")[4]

Where the older generations had escaped to the Indies, the younger one found refuge in education. It was the father, George, otherwise so narrow-minded and repressive, who encouraged this, his "mania" for education making it something like a precondition for salvation—an education that included the girls as well as the boys; one of his daughters went to Oxford on a scholarship and became the principal of a college in Toronto. His son Edmund (the father of the Knox brothers of this volume), also on a scholarship, received an excellent classical training at Saint Paul's; he later remembered with satisfaction that it cost his family all of one shilling, the obligatory tip given to the porter by a new student. The classes were accompanied by daily beatings (this too seemed to be obligatory), but these were mild, "largely owing to the absent-mindedness of the High Master." Saint Paul's was followed, again thanks to a scholarship, by Corpus Christi, Oxford, where Edmund received three Firsts (the highest honors) in Greats (the classics and philosophy), Law, and Modern History.[5]

Ordained and elected a fellow of Merton College, Edmund rejected the dour low-church Anglicanism of his father, preferring the Quaker tradition of his mother, which he transformed into a humane and genial Evangelicalism. He even developed a taste for novels (for Austen and Trollope especially). Although college fellows were generally not allowed to marry, at just about this time Merton amended its statutes to permit the marriage of several fellows. Edmund took advantage of this dispensation to marry, in 1878, Ellen Penelope French, the daughter of the rector of a neighboring church. Six years (and four children) later he left Oxford to take up a curacy in Leicestershire.

Ellen brought to the family a very different kind of religious background, reminding us once again of the extraordinary diversity not only of the Anglican ministry but of the Evangelical as well. Her father, Thomas French, was almost a parody of the religious enthusiast, "a saint," Fitzgerald tells us, "holy in the noblest sense of the word, and as exasperating as all saints."[6] The son of a comfortable, conventional clergyman, he too had gone to India—not, like George Knox, to serve as a chaplain to the English community, but rather as a missionary to the natives. Living a life of extreme austerity, reading the Bible to lepers and preaching to the pagans, he somehow found the time and energy to master seven Indian dialects, marry the daughter of a wealthy Quaker family, and sire eight children. After brief stays in England, he returned to India, leaving his family behind. Appointed Bishop of Lahore, he served there until 1889 when ill-health obliged him to return to England. Within a year he found his way back to the Middle East, this time without position or authority. Dressed as a Muslim, he preached at the gate of the mosque or in the bazaar, handed out Bibles to the natives, and died in Muscat (of near starvation, among other things) in 1891, at the age of sixty-six. (That same year Edmund's father died in far more comfortable circumstances in England.)

It was in 1891, too, that Edmund left his agreeable country parish for an industrial district in Birmingham. He welcomed it as an opportunity to serve in a larger, more challenging world, but it was a wrench for his family—four boys and two girls between the ages of ten and three, a happy, boisterous group (very different from the household in which Edmund himself had grown up). The new vicarage, a small house in a typically dark, narrow, and smoke-begrimed street, could not have been more different from their old rambling, cheerful country house. The children adapted well to their new quarters, but their mother was not so fortunate. Ailing since the birth of her last child, she died within a year. The children were then dispersed among relatives, only the oldest, Edmund, remaining at home with his father and an aunt. The two girls, Winifred and Ethel, and one of the boys, Dillwyn, had the misfortune to be sent to a widowed great-aunt in Eastbourne, who had the temperament of their grandfather and whose Protestantism was "of the 'black' variety." The younger boys, Wilfred and Ronald, fared better at the home of an uncle, an easygoing vicar in a country parish in Lincolnshire, an Evangelical of the "sweet and primitive" kind, who managed to share their childish pleasures while cramming into them, almost unwittingly, it seemed, an impressive amount of learning. "The boys," Fitzgerald observes, "were beginning to resemble savages, speaking Latin and Greek."[7]

When the father was appointed Suffragan Bishop of Coventry, four years later, "it became evident," he said, "that I must marry again," for the sake of the diocese if not his children. He found a suitable candidate in Ethel Newton, a vicar's daughter. Fortunately for him, and, more, for his children, this young woman (she was twenty-seven, twenty years younger than he) was not only familiar with the role she had to play; she was also good-looking, good-natured, and cultivated. Although she had no formal education, she learned classical Greek "simply because she wanted to." One of the family jokes was the diary entry on her wedding day: "Finished the *Antigone*. Married Bip [Bishop]."[8]

With the Bishop's remarriage, the family was happily reunited, "Mrs. K.," as the children called her, adapting to a life far more austere than the luxurious one to which she was accustomed. (Although her father was very rich, he made it a matter of principle not to settle money on his daughters when they married.) She also managed to cope with children who were far more argumentative and unconventional than her own siblings. It was a cheerful household but also an earnest one, for all the children (with the exception of the oldest, Ethel, who was somewhat retarded) crammed for scholarships, a preparation "so intensive," Fitzgerald says, "as to be only just over the borderline of sanity."[9]

All the children did get scholarships, and all to elite schools: Edmund to Rugby and Corpus Christi College, Oxford; Winifred to Lady Margaret Hall, Oxford; Dillwyn to Eton and King's College, Cambridge; Wilfred to Rugby and Trinity College, Oxford; and Ronald to Eton and Balliol College, Oxford. But this is all they had in common. For the rest, while they remained loyal to each other as a family, their lives, careers, temperaments, and, above all, religious affiliations took them in very different directions.

Penelope Fitzgerald, a skillful (as well as wonderfully engaging) writer, succeeds in intertwining the lives of the brothers at each stage of their careers, thus keeping them intact as a family while allowing them to diverge as individuals. The diversities of career are easily identified: Edmund, editor of *Punch*; Dillwyn, cryptographer; Wilfred, Anglo-Catholic priest; Ronald, Roman Catholic priest. But the devil—or God, in this case—is in the details, and the details of their respective lives and minds make for a fascinating saga.

Edmund, the oldest, was also the first to disappoint the father. His scholarship at Corpus Christi was suspended for "frivolous and extravagant" behavior (climbing in after hours over spiked walls, organizing extracurricular and unauthorized entertainments, spending more time at dining clubs than at lectures), and he was reinstated only after he paid a fine and did penance by mastering the whole of Herodotus and Plato's *Republic*. After completing the course of studies and passing the first examination for an honors degree, he left Oxford without any degree, having decided to become a writer. He had a special talent for light verse; there was no word, he boasted (and frequently demonstrated to the amusement of his family and friends) for which he could not find a rhyme. After brief stints teaching at a preparatory school in Manchester and as a subeditor on *Pall Mall Magazine*, he became a regular contributor to *Punch* under the pen-name "Evoe."

This was hardly the career the father had envisaged for his namesake, but still more disturbing was the young man's religious skepticism, or, at best, indifference. The bishop was only slightly mollified by his son's marriage, in 1912, to the daughter of the Bishop of Lincoln, which was suitably reported in the local paper under the headline, "Bishop's Son Weds Bishop's Daughter." With the outbreak of war, Edmund, then thirty-four and the father of a one-year-old, joined the army. Wounded in the battle of Ypres in 1917, he was invalided home. He resumed writing for *Punch* (parodies as well as verses), joined the regular staff (with a regular income) in 1921, and served as editor from 1932 to 1945. It might have been said of him, as was said of the previous editor of *Punch*, that "he is the kind of man who doesn't take his humour seriously."[10] But he did take it seriously in at least one respect. Under his editorship the magazine was notable not only for its distinctive wit and humor (so distinctive that it was nearly incomprehensible to Americans) but also for its progressive stance on social issues and its consistent hostility to Nazism. After the war, with his retirement from *Punch*, he continued as a freelance writer and as a local celebrity in Hampstead Heath, where he had moved with his second wife (his first having died before the war). He long outlived his younger brothers, dying in 1971 at the age of ninety.

If Edmund's profession and irreligion took him far from the world of his father, Dillwyn's circle of friends and more aggressive irreligion were a much greater rupture. At Eton, Dillwyn became what Fitzgerald calls a "ferocious agnostic"—ferocious atheist, might be more accurate. With his great friend and classmate John

Maynard Keynes, he undertook "experiments, intellectual and sexual, to resolve the question of what things are necessary to life"—things that most emphatically did not include religion. His friendship with Keynes, and presumably their experiments, were continued at King's College, where a word was coined for Dillwyn—"noxian," meaning "noxious and anti-Christian."[11] Unlike Keynes, he turned down an invitation to join the Apostles, the secret (or not so secret) society that had the highest quotient of homosexuals as well as intellectuals. But he was very much part of that milieu, "expanding cautiously," as Fitzgerald delicately puts it, "in the Apostolic friendship."[12] If he was not himself overtly homosexual, he attracted those who were undeniably so, including Lytton Strachey who frankly declared his love for him, which was apparently unrequited.

Dillwyn's main intellectual passion, then and later, was Greek poetry, and he was delighted to assist his mentor, the renowned Greek scholar Walter Headlam, to prepare a definitive edition of the poet Herodas and decipher some papyrus fragments of his poems. (Fitzgerald neglects to mention the fact that Herodas was known, if at all, for his bawdy verses.) That project earned Dillwyn a fellowship at King's College. With the outbreak of war, rejected by the army because of his bad eyesight, he was recruited by naval intelligence to join the band of cryptographers charged with breaking the German war codes. The head of his department, wondering why the Germans did not suspect that their code had been compromised, could only suppose that it was because of "the English reputation for stupidity." (But the head, Fitzgerald wryly notes, was a Scotsman.)[13] In fact, the work called upon the imagination and patience of very talented men and women, among whom Dillwyn was perhaps the most gifted, applying to this task the same talents that had proved so effective in the explication of obscure Greek meters and the reconstruction of papyrus fragments.

Instead of returning to Cambridge after the war, Dillwyn remained at the Foreign Office as a cryptographer. He found time, however, to publish his edition of Herodas as well as another even more esoteric work of Greek scholarship. Like Keynes, he eventually married and, unlike him, had two sons (one of whom was named Maynard after his godfather). In the 1930s he was largely responsible for breaking the German code known as "Enigma," and in the early years of the Second World War, stationed at Bletchley, he had the distinction of decoding the "Enigma Variation," which played a crucial role in several engagements during the war. He himself did not survive the war, dying of cancer in 1943.

It is hard to know which of the sons was more displeasing to the father: the two older ones who were conspicuously lacking in religious faith, or the two younger ones whose faith, as the bishop thought it, was excessive and perverted. At Rugby, Wilfred found himself obsessed with the "social question," as it was called, the problem of poverty, and became a socialist à la Ruskin and J. F. D. Maurice. Hoping to remove him from the "noxian" influence of Dillwyn, his father encouraged him to go to Oxford rather than Cambridge. There, after experiencing a temporary loss of faith, he recovered sufficiently to consider entering the priesthood. That was small consolation for his father, because Wilfred, like his younger brother Ronald, was a "Romaniser," drawn to the Anglo-Catholic movement whose rituals and sacraments were anathema to an Evangelical like his father. As if this were not distressing enough, he was attracted to that sect of high-church Anglicanism, led by William Temple and George Lansbury, which was infused with a strong social as well as religious mission. Wilfred, then resident at the Trinity Mission in the East End, felt obliged to inform his father that he was a Christian socialist and, worse, a member of the Labour party. (The trade union meetings, he later recalled, where they discussed the best means of redistributing the means of production, took place in cocoa-rooms in the district, cocoa being "the great conspiratorial drink" of the time.)[14]

Shortly before the war, preparing for his ordination, Wilfred voluntarily (this was not required of the Anglo-Catholic priesthood) took a vow of celibacy, and of poverty as well. Unable to serve as a chaplain in the army because of the prejudice against Anglo-Catholics, he worked in the intelligence branch of the War Office, where his two brothers were already installed. After the war, seeking a community of like-minded souls, he joined the Oratory of the Good Shepherd in Cambridge, a religious brotherhood of unmarried priests and laymen, where piety and eccentricity thrived together. "It is fortunate for us," one of the superiors declared, "that loving and liking are not the same thing. We are not called upon to like our neighbour, but to love him"—upon which Fitzgerald observes that this comment shows "how practical unworldliness can be."[15] When Wilfred was not gardening (his favorite activity), he wrote a book on meditation and prayer and scholarly works of apologetics and theology, one of which, *St. Paul and the Church of the Gentiles*, earned him a fellowship in the British Academy. With the closing of the Oratory house in the early days of the Second World War, he became chaplain at Pembroke College, where he taught undergraduates and ministered to them in his usual devoted but eccentric fashion. "He was the sort of man," one of his students said, "who understood every natural joy and sorrow that we could feel at that age, but couldn't find his own collar-stud." (Fitzgerald corrects the record: "Wilfred never had any collar-studs; he used a paper-clip.")[16] Malcolm Muggeridge, a later editor of *Punch*, remembered seeing Wilfred in Cambridge at a Eucharist service on a very cold morning with a hot-water bottle under his vestments, giving him "a slight air of pregnancy."[17] Wilfred died in 1950, like Dillwyn, after a painful bout of cancer.

Where Dillwyn had discovered atheism at Eton, Ronald, the youngest of the brothers, discovered Anglo-Catholicism. Reading a history of the Tractarian movement, he later recalled, he "trembled for Newman, mourned for him as lost to the Church, and rose with the knowledge that somewhere, beyond the circles I moved in, there was a cause for which clergymen had been sent to prison and nobles lives spent; a cause which could be mine."[18] His father, for whom Tractarianism was almost as bad as Romanism, hoped that the youngest of his children (and his favorite) would outgrow this heresy. But Ronald was no more obliging than the others. A brilliant speaker and debater, witty, high-spirited, extremely sociable and popular, he had offers that would have brought him into the world of high politics. Instead he accepted a fellowship at Trinity College and became the center of a cult of high-church Anglicans. As private tutor to the young Harold Macmillan (who had just left Eton), he introduced the future prime minister to "Ronnie's religion," as it was called.[19] But he was shortly dismissed by Mrs. Macmillan when he refused to refrain from speaking about religion to her son. When Macmillan came to Balliol, their friendship resumed.

In this and other of Ronald's friendships (as in Dillwyn's), there are at least intimations of homosexuality. Evelyn Waugh, in his biography of Ronald Knox, mentions the much-sought-after boy at Eton whom Ronald "loved" and whom he established in his "little court of troubadours."[20] Similarly, Fitzgerald speaks of his intense feelings for one of his students at Trinity, Guy Lawrence, "very fair, very handsome and highly strung," whom he helped nurse through a nervous breakdown. Although she too (like Waugh), makes it clear that Ronald "loved" his friends, and Guy above all, she is confident that these friendships, although "deeply emotional," were "in no way sensual," and "physical presence was in no way part of them."[21] Perhaps it was because Ronald did not have that confidence that he chose, when ordained as an Anglican priest in 1912, to take the vow of celibacy (as Wilfred did about the same time).

"Between ourselves, Winnie," the bishop once remarked to his daughter, "I cannot understand what it is that the dear boys [Wilfred and Ronald] see in the Blessed Virgin Mary."[22] Fitzgerald explains that while Wilfred was drawn to the rites and dogmas of Anglo-Catholicism from a need for communal "wholeness," Ronald did so from a regard for "authority." "If you have a sloppy religion," Ronald reasoned, "you get a sloppy atheism."[23] Anglo-Catholicism was the least sloppy form of Protestantism, but still too sloppy for his taste. In 1917, after agonizing for years over whether "to pope," Ronald was received into the Catholic church and ordained as a priest two years later. To the family, Fitzgerald says, "Ronnie was 'lost,'" divided from them by "an invisible door of iron."[24]

As a secular priest unattached to a religious order or parish, Ronald's first assignment was as a teacher of Latin in a seminary and boys' school in Hertfordshire. Although he performed ably, it was a world he did not fit into comfortably. He was happier vacationing with Lord and Lady Lovat at their castle in Scotland, and writing the light essays and columns that earned him the tribute, by the *Daily Mail*, of being "the wittiest young man in England."[25] In 1926 he was pleased to be appointed University Chaplain for Catholics at Oxford, which gave him more time to write the articles and books (including detective stories) that were making him something of a celebrity, and, not unimportant, were supplementing his modest chaplaincy stipend. (Evelyn Waugh, describing his detective novels as ingenious, scrupulous, and logical, added, in his usual misogynic fashion, that "very few women have ever enjoyed them.")[26] But these distractions began to pall, and he became disaffected with students who were obsessed, as he saw it, with sex, travel, and European politics, in that order. Out of sorts with the young, he was also out of sorts with his times. He liked to think of himself not as middle-aged but as "medieval," and refused to have anything to do with such modern contraptions as airplanes, telephones, or movies; the last good invention, he insisted, was the toast rack. (He relented somewhat in his old age, traveling to Africa by plane and even going to a movie there.)

Resigning the chaplaincy in 1937, and giving up novel writing as well, he took up residency at the Acton estate at Aldenham in Shropshire (on the invitation of Lady Acton, the wife of the grandson of the great historian). There he devoted himself to his grand enterprise, a new translation of the New Testament. The translation was not an unequivocal success. Conceived as the work of a commission, it was taken over, in effect, by Ronald, who consulted his colleagues only when he was confronted with some exceptionally obscure passage. Completed in 1942, its publication was delayed for three years until it was finally, and evidently reluctantly, accepted by the hierarchy as an authorized version. While it sold moderately well, it received enough scholarly criticism to make it, his biographer says, an "exercise in humility"; Ronald jocularly promised that, on his deathbed, he would forgive his reviewers.[27] (He was spared an even more trying exercise in humility: the publication after his death of two more scholarly authorized versions of the New Testament.)

When the Actons closed their Aldenham home after the war, Ronald was installed as chaplain (and paying guest!) at the Asquith estate in Somerset, where he continued to write books on a variety of subjects. Oddly enough, Fitzgerald does not mention the most interesting and best known of these, *Enthusiasm*, a study of charismatic movements in the seventeenth and eighteenth centuries. Published in 1950, it was a book he had been working on intermittently for three decades. He himself was dissatisfied with it; having gone through so many revisions and changing viewpoints over the years, it was, he disarmingly confessed in the preface, a "hotchpotch."[28] Yet it was reasonably well received and is still in print. In print as well are paperback editions of several other books, including the New Testament translation reissued as recently as 1998, and a volume of selections from his works under the title *Quotable Knox*. At his death in 1957, he had the distinction of being England's most famous Catholic priest—"a normal, pipe-smoking, income-taxed Englishman," Fitzgerald observes, "not a Jesuit, not a mystic, no black-coats, no sweeping gestures."[29] Not quite, however, your normal Englishman. A reader of Waugh's biography may remember him, in his last years, as a brilliant eccentric—a crossword addict who challenged himself by doing the *Times* crossword by reading only the horizontal clues, filling in the perpendiculars by guesswork, and then verifying them by their clues.

One of the remarkable things about this family is that, in spite of all their differences on matters of supreme importance to them— matters of life and death, of redemption and salvation—they continued to remain a family. Although the bishop cut Ronald out of his will and did not attend the ceremonies at which one son was made an Anglican priest and another a Catholic one, they all continued to meet—to argue vehemently, to be sure, but also to share familial joys and sorrows. Even as the bishop, in retirement in Kent, wrote tracts refuting Anglo-Catholicism and defending the traditional Prayer Book, he welcomed his errant sons on their occasional visits home. In his memoirs, published two years before his death in 1937, he reflected upon his relationship with his curious assortment of progeny: "I have not succeeded, as my father succeeded, in bringing my children up entirely in their father's faith, and for this I take no small share of the blame, so far as it is blame, to myself." He recalled Ronald, as a schoolboy, once completing a

Greek phrase with the line, "It is our boast that we are far ahead of our parents."

> These words [the bishop commented] seem to me to embody, at once, the effects of a Public School education, the spirit and temper of the age in which my children grew up, and the exceptional vivacity of their character. They were determined to be better than their parents had been, and to do better than their parents had done, and to live in the spirit of the restless first decades of the twentieth century. Who shall say that this ambition was in itself wrong or unnatural? That it led some of them in directions often very costly to those whom they loved and who loved them, cannot be denied, and here I find the saddest of the experiences and remembrances of my life, the records of the most humiliating of my failures.

He concluded, in a spirit of Christian humility—and more, of genuine personal gratitude: "Against these I set the treasure of the full and over-flowing measure of my children's love, surpassing all that I deserve."[30]

It is a poignant commentary by a father who was fully appreciative of the abilities and achievements of his four remarkable sons, each of whom was distinguished in his own right, and each of whom was an implicit rebuke to himself. It is also a poignant commentary on the sons themselves. The memoir was written when the sons were middle-aged and the "directions" of their lives set. But if their ambition was "to do better than their parents had done," it is not clear that they succeeded, either then or later. And if the father had cause to regret the failures of his life—the inability to hand down to his sons the religious legacy he had received from his father—the sons had reason to recognize their own failures.

None of them, not even the bishop, set great store on titles. Yet it must have occurred to his two priest-sons, as to the father, that neither of them attained the distinction of a bishopric, which had come almost effortlessly to their father (and grandfather as well). Ronald, the best known of the brothers—probably the best-known English Catholic at the time (and the best-known convert since Cardinal Newman), might have been expected to acquire that title. Yet he never attained a high position in the church, the title "Monsignor" being a purely honorific one bestowed upon him late in life. The hierarchy never quite trusted or respected him, perhaps because of his secular, irreverent writings, perhaps because of his opposition to the Modernist theology that was gaining favor in the church. And his most ambitious work, the translation of the New Testament, proved to be a very dubious achievement.

Nor did the two older sons, outwardly so successful, enjoy an unequivocal satisfaction in their lives and careers. Edmund reached the pinnacle of his profession as editor of *Punch*—at a time, however, as he was painfully aware, when that brand of humor was already beginning to be perceived as quaint and provincial; nor was this, the prewar and war years, the most auspicious time to put out a humor magazine. Dillwyn, for his part, had notable triumphs as a cryptographer but not as the Greek scholar that was his true avocation, if not vocation. It is not clear why he did not, after the First World War, return to Cambridge or accept the professorships elsewhere that had been offered him, which might have given him the opportunity to produce something more memorable than two rather obscure monographs.

Describing one summer vacation while Edmund was at Oxford, Fitzgerald tells us that he "fell into the melancholy which lay in wait for all the brothers"[31]—Edmund, the witty, fun-loving, future editor of *Punch*, who was about to lose his scholarship because he was enjoying himself too much. The tendency to melancholy, treated delicately, almost casually, appears as a refrain throughout the book, as one brother after another passed through, as Wilfred did, a "black night of the soul."[32] Malcolm Muggeridge, who knew them personally (with the possible exception of Dillwyn), speaks of them as being "God-haunted," some "negatively," rejecting the God that haunted them, others "positively," serving that God in their different ways.[33] This perception comes from someone who was himself "God-haunted," having experienced, late in life, a deeply moving religious conversion. Whatever the nature of the Knox melancholia, it gives an added dimension and depth to their lives and careers.

But this book is more than a chronicle of a fascinating family. It is the chronicle of several generations of Englishmen who defy the usual stereotypes of Englishmen in general and of the religious in particular. It is a dramatic revelation of the extraordinary variety of types contained within the familiar rubrics: Evangelical bishops as various as the staid and sensible Bishop of Manchester and the saintly ascetic Bishop of Lahore; Anglo-Catholic priests like Wilfred, the Christian Socialist and Labour party enthusiast, who was hardly the typical Anglican high-churchman; and Roman Catholic priests like Ronald who rejected Modernism but had an irreverent streak that made him suspect among the orthodox. (One wonders what the historian Lord Acton would have made of the rather worldly priest who took up residence at Aldenham and supervised a translation of the New Testament that was conspicuously below the historian's standard.)

It is not only religious stereotypes that are belied: it is class stereotypes as well—most notably the stereotype of the upper-middle-class Englishman. The Knoxes were undeniably upper middle class, even though some of them were quite poor. This is a salutary reminder that, in Victorian England as in twentieth-century England, there was no necessary correlation between class and income. Neither was there any necessary correlation between class and intellectual or spiritual disposition. Having gone to the best schools (where they seemed not to have suffered any stigma from being on scholarships), they managed to espouse wildly different beliefs, pursue very different careers, and lead utterly different lives. Fitzgerald does not dwell on the theme of class, but she does make much of education, which is itself a commentary on class.

Perhaps the only quality the grandfather and father had in common was their "mania" for education. Describing the intensive cramming for scholarships, Fitzgerald explains that "in this family which breathed the air of scholarship, but had constant difficulty in making ends meet, education was the key to the future." It was the means by which the children could achieve the careers the bishop anticipated for them: "Winnie was destined for University and, surely, for a brilliant clerical marriage, the three elder boys for the Civil Service, Ronnie for the Evangelical ministry."[34] The obvious irony is the failure of the bishop's expectations. But perhaps more interesting is the fact that he (like his father before him) should have looked to education, rather than to family and social connections, for the welfare of his children. And not just the nominal education that would ensure a respectable life (the pass degree that was the English equivalent of the American "gentleman's C") but nothing less than a First.

To an American, this is a familiar scenario. But it is one associated with a poor immigrant family seeking to assimilate itself into a new country and culture, rather than a native, well-established, upper-middle-class family. It is all the more surprising to find this in England of all countries, and late-Victorian England at that, which was reputedly so class-ridden, where class distinctions and privileges were presumably decisive. For the Knox family at least (and perhaps for many more than one might think), class was not at all the determining factor in their lives. This is what makes this family so fascinating. Character and beliefs, not social and material interests, were what made the brothers so distinctive and so memorable.

There are a few, but not many, biographers worthy of their subjects. Almost by definition, the subject of a biography is more important, more notable, than the author of the biography—else the subject would not warrant a biography. At least so it was until recently, when biographers have begun to take it upon themselves to celebrate the "little," the "ordinary" man or woman—in the process celebrating themselves for being so broad-minded and largehearted. The Knox brothers, however, have found their equal in their biographer, so that this book is as much a tribute to the author as to the subjects. (It was reissued shortly after her death.)

Penelope Fitzgerald was sixty when this book appeared. Her first, published two years earlier, was a biography of the Pre-Raphaelite artist Edward Burne-Jones; her second, a mystery, was written to entertain her dying husband. Although she discovered her vocation late in life, the book on the Knoxes, like her earlier ones, is the work of an assured writer, displaying the dry wit and irony she inherited from her father, the editor of *Punch*, as well as the learning and play of mind characteristic of all the family. These qualities are abundantly evident in her later novels as well. In an introduction to Jane Austen's *Emma*, Fitzgerald remarks of Emma (the character, not the book) that "she has the potentialities of a best-selling novelist."[35] A perceptive reader of *The Knox Brothers* might have predicted that its author also had the potentialities of a best-selling novelist. Like Austen, Fitzgerald manages, in her nonfiction as in her fiction, to be ironic, even sardonic at times, without being in the least ungenerous or unsympathetic. She never parades her own cleverness at the expense of her characters; she never gives way to muckraking or sensationalism. The only fault one may find in this book is the scrupulous exclusion of herself from the narrative, depriving us of her own memories of this memorable family. (Her one concession to familial acquaintance is her referring to the brothers by their family nicknames.)

If there is a melancholic note in this book, as in her novels, it is because she herself shares that Knox trait. "I have remained true to my deepest convictions," she told an interviewer shortly before her death. "I mean to the courage of those who are born to be defeated, the weaknesses of the strong, and the tragedy of misunderstandings and missed opportunities, which I have done my best to treat as comedy, for otherwise how can we manage to bear it?"[36] She was obviously reflecting on her own life, about which she has been admirably reticent, speaking of it only reluctantly and elliptically to insistent interviewers. Married to an alcoholic—a major in the Irish Guards, trained as a barrister but working, when he worked, as a travel agent (he "didn't have much luck in life," she delicately put it)[37]—she became the family provider, taking lowly jobs with the Ministry of Food and the BBC, working in a bookstore, editing a small literary journal, teaching at a school for child actors, and moving frequently to ever cheaper accommodations. (When their barge sank, the family moved into public housing.) One is reminded once again of the vagaries of class; Fitzgerald was, after all, the granddaughter of not one but two bishops and the great-granddaughter of yet another.

Readers of her novels will find these work experiences and settings familiar. What they will not find in them is much discussion of religion. She told one interviewer that she had strong religious beliefs and regretted having not made this altogether clear in her novels.[38] But she did make it abundantly clear in *The Knox Brothers*. Not clear, to be sure, theologically or denominationally. Whatever her personal creed, her sympathies were sufficiently catholic (with a lower-case "c") to permit her to appreciate the transports and torments of each of her "God-haunted" characters. Alluding to the "black night of the soul" that Wilfred passed through during the war years, she went on to say that it was "no less painful to a Christian because so many have experienced it."[39]

That quiet observation, made almost in passing, is testimony to her own religiosity and sensibility.

A few years before Fitzgerald's death in 2000, another distinguished novelist, A. S. Byatt, wrote an appreciation of her that can now serve as a memorial tribute. Her later novels, Byatt said, showed her to be "Jane Austen's nearest heir, for precision and invention." They also evoked what Henry James called "the imagination of disaster," an imagination that was at the same time tragic and comic. And religious as well, for it was the "religious understanding of the individual," the individual understood as "body and soul," that permeated her novels. (Byatt casually remarked upon the fact that she first met Fitzgerald when they were both teaching at a tutorial school in the 1960s!)[40]

Annan concluded his essay on the "intellectual aristocracy": "Here at any rate seems to be an aristocracy that shows no signs of expiring."[41] Half a century later, that aristocracy was alive and well in the person of Penelope Fitzgerald, a worthy descendant of the Knox clan.

Michael Oakeshott
The Conservative Disposition

🙡 In 1950, in the preface to *The Liberal Imagination,* Lionel Trilling made the pronouncement that haunted American politics for almost half a century—still haunts America in some circles. "In the United States at this time liberalism is not only the dominant but even the sole intellectual tradition." This is not to say, he added, that there was no impulse to conservatism; indeed there were probably stronger such impulses than we knew. Those impulses, however, did not, with rare exceptions, express themselves in ideas, but "only in action or in irritable mental gestures which seek to resemble ideas."[1]

Trilling was right about America in 1950. But in England at that time there was one important thinker who did speak and write and teach in the name of conservativism, and who made conservatism a respectable and lively subject. It was a special kind of conservatism that Michael Oakeshott espoused—what Trilling would have called a "conservative imagination," or, as Oakeshott himself preferred, a "conservative disposition"—a temper of mind rather than a set of ideas, a spirit and attitude rather than a philosophy or creed.

From any conventional point of view, Oakeshott's career was full of anomalies. Having read history as an undergraduate at

Cambridge in the early 1920s, he went on, after a period of study abroad, to become a lecturer in history there for fifteen years until the war, and another four years afterward. (He enlisted in the army as soon as war broke out—he was then thirty-seven—serving first as a gunner and ending as the commander of a squadron.)* In all those years as a lecturer in history, and a very popular one, he never wrote a work of history or even a historical essay, although he did review some books on history and wrote an essay on the "activity" of being a historian.[3] His only important work during this period was on philosophy, *Experience and Its Modes,* in 1933. When he was appointed to a chair at the London School of Economics in 1951, it was neither to the chair of history nor of philosophy but of political science. In his inaugural lecture he paid tribute to the previous occupants of that chair, Graham Wallas and Harold Laski. He did not dwell on the obvious irony of the situation: that a self-avowed conservative should be taking the place of two notable socialists in an institution generally regarded as the citadel of socialism. He did allude to the fact that while his two predecessors were firmly confident of the truth of their teach-

---

*Peregrine Worsthorne, the English journalist, recalls meeting Oakeshott in the army:

> I first met him in Holland when he was the unit adjutant and I a newly-joined young subaltern fresh from Cambridge, and full of undergraduate arrogance. Such was Oakeshott's modesty and reticence that he never let on that he was also from Cambridge where he had been a famous pre-war don, author of what was already a classic work. Having no idea who or what he was, I used to lecture him ceaselessly in the mess, while he sat back giggling encouragement to my wildest flights of intellectual absurdity. We even shared a tent together for a while, which gave me even more opportunities to air my views, far into the night, still in total ignorance of his true identity. Not until I returned to Cambridge after the war, and attended my first lecture, did the penny drop. For there at the podium stood the self-same Oakeshott, with a crammed audience hanging on his every word.[2]

ings, he himself was a thoroughgoing skeptic. But he did not follow through on the paradox that a skeptic about political "science" should hold the professorship of political science.

One might be inclined to give Oakeshott the title of political philosopher rather than political scientist, were it not that he was equally skeptical of the usual claims of political philosophy—skeptical, indeed, of the possibility of any legitimate relationship between philosophy and politics. The philosopher, he insisted, has no practical lessons for the politician or the student of politics, except perhaps the lesson that politics is and should be totally independent of philosophy. "Political philosophy," he announced in his inaugural lecture, addressing the most highly politicized university in the country, "cannot be expected to increase our ability to be successful in political activity. It will not help us to distinguish between good and bad political projects; it has no power to guide or to direct us in the enterprise of pursuing the intimations of our tradition."[4]

Abjuring both political science and political philosophy, as these disciplines are normally understood, Oakeshott nevertheless acquired a small but distinguished body of admirers, not only in the academy but among journalists, writers, and public figures. He had nothing like the influence of Harold Laski, at home and still less abroad. Oakeshott's appeal was to a much more limited circle. But he was unquestionably the best-known and most respected intellectual spokesman for British conservatism. He resigned from the chair at the London School of Economics in 1969 but remained very much a presence in England until his death in 1990.

Oakeshott achieved this eminence with what might seem to be a modest body of work. Unlike Laski, who wrote voluminously and encyclopedically, Oakeshott's oeuvre is relatively slight. *Experience and Its Modes*, a systematic philosophical treatise, was a remarkable accomplishment for a man of thirty-one, presaging an illustrious and productive career. Yet for more than forty years, until the publication of *On Human Conduct* in 1975, he wrote nothing else remotely like it. During the thirties he published an essay a year and a volume of readings, apparently intended as a textbook, *The Social and Political Doctrines of Contemporary Europe*. He was somewhat more prolific after the war, editing Hobbes's *Leviathan* with a substantial introduction in 1946, and averaging an essay or two a year for the following decade and a half. These essays, as well as his warm personal relations with friends and students, brought him a devoted and influential group of disciples. But not until 1962, with the reprinting of ten of these essays in *Rationalism in Politics*, did he finally attract the attention of a larger public. His later works—*On Human Conduct* in 1975 and a small volume of essays, *On History*, in 1983—were respectfully received but did not generate the excitement of *Rationalism in Politics*. In any case, his reputation by then was firmly established.*

These apparent anomalies—the political philosopher who had so limited a view of the task of political philosophy, the intellectual who was so reluctant a producer of intellectual goods, the master who acquired disciples seemingly effortlessly—were, of course, no anomalies at all. They were perfectly in character, entirely consistent with the conservative disposition as Oakeshott himself understood it. It was also in character that, having written so little about the classics of political thought (with the exception of

---

*His reputation, that is, among the cognoscenti. The first printing of *Experience and Its Modes* was one thousand copies, and was sold out only after thirty-one years. A second edition of a thousand copies in 1966 went out of print after three years and was reissued in 1978. Even *Rationalism in Politics* had a modest sale, with a first printing of five thousand copies; a small paperback edition appeared in 1967, and a library edition of a thousand copies in 1974.[5]

Hobbes), he entitled one book co-authored by him *A Guide to the Classics*—the "classics" he had in mind is suggested by the subtitle, "How to Pick the Derby Winner." (His co-author, Guy Griffith, a colleague at Cambridge, was a Byzantine scholar.)* If the title was facetious, the contents were serious enough, or at least as serious in Oakeshott's scheme of values as any other subject occupying a civilized man. His admirers take delight in the fact that he was a racing man and the owner of a racing horse, and in his disdain for academic solemnities and proprieties. They regard this as existential confirmation of his philosophy, his conviction that all activities, politics as much as racing, are to be understood in their own terms and enjoyed for their own sakes rather than subsumed under rationalist categories and made to serve utilitarian ends.

The title essay of *Rationalism in Politics* first appeared in 1947 and set the tone, if not the theme, for the rest of the volume. For Oakeshott, Rationalism is the great heresy of modern times. (He generally capitalized "Rationalism" and lower-cased "conservatism," which is itself a commentary on his use of those terms.) The Rationalist, taking reason as his only authority, is necessarily hostile to any other authority: tradition, habit, custom, prejudice, common sense. It is the nature of the Rationalist to be at the same time skeptical and optimistic: skeptical because "there is no opinion, no habit, no belief, nothing so firmly rooted or so widely held that he hesitates to question it and to judge it by what he calls his 'reason'"; and optimistic because he "never doubts the power of his 'reason' (when properly applied) to determine the worth of a thing,

---

*Originally published in 1936, this was the only book Oakeshott bothered to revise when it was reissued in 1947. Even the title was changed, to the dismay of the aficionados who enjoyed the pun. *A New Guide to the Derby* may have sold more books, but it lacked the insider jest of *A Guide to the Classics*.

the truth of an opinion or the propriety of an action."[6] The Rationalist has no respect for the seemingly irrational vestiges of the past, and little patience with the transitory arrangements of the present. He has only an overwhelming yearning for a future in which all will be made orderly, reasonable, of maximum utility and efficiency. And he would like this future to be realized as soon as possible. His is the politics of "destruction and creation" rather than of "acceptance or reform."[7] He wants no patch-up jobs, no tinkering with this or that, still less the kinds of changes that come about without the direct, conscious, rational intervention of men. He sees life (social and political affairs as well as the life of the individual) as a series of problems to be solved, of felt needs which have to be instantly satisfied. And they can be solved and satisfied only by a set of rationally devised techniques that are of immediate, universal, and certain application.

Although Oakeshott puts the Rationalist's "reason" in quotation marks, as if it were a spurious kind of reason, he does not specify any other kind of reason to which the non-Rationalist can lay claim. But he does so implicitly in identifying the Rationalist's "reason" with "technical knowledge" in contrast to "practical knowledge." "The sovereignty of 'reason,' for the Rationalist, means the sovereignty of technique." But there is another kind of knowledge, practical knowledge, which "can neither be taught nor learned, but only imparted and acquired," and which cannot be laid down in rules and precepts because it involves a sensitivity, artistry, and intelligence that come from long exposure to traditions and habits that have proved themselves in practice.[8]

Oakeshott is often accused of being "elitist." But there is nothing precious or recondite in his notion of practical knowledge. His metaphors and analogies are thoroughly commonplace. They come from cooking, racing, gambling, carpentry, sports, love—activities common to all people, although not all people excel in all of them.

He concedes that there is some degree of technical knowledge involved in these activities; this is why there can be manuals of cooking, gambling, even lovemaking. But to think that such manuals are any substitute for practical knowledge is the modern fallacy. The author of one such manual, he recalls—he coyly refrains from identifying himself—had gone to some pains to point out that there are no precise rules for picking a Derby winner, no shortcuts for the firsthand familiarity with horses which was once more common than it is today and which makes for a kind of intelligence that no amount of rules can supply. Yet some readers of the manual—"greedy, rationalistic readers, on the look-out for an infallible method"—thought they had been "sold a pup" because the book did not bring them up to the level of men of genuine knowledge who had long and intimate experience of racing and betting.[9]

Oakeshott rarely speaks of liberals or liberalism, probably because he himself has too high a regard for liberty to apply those honorific labels to his antagonists. But it is obvious that in describing rationalism, and in characterizing it as the prevalent mode of thought in our time, he has in mind what today is normally called liberalism. And he has no hesitation in speaking of himself as a conservative and in praising the virtues of the conservative disposition. The most explicit statement of this disposition is the essay "On Being Conservative," written in 1956, a counterpart to "Rationalism in Politics" written almost a decade before. After his uncompromising indictment of the Rationalist mentality, he may have felt it necessary to provide a positive statement of an alternative mode of thought and behavior. Yet even without this essay, the alternative is abundantly clear in everything he wrote. And that alternative is always in the form of a disposition rather than a creed.

Oakeshott does not defend philosophical doctrines or even take political positions in the usual fashion. Instead he defines the conservative in terms of attitudes and habits of mind and conduct that pervade all aspects of life. This disposition is exhibited in personal more than public affairs, in the intimate, daily activities of life more than in the large political decisions. It has, to be sure, political implications, and Oakeshott does not hesitate to spell these out. But politics, he insists, is only a small part of life and not the most important part. Only the Rationalist, wanting to effect large social changes, inflates politics and thus deflates man's humanity.

The key word describing the conservative disposition is "enjoyment." Where the Rationalist, pursuing reason, is always lusting after something that is not, the conservative prefers to enjoy whatever is. He enjoys family and friends as he also enjoys his liberties; he is loyal to them as they are, and is not discontented because they are no better than they are. The popular conception of the conservative is of a person who idolizes the past; for Oakeshott, the conservative is one who esteems the present and therefore values whatever the past has bequeathed to the present. He esteems the present not because it is more admirable than any conceivable alternative but because it is familiar and for that reason enjoyable. And enjoying the present, he realizes how much he would lose if it were gone. Oakeshott admits that if the present were arid, if there were little or nothing in it to enjoy, the conservative disposition would be inappropriate. But the present is rarely, he finds, intolerable, except to those who are ignorant of the resources of their world and of the opportunities for enjoyment, or to those who are so captivated by the Rationalist impulse, the desire to make the world conform to their ideal, that they see the present only as a "residue of inopportunities."[10] If the old are more apt to be conservative than the young, it is not, as the young are inclined to think, because the old are more fearful of what they might lose by change but because time and maturity have taught them the value of what they have.

Unlike the stereotypical conservative, Oakeshott's conservative is not averse to change as such. He recognizes both the need and the inevitability of change. The question is how to accommodate change. The conservative proposes to do so by small doses rather than large, out of necessity rather than ideology, gradually, slowly, incrementally, naturally, with a minimum disruption of life. Unlike the Rationalist who thinks innovation to be a good thing in itself, the conservative regards it as a deprivation, a loss of something familiar, regrettable even when necessary. To him all innovations are inherently equivocal, a compound of gain and loss, and not only because of their unanticipated consequences but also because of their predictable effects, the fact that a change in any part of life inevitably brings with it a change in the whole texture of life. Thus the true conservative resists unnecessary changes and suffers necessary ones.

> The disposition to be conservative is, then, warm and positive in respect of enjoyment, and correspondingly cool and critical in respect of change and innovation: these two inclinations support and elucidate one another. The man of conservative temperament believes that a known good is not lightly to be surrendered for an unknown better. He is not in love with what is dangerous and difficult; he is unadventurous; he has no impulse to sail uncharted seas; for him there is no magic in being lost, bewildered or shipwrecked. If he is forced to navigate the unknown, he sees virtue in heaving the lead every inch of the way. What others plausibly identify as timidity, he recognizes in himself as rational prudence; what others interpret as inactivity, he recognizes as a disposition to enjoy rather than to exploit. He is cautious, and he is disposed to indicate his assent or dissent, not in absolute, but in graduated terms. He eyes the situation in terms of its propensity to disrupt the familiarity of the features of his world.[11]

It is typical of Oakeshott that he should introduce the subject of politics only midway in his essay "On Being Conservative." But this is entirely fitting in his scheme of things. The conservative disposition is an attitude toward life rather than a particular mode of politics, and politics itself is defined and limited by that disposition. Like everything else in life, politics is a matter of experience and habituation. "Political education" is not an indoctrination or even elucidation of political principles but rather the elucidation of the traditional practices and activities characterizing a nation's actual political life. Similarly, government is an activity rather than a system, and a narrowly conceived activity at that: "the provision and custody of general rules of conduct, which are understood, not as plans for imposing substantive activities, but as instruments enabling people to pursue the activities of their own choice with the minimum frustration."[12]

The purpose of government is not to bring order out of the disorder of society, for society is inherently in a condition of disorder, consisting of a multitude of people engaged in a great variety of activities, acting out of a multiplicity of motives, interests, passions, reasons. Government is not intended to direct these activities to a more coherent or rational end, or to instruct or edify the people, or to make them happier or better. The function of government is nothing more nor less than the function of ruling, in the sense in which an umpire may be said to rule, by administering the agreed-upon rules of the game without himself playing in the game; or in which a chairman presiding over a debate rules, by seeing to it that the disputants observe the rules of order without himself participating in the debate.

This limited role of government commends itself to Oakeshott not because it derives from some philosophical or political principle—the idea, for example, that freedom of choice is an absolute value, or that truth and goodness emerge only from the unfettered diversity of activity and opinion. (Oakeshott does not mention Mill by name, but it is clear that at this point he is dissociating himself from the argument of *On Liberty*.) The conservative has little use for government because he thinks that most people are inclined to make their own choices and find their happiness in doing so, that they pursue a variety of enterprises and hold to a variety of beliefs, and that life reveals no large design but only an incessant, changeful, multitudinous activity. Under these conditions, the function of government is simply to make and enforce those rules of conduct that are themselves part of these facts of life. With such rules (as distinct from the Rationalist's contrived rules), the conservative is comfortable, both because they are familiar and because they leave him free to do what he wants to do. These are the rules "it is appropriate to be conservative about."[13]

If this modest conception of government—as umpire or chairman—distinguishes Oakeshott from most modern liberals, it also distinguishes him, and quite as sharply, from many conservatives. He makes short shrift of those conservatives who rely not upon a disposition but upon a principle or creed: the idea of God, or original sin, or natural law, or organic society, or the absolute value of the human personality.* To Oakeshott, these or any other principles intended to legitimize the social order are "highfalutin metaphysical beliefs." They are not only unnecessary; they are potentially dangerous because, like any other Rationalist ideal, they tempt government to do more than it should do, "to turn a private dream into a public and compulsory

---

*Unlike many conservatives, he has little use for Edmund Burke, linking him together with Bentham as Rationalists—in Burke's case because of his "metaphysical" belief in religion, natural law, and an organic society held together by the bonds of that "great primeval contract of eternal society."[14]

manner of living." Oakeshott's warning, "the conjunction of dreaming and ruling generates tyranny," applies as much to the conservative Rationalist as to the liberal Rationalist.[15]

That Oakeshott is as far removed from these rationalistic conservatives as he is from the most rationalistic liberals is most evident in his attitude toward religion. One might expect him to be personally skeptical about the existence of God, of a providential social order, or of a divinely ordained morality, and at the same time sensible of the power of these beliefs, their deep roots in the habits, institutions, and activities of ordinary life. Other thinkers have managed to combine private disbelief (or a suspension of belief) with a high regard for the public dimensions of belief—not as a Machiavellian strategy for social control but out of a proper deference to the opinions and behavior that have long characterized civilized life. Oakeshott especially, one might think, would be respectful of religious sensibilities and impatient with the Rationalist mentality that is aggressively secular, regarding religion as regressive and oppressive. The concluding sentence of his essay, "On Being Conservative," has the conservative "at home in this commonplace world."[16] One might read this as an invitation to be at home in the religious beliefs and practices which, however attenuated, are still an important part of this commonplace world, perhaps as important a part as the horse racing, betting, cooking, fishing, and other homely activities Oakeshott dwells on so lovingly.

Yet in that essay, when Oakeshott briefly alludes to religion, he does so begrudgingly. He tolerates religious institutions not as a means of giving expression and actuality to religious faith but rather as a means of restraining that faith. Conservatives, he grants, "might even be prepared to suffer a legally established ecclesiastical order; but it would not be because they believed it to represent some unassailable religious truth, but merely because it restrained the indecent competition of sects and (as Hume said) moderated 'the plague of a too diligent clergy'." Religious beliefs—God, divine law, a providential order—are dealt with dismissively, as yet other examples of "highfalutin metaphysical beliefs." What is called for is a "mood of indifference" that will "rein in" one's own beliefs and tolerate even "what is abominable." Such a mood, Oakeshott explains, is not suited to the young; it can be sustained only by the mature—and, he might have added, by those of little faith, or, better yet, of no faith.[17]

Experience and Its Modes has a very brief discussion of religion—four pages in a 350-page work, which suggests the relative weight Oakeshott gives it in the totality of human experience. At one point he credits religion with being "practical experience at its fullest." But he then goes on to say that, as distinct from other forms of practical experience, religion is always characterized "by intensity and strength of devotion and by singleness of purpose." Several pages later, distinguishing between practical truths that are conducive to freedom and practical errors that "enslave," "mislead," or "endanger" our lives, he puts religion in the latter category. A footnote quotes Hume: "Generally speaking, the errors of religion are dangerous; those of philosophy only ridiculous."[18]

One can understand Hume's fear of the practical "dangers" of religion. He was close enough to the Puritan experience, and a witness in his own day to the Methodist revival (*A Treatise on Human Nature* was published the very year of that revival), to feel a lively sense of the power of religion, of the passion it might evoke and the divisive effect it might have upon society and the polity. But Oakeshott, priding himself on his practical common sense, could hardly share that fear—not, at any rate, in the England of his own time. It might be that he was foreseeing the religious passions that were later to be unleashed in other parts of the world. Yet he does not presume to speak or philosophize for the whole world. On the contrary, he is insistent that only in his world, his kind of civilization, is the conservative disposition appropriate.

Oakeshott's last major work, *On Human Conduct*, in 1975, exhibits a greater tolerance, even sympathy, for religion. It is now seen as providing a faith that reconciles us to the "unavoidable dissonances" of the human condition. And not only the familiar contingencies of life—infirmities and miseries, disasters and frustrations, culminating in death itself—but the inevitable wrongs that we ourselves perpetrate. By substituting the sense of sin for that of guilt, religion deprives wrongdoing of its fatality without diminishing its enormity; it creates "a refuge from the destroying Angst of guilt." And it reconciles us to a still greater dissonance of the human condition: the haunting sense of hollowness and futility, of nothingness. Each religion reflects, in its own "idiom of faith" and in the "poetic quality" of its images, rites, and observances, the "civilization of the believer." And each invites us, in its own way, to live "so far as is possible, as an immortal."[19]

It is a sensitive and moving account of religious faith that Oakeshott has now given us, and one in keeping with the conservative disposition that he has described elsewhere. It is, however, all too brief, several pages introduced almost as an afterthought: "To this consideration of moral conduct I will add a brief recognition of religious belief: not to do so, however inadequately, would be to leave this account of human conduct inexcusably incomplete."[20] As an account of "human conduct," it is still incomplete, for it dwells almost entirely on religion in the existential sense, the religious impulse or sensibility, rather than the creeds, practices, and institutions that make of religion a communal and historical reality instead of a merely personal or emotive one.*

---

*This cursory treatment of religion is all the stranger because he had once been more attentive to religion. His first publication, in 1927, was a ten-page pamphlet originally given as a talk, *Religion and the Moral Life*. After reviewing the commonly held views of the relationship of religion and morality, he concluded that there was at least a historical relationship between "our moral life

In morality, as in politics, Oakeshott is chary of anything that might suggest a conscious, deliberate system of principles and practices. Just as the polity is ill advised to pursue conscious social ideals, so the individual is ill advised to pursue conscious moral ideals, the Rationalist fallacy lying in both the consciousness and the pursuit of those ideals. And just as the polity does not depend on any idea of divine or natural law, so morality does not depend on religious authority, moral sense, conscience, or even the "habit of reflective thought." All it does depend on is the "habit of affection and conduct." "We acquire habits of conduct, not by constructing a way of living upon rules or precepts learned by heart and subsequently practised, but by living with people who habitually behave in a certain manner: we acquire habits of conduct in the same way as we acquire our native language."[22]

The parallel between morality and politics would seem to falter at one point. In politics, a reliance on habit, as Oakeshott understands it, tends to limit the role of government and give greater latitude to the individual. In morality, a reliance on habit is apt to enhance the role of society (although not of government) and to restrict that of the individual. Moral habituation is, after all, a training in social conformity. To the extent to which it succeeds, it would seem to gainsay the variety and individuality that conservatism—Oakeshott's conservativism—is designed to promote. Oakeshott denies that this is necessarily the case. The "moral eccentric," he insists, is in no way excluded from the framework of the moral life. On the contrary, the impulse to dissent derives from the moral tradition itself. "There is a freedom and inventiveness at

---

today" and "what we understand the Christian view of life to be." He never reprinted this pamphlet. Nor did he choose to reprint his only other essay on religion, written the following year: "The Importance of the Historical Element in Christianity."[21]

the heart of every traditional way of life, and deviation may be an expression of that freedom, springing from a sensitiveness to the tradition itself and remaining faithful to the traditional form."[23] The deviant, even while he is protected in his deviancy, does not constitute a threat to the moral life, any more than a change in moral habits is a threat to morality. Since the moral life is not conceived of as a system, since it does not depend upon any set of rational principles, the abandonment of any part of it does not entail a collapse of the whole. The moral life goes on, with all its deviations, anomalies, and irrationalities.

Oakeshott's image of the moral life is attractive and plausible—or was so at the time he so eloquently argued for it. "Rationalism in Politics" was first published in 1947, and the other essays in the book of that title appeared between then and 1962, when the book was published. Some critics at the time said it reflected the temper of the fifties but was inappropriate to the sixties. The critique of rationalism—so this argument went—was congenial to those who had been disenchanted by the postwar Labour government, with its often blundering experiments in social engineering, its irritating paternalism, its mean-spirited austerity. But to the generation of the sixties, having little respect for traditional habits and institutions, seeking radical solutions to what seemed to be intolerable inequities, Oakeshott sounded passive and querulous, committed to an outmoded and unjust status quo.

There is something in this identification of Oakeshott with the fifties and his dissociation from the sixties. But it is not quite what his critics were then saying. It was not the advent of a new social consciousness that made Oakeshott seem irrelevant. On the contrary, that turn of affairs made his admonitions all the more timely, for beneath the surface of dissent lay a new form of rationalism, an impatient and imperious temper that sought quick and easy answers to difficult and complicated situations. In this sense, Oakeshott brilliantly anticipated the sixties. In the rationalist reformism of the late forties and fifties he saw the intimations of the rationalist radicalism of the following decade. And his critique of rationalism applied to both.

There came a point, however, when events seemed to overtake him. By the late sixties it was becoming apparent that something like a moral revolution was taking place. Moral deviancy was being popularized and democratized, so that it was not the occasional eccentric or sect but an entire generation that appeared to be rejecting traditional "habits of conduct," indeed, rejecting the very idea of "moral habituation." From sporadic excesses of rhetoric and behavior, the counterculture developed into an antagonism to all "hegemonic" political authorities and social institutions as well as a disdain for the traditional, habitual modes of thought and conduct that sustained society. A generation that prided itself on being "alienated" was not inclined to look tolerantly upon the familiar, to enjoy the present for what it is, to accept the facts of life and make the best of them, still less to respect the informal rules of conduct that govern society, obviating the need for formal rules imposed by government.

Oakeshott may not have anticipated the full nature and extent of the moral revolution that emerged in the late sixties and the decades that followed. (And he would have objected to the term "revolution" as being too dramatic, too uncompromising and obdurate.) But he was hardly unaware of the potentialities for anarchy and subversion. His "disposition" was optimistic but not naive. A year before "Rationalism in Politics" (the essay, not the book), he wrote a seventy-five-page introduction to Hobbes's *Leviathan,* which foreshadows some of the themes of the later essay. It is interesting that Hobbes, the most provocative of modern thinkers, should have been the first subject Oakeshott chose when he returned to the university after the war. With great subtlety he analyzed and finally absolved this "alleged apostle of absolutism" of many of the faults other commentators had found in him.[24] But he did not entirely acquit him of the failing of all political philosophers—a rationalism that was profoundly pessimistic.

> It is characteristic of political philosophers that they take a somber view of the human situation: they deal in darkness. Human life in their writings appears, generally, not as a feat or even as a journey, but as a predicament: and the link between politics and eternity is the contribution the political order is conceived as making to the deliverance of mankind. . . . Man, so the varied formula runs, is the dupe of error, the slave of sin, of passion, of fear, of care, the enemy of himself or of others or of both—*O miseras hominum mentes, O pectora caeca*—and the civil order appears as the whole or a part of the scheme of his salvation.[25]

This was written by a man who had good reason to take "a somber view of the human situation," having just returned from a devastating war waged against a regime guilty of the most monstrous tyranny and atrocities. Yet the lesson he drew from that experience was not "dark" or even dreary. Instead he apparently found "salvation" in an England that had fought and won the war honorably and could now revert to a natural "civil order," an order that did not have to be imposed artificially as a "deliverance" from the inherent evils of human nature but was rather the normal condition of a "civil" and civilized people.

Perhaps one reason Oakeshott acquired the admirers and disciples he did during this postwar period was in reaction to those wartime experiences and in gratitude to a society that did not have to "deal in darkness." Later, when that tranquility was disturbed by the counterculture—and, even more, by a counterculture that seemed to be becoming the dominant culture—some of those admirers and disciples began to have second thoughts, to suspect that the conservative disposition is inadequate to cope with these turbulent times, indeed, that any "disposition" is inadequate. These admirers, friendly critics now, continue to share Oakeshott's distrust of the rationalism characteristic of much political philosophy, a rationalism that converts philosophy into ideology, ideology into "praxis," and "praxis" into aggressive political actions and an intrusive state. But they also believe that the critique of rationalism can be carried too far, that reason does not necessarily degenerate into rationalism, nor ideas into ideologies. In the moral vacuum created by the absence of "habits of conduct," reason and ideas—and philosophy, religion, education, even inculcation—may be the only means of re-creating lost values and perhaps eventually restoring a "disposition" that no longer requires the active intervention of mind and will.*

In one of his most eloquent essays, "The Voice of Poetry in the Conversation of Mankind," written in 1959, Oakeshott describes the kind of conversation that constitutes civilized discourse and that has its analogue in all civilized relationships.[26] Conversation, he says, may have intervals of reasoned argument, but it cannot be that entirely or even largely. It must be hospitable to plays of fancy, flights of speculation, irrelevancies, and inconsequentialities. It

---

*But not all his admirers have become critics. Oakeshott has retained a core of devoted disciples, in England, America, Australia, and elsewhere, who keep his ideas alive and his books in print. All his books (with the exception of the *Guide to the Classics*, which, unlike most classics, became hopelessly dated) have been reprinted, most of them since his death, and many are available in paperback as well as hardcover. There are also selections of essays and lectures by him that had not been previously published, as well as several books and collections of essays about him. (Since the turn of the century, five books by or about him have appeared, and several are scheduled for future publication.) A Michael Oakeshott Association conducts annual conferences, the papers of which are then published.

speaks in many voices, recognizes no authority, requires no credentials. It asks of its participants only that they have the ability to converse and the good manners to listen, not that they reason cogently, make discoveries about the world, or try to improve it.

This essay is as elegant, urbane, and witty as the ideal of conversation conjured up in it. It also recalls the Oakeshott I knew, with whom conversation, even controversy, was a sheer delight. He did not avoid disagreement; there was nothing wimpish about him. But he confronted it with such good nature and good humor that he always won the argument (he would never, of course, have called it that) by default, so to speak. It is not often that the person and the philosopher are so totally congruent. The "conservative disposition"—the disposition to enjoy what is rather than pining for what might be, to appreciate the givens and the goods of life without wanting to subject them to social or political validation—this is a perfect description of his own temperament. He was charming, gracious, debonair, to women always gallant, even dashing, although in a thoroughly unassuming, unpretentious manner.

Oakeshott's conservatism, like his temperament, is something of a rarity these days. It puts a great value on liberty and individuality, but it is not libertarian in the free-market sense, if only because he himself paid little attention to economics. It respects tradition, custom, norms of conduct, but it is not social conservatism as we now know it, for it is more open, adventurous, less moralistic and religious-minded. And it is far too wary and skeptical of government to fall into the neoconservative camp. Yet it still speaks to us today, not as a practical philosophy—but then Oakeshott did not think of philosophy as a practical enterprise—but as a disposition that reminds us of more tranquil times, and which may still serve as a corrective to the more rigorous and strenuous modes of thought and conduct called for in a world that is anything but tranquil.

Winston Churchill

"Quite Simply, a Great Man"

~✺~ The eminent English historian Geoffrey Elton once wrote:

> When I meet a historian who cannot think that there have been
> great men, great men moreover in politics, I feel myself in the
> presence of a bad historian; and there are times when I incline to
> judge all historians by their opinion of Winston Churchill—
> whether they can see that, no matter how much better the details,
> often damaging, of man and career become known, he still re-
> mains, quite simply, a great man.[1]

In the United States we are re-remembering our great men. After years of being told by learned historians that history is not
made by great men—that it is made by forces (economic, social,
demographic, geographic) beyond the control of individuals, that
the very words "great men" are an aspersion on all the ordinary
people, the "anonymous masses" whose names do not figure in the
pages of history, to say nothing of the women, great and not great,
who are thereby expunged from history (the very idea of greatness
is maligned as masculine, thus sexist)—we are now being deluged
with best-selling books on our great men, most notably, the
Founders and Abraham Lincoln. These are not, as they might once

have been, muckraking books, exposing the clay feet (or, more often, the libidinous impulses) that make these men seem less great. Nor are they hagiographic works designed to make them not so much great men as supermen. They are, in fact, good, solid, scholarly, and, not least, readable volumes that establish their subjects' title to greatness not so much by virtue of their personal qualities, although these are no small part of it, but by their role in history, in the founding and shaping of the nation.

In the aftermath of the most devastating terrorist attack in our history, we had occasion to remember another great man, who was not one of our own (although he liked to remind us that his mother was American). As we embarked on the war against terrorism, we were admonished to recall the courage, determination, and heroism of Winston Churchill in his (and our) war against Nazism. Commentators on September 11th repeatedly invoked his name, and newspapers devoted entire articles to him, quoting his more memorable pronouncements and recalling his bravery and bravado during the war. An electronic count of references to him in print alone during the first week after the attacks came to more than a thousand, not including television, radio, and speeches. It was startling to hear the president, not known for his rhetorical deftness, being commended for his Churchillian addresses to the nation. A passage in one speech—"We will not waver; we will not tire; we will not falter; and we will not fail"[2]— clearly echoed Churchill's famous speech of February 9, 1941: "We shall not fail or falter; we shall not weaken or tire."[3] It was not surprising to hear the secretary of defense, the deputy secretary of defense, even the secretary of health and human services quoting Churchill. But it was bizarre to hear his words rendered in the accent and intonation of the mayor of New York; "Churchill in a ball cap," Churchill's grandson (another Winston), dubbed him.[4] Rudy Giuliani not only quoted Churchill; he was repeatedly likened to him as he walked amid the rubble of the World Trade Center, honoring those who lost their lives there and comforting their survivors. "Who Knew Rudy Was Churchill?" read the headline in one newspaper.[5] And so it went through one crisis after another. When anthrax caused the closing of the House of Representatives for a few days, a historian might be reminded of Churchill's reaction to the bombing of the House of Commons: "This Chamber must be rebuilt—just as it was! Meanwhile, we shall not miss a single day's debate through this."[6]

The British—*pace* Elton—have not always been so respectful of Churchill. In 1995, to commemorate the fiftieth anniversary of the victory over Germany, the British Education Department prepared a video to be distributed to all primary schools. The thirty-four-minute video contained a single fourteen-second reference to Churchill, a remark uttered by a child: "People thought he helped the war end in Britain."[7] In the twenty-four-minute video for secondary schools, he was mentioned exactly once: "Though defeated, Mr. Churchill is proclaimed a great war leader"; this was followed by the comment that his defeat allowed the Labour party "to use profits from state-owned industries to finance better public services, such as health care."[8] A survey a few weeks later showed that one in three British schoolchildren had no idea who Churchill was; guesses ranged from an American president to a songwriter.

Fortunately the Education Department's cavalier treatment of Churchill does not extend to biographers who continue to write about him, sometimes disparagingly ("revisionist" accounts that criticize him for not making peace with Hitler earlier) but more often respectfully. Nor is it reflected in the reading public who continue to make best-sellers of many of these books (especially of the appreciative ones). The bibliography of works by and about Churchill contains some three thousand entries, including the authorized (definitive, one would normally say, except that in the case of Churchill nothing is definitive) eight-volume biography by Randolph S. Churchill and Martin Gilbert, with its thirteen companion volumes of documents and many more to come. Among the more notable biographies are the first two volumes of William Manchester's projected trilogy (the final volume will not be completed), and, in the final decade of the century alone, books of substantial length by Gilbert (over a thousand pages), Clive Ponting, John Charmley, Henry Pelling, and Norman Rose, in addition to half a dozen shorter works, books on particular aspects of Churchill's life, and volumes of essays. And then there are all the books by Churchill himself, most of which are in print, in paperback, and often in audio cassettes as well. John Plumb, himself a best-selling historian and sensitive to such matters, once observed that Churchill "sold more books on history than any historian in this century and perhaps any century."[9]

Two biographies of Churchill appearing in the same year, 2001, by Geoffrey Best and the late Roy Jenkins, make for a nice counterpoint. The first, of modest length, is by a professional historian—professor of history at St. Antony's College, Oxford, and the author of scholarly works on Victorian Britain and, more recently, on modern warfare. The second, three times longer, is by a professional politician—a longtime member of Parliament who is also a prolific writer and biographer.[10] Both authors are of an age to remember Churchill during the war. As a schoolboy, Best listened to Churchill's speeches as "quasi-religious events" and was so impressed that he requested a volume of them as a school prize.[11] Jenkins was introduced to Churchill by his father, a Labour member of Parliament, in the temporary quarters of the Commons after the old chamber was destroyed by bombs.[12] Half a century later the historian has given us a spirited, illuminating, and very readable biography of "the greatest Englishman of the twentieth century," "the saviour of his country,"[13]* while the politician/writer has produced a much more ponderous and far less reverent tome.

Jenkins's account of how he came to his subject is instructive. Having just completed a prizewinning biography of Gladstone, he was casting around for his next project—a "big subject" worthy of its predecessor; anything less, he said, would be like ambling up Snowdon after an expedition to the Himalayas. (The mountain-climbing metaphor also appears in the preface to his Gladstone biography, where he compared that task to climbing the Matterhorn.) Only Churchill met that requirement; indeed, he now decided, Churchill was "marginally ahead" of Gladstone.[15] (In his earlier book, Gladstone was "the most remarkable specimen of humanity" who ever served as prime minister.[16]) Because of his own parliamentary and ministerial experience—like Churchill, he was not only a member of Parliament but also a sometime home secretary and chancellor of the Exchequer—Jenkins believed himself to be uniquely qualified to write a biography of Churchill. Like Churchill, too, he managed to be a prolific and successful writer even as he pursued an active political career.

Unlike Churchill, however, Jenkins was a member of the Labour party before resigning to found the short-lived Social Democratic party (and to serve as the first president of the European Commission in Brussels). And his writings, particularly his biography of Gladstone, have the effect of distorting his study of Churchill. Jenkins's Churchill is haunted by Gladstone's ghost. Again and again we are reminded of the parallels (some rather far-fetched) in the lives and careers of these two eminences.[17] Yet it is

---

*When Isaiah Berlin, in 1949, praised Churchill as "the saviour of his country, a mythical hero who belongs to legend as much as to reality, the largest human being of our time," Churchill wryly observed that it was "too good to be true."[14]

not the Liberal Gladstone who bears comparison with Churchill but the Tory Disraeli (whom Jenkins mentions only in passing).

Temperamentally and politically, Churchill was cast in the Disraelian mode—romantic, flamboyant, and eccentric; paternalistic, nationalistic, and imperialistic.* If Gladstone was a "little Englander," Churchill, like Disraeli, surely deserves the title of "great Englander." Whereas Gladstone was essentially a Manchester liberal, Churchill, like Disraeli (and like his own father), was a Tory Democrat. (It was Randolph Churchill who founded the Primrose League, named in honor of Disraeli, the primrose being his favorite flower. One of Winston's first political acts as a schoolboy was to join the Primrose League.) Gladstone, his contemporaries suspected, saw himself as the emissary of God on earth; Churchill, again like Disraeli, preferred to think of himself as the emissary of the English nation. Gladstone was notoriously humorless, priggish, moralistic; Churchill was witty, irreverent, ironic. (There are entire books on Churchill's "wit and wisdom," and scores of other witticisms that circulated privately because they were too ribald for publication.) Disraeli would have been amused, and Gladstone appalled, by Churchill's famous quip, "I am ready to meet my Maker. Whether my Maker is ready to meet me is another question." Asked to elaborate on his religious belief, Churchill quoted a character in one of Disraeli's novels: "Sensible men are all of the same religion." Pressed further, he cited Disraeli again: "Sensible men never tell."[19] (In fact, the quip originated with Lord Shaftesbury over a century earlier.)

---

*In his biography of his father, Churchill paid tribute to Disraeli as the progenitor of Tory democracy. Toward Gladstone he made a determined effort to be respectful, describing him as "courtly" but also quoting a speech by Randolph Churchill savagely ridiculing him for his sanctimoniousness and self-promotion.[18]

It is often said that had Churchill died in 1939, at the ripe age of sixty-five (outliving his father by almost twenty years), he would be remembered, if at all, not as a hero but as yet another politician, and (like his father) a failed politician to boot. If that were so, it would do a grave injustice to a man who was always larger than life. He lived his life with a vigor and passion exhibited by few men. And he wrote about it even as he lived it—not narcissistically, like so many memoirists of our own time, but historically, so to speak, fully conscious that in writing about himself he was writing about his country and his times. By 1939 Churchill had written three books about his military experiences in India and Africa in the late 1890s, a memoir of his early life, a two-volume biography of his father, a four-volume life-and-times of his ancestor, the first Duke of Marlborough, a five-volume history of the First World War and its aftermath, a four-volume history of the English-speaking peoples (published very much later), several other books about his experiences and contemporaries, and one (happily, only one) novel, *Savrola*—all of this in addition to the steady stream of newspaper articles from which he derived a substantial part of his income, the innumerable speeches delivered in and out of Parliament (three volumes of which were published before 1939), and the voluminous correspondence, with his wife most notably but with others as well. During all this time he was an active (too active, many complained) member of Parliament, often in high position in the cabinet.

In retrospect, of course, we can recognize in that pre-hero, pre–World War II Churchill the distinctive features of the character we now know. His biography of the Duke of Marlborough is not simply a testament of ancestral piety or pride (it does not ignore the duke's less reputable aspects, his self-aggrandizement and self-enrichment, although it dwells upon them less than most biographers). It is rather an account of the military and diplomatic

achievements that Churchill admired and, perhaps, hoped to emulate. He cherished the Blenheim estate that was his only material
heritage from that aristocratic lineage (the family fortune had long
since been dissipated), at least in part because of the memory of the
Battle of Blenheim itself. Marlborough's victory in what proved to
be one of the decisive battles in the War of the Spanish Succession
had altered the balance of power in Europe, signaling the end of
the French dominion and the beginning of the British. "England's
Advance to World Power" is the title Churchill later gave to this
period in his *History of the English-Speaking Peoples*, paying tribute
to the ancestor who had "rendered glorious" one of the great reigns
in English history.[20]

We can also see something of the later Churchill in his own father. Lord Randolph Churchill once quipped that Gladstone was
"an old man in a hurry."[21] It was more true to say that Randolph
himself was a young man in a hurry. He announced his engagement
to Jennie Jerome, daughter of an American financier, three days after they met; they were married eight months later (a delay occa-
sioned by their fathers' squabbling over the dowry); and Winston
was born seven months after that (prematurely, owing to a riding
fall by his mother). In that year, 1874, Randolph, then twenty-five,
acquired not only a son but also a seat in Parliament (like his father before him). Ten years later he was chancellor of the Exchequer and leader of the House of Commons in Salisbury's
government. Ten years after that, at the age of forty-five, he was
dead. If Winston Churchill was also very much a young man in a
hurry, it may have been because he suspected that, like his father,
he would have little time to achieve the prominence he sought.

There was much else in the life of the father that presaged that
of the son. Randolph Churchill was the most successful orator (or
demagogue, his critics had it) of his time, the most famous (or pub-
licity-seeking) member of his party, the boldest (or most irrespon-

sible) theoretician, a lively (or insolent) conversationalist, and a great (or cruel) wit—traits that have also been attributed to the son. The father was also a failure in politics (having had to resign as chancellor after the defeat of his first budget), as his son was thought to be before 1939. In one respect, however, the two differed markedly. Randolph was even more a failure as a father than as a politician. Many years later, toward the end of a long dinner together, Winston remarked to his own son, another Randolph: "We have this evening had a longer period of continuous conversation together than the total which I ever had with my father in the whole course of his life."[22] (He was twenty when his father died.) He might have said the same of his mother. A great beauty and an active socialite, she had little time for her husband (it was rumored that Winston's younger brother had a different father—there are several plausible candidates for that role), and even less time for her son. "She shone for me like the Evening Star," he later wrote. "I loved her dearly—but at a distance."[23] A constant refrain in his letters from school is the pathetic and almost invariably vain wish that she visit him occasionally or that she be at home when he returned on holiday. It was his old nanny to whom he paid tribute, on her death, as "my dearest and most intimate friend during the whole of the twenty years I had lived."[24]

The biographer of Churchill is always competing with his subject, who wrote so voluminously and movingly about his own life. Churchill's memoir, *My Early Life*, gives a memorable picture of his childhood and schooling (boarding schools, of course): his first school brutal even by the standards of the day (the severity of the flogging, he later recalled, would not have been tolerated in any reformatory for delinquent children); the second physically less disagreeable (although the food was even worse) and intellectually less rigorous. Then there was Harrow, where he did not at all distinguish himself in the classics, which were supposedly the mark of an educated man, but where he acquired other traits that were to serve him well—a love of history, of English literature, and of the English language. These talents did not quite prepare him for Sandhurst, the military academy, which he entered after three tries, but which he graduated from (in December 1894, weeks before his father's death) well near the top of his class. Commissioned as a second lieutenant in the cavalry, he embarked on a military career combined, most improbably, with a career in journalism, leading, again improbably, to an extraordinary career in politics.

While still at Harrow, Churchill wrote to his aunt: "If I had two lives I would be a soldier and a politician. But as there will be no war in my time I shall have to be a politician."[25] Churchill soon found his war, or rather a series of wars. During the winter season of leave in 1895, while most of his fellow officers were hunting, he volunteered with the Spanish force engaged in suppressing the nationalist rebels in Cuba. This was his first rather desultory experience of warfare (and the beginning of his lifelong addiction to Cuban cigars). Returning to his regiment in India, he had a more serious taste of war on the north-west frontier, and, more serious still, as a volunteer in the Sudan where he participated in what is generally agreed to be the last great cavalry charge in British history.

An active officer in his regiment, Churchill also served as a war correspondent covering the battles in which he himself was engaged, and he then proceeded to write books about those engagements. It may have been fame and money that helped inspire both his writing and his military adventures. But there is no doubt of his bravery and his evident attraction to danger itself, to the glamour of war and the imperial enterprise served by war. He also somehow managed to find time, when not fighting or writing (or drinking or playing polo), to read—not casually, for distraction, but systematically and purposely, as if to compensate for the education he had failed to get in school. He started with the obvious masters, Gibbon and Macaulay, and then went on to Plato, Aristotle, Schopenhauer, Malthus, Darwin, Adam Smith.

"If I had two lives . . .," he had written as a schoolboy. Having led the first of those lives as a soldier, he was ready for the second as a politician. Resigning from his regiment early in 1899, he returned to England to stand for, and lose, a by-election. He then temporarily retreated to his other life, wangling an assignment (in spite of an official decree against just that) as both an officer and a correspondent in the Boer War. This had the unintended effect of furthering his parliamentary career. During a skirmish on the armored train that was taking them to their regiment, he and other officers were captured by the Boers. After a month of imprisonment, he alone managed to escape and make his way to the front where he took part in some hard-fought battles. Returning to England six months later as a celebrity, he had no difficulty winning a seat in Parliament.

Churchill brought to Parliament the same combative spirit he had displayed in war. A Conservative like his father, he soon found himself (again like his father) at odds with some of his colleagues, and for some of the same reasons. He did not then call himself a Tory Democrat, but that label accurately describes his early parliamentary career. His break with the Conservatives in 1904 is usually attributed to his ardent support of free trade as opposed to the protectionism that was gaining strength in the party. But free trade for him was a social rather than an economic issue. Protectionism, he said, meant "dear food for the million, cheap labour for the millionaire."[26] His last speech before crossing the aisles was in support of a bill to strengthen trade unionism. Speaking without notes, he lost the thread of his argument after three-quarters of an hour and had to sit down without completing the sentence: "It lies with the government to satisfy the working classes. . . ."[27] Soon afterward he ostentatiously took the seat that had been occupied by his father in opposition—a seat, as it happened, next to Lloyd George.

With the victory of the Liberal party in 1906, Churchill started the ten-year climb upward in his new party, from the Colonial Office to the Board of Trade, the Home Office, and finally the Admiralty. His father's Tory Democracy had evolved into the "New Liberalism" of the prewar period, a social-minded, reformist liberalism that Churchill enthusiastically endorsed and that resulted in such innovations as old-age pensions, labor exchanges, the regulation of sweated industries, minimum wages for specified industries, and unemployment and health insurance as provided in the National Insurance Act. (The latter was not passed until 1911, by which time Churchill was at the Admiralty, but the details had been worked out by him long before.) Some historians regard these measures as the precursor of the welfare state. Churchill himself spoke of them at the time as "a big slice of Bismarckism over the whole underside of our industrial system."[28] (A quarter of a century earlier, Randolph Churchill had defended Tory Democracy as a substitute for Bismarck's "state socialism."[29]) With his customary bravado, Churchill anticipated and went well beyond the other major act of 1911 limiting the House of Lords. He proposed instead the total abolition of the upper house, or at the very least a reconstituted body made up of elected members who had demonstrated their commitment to public service.

The more memorable event of this period was Churchill's marriage in 1908, after a whirlwind courtship (again, like his father) to Clementine Hozier, ten years his junior, the beautiful and gifted daughter of a titled but rather impecunious family. Unlike his father's marriage, this was an unmitigated success—"one of the most remarkable marriages," Best remarks (after a review of the possible contenders), "of any great man in twentieth-century political public life."[30] It was also, perhaps, the most documented marriage of the century, since the two were often apart and were inveterate letter writers. If most of their children were not as successful in their domestic lives as he—of the four, only the youngest, Mary, had an untroubled life—it was not because of any lack of love or attention by their parents; on the contrary, some regarded the Churchills as overly indulgent parents.

Churchill's role at the beginning of the First World War, Jenkins observes, was a "mini dress rehearsal" of the first years of the Second World War.[31] That rehearsal actually started before the outbreak of the war, because it was then, in opposition to his colleagues, that he anticipated and tried to prepare for the war. As head of the Admiralty, he increased the naval budget, improved the conditions of the seamen, and introduced important technical innovations. But the failure of the Dardanelles campaign, for which he was held responsible, and the formation of the National Government in 1915 led to Churchill's demotion to the lowest of cabinet positions, the chancellorship of the Duchy of Lancaster. It was then, during a brief period of depression, that he began to paint, a hobby that was to become something like an avocation.

But he soon found something more active to engage him. Resigning the chancellorship, he joined his old regiment with the rank of major. His time with the expeditionary force in France was brief—something less than six months, with short leaves home. A biographer is tempted to dwell on his letters to his wife, containing requests for brandy, chocolates, Stilton cheese, sardines, ham, slabs of corned beef (but not "fancy tinned things"), interspersed with moving messages of love and stoic reflections on life and death.[32] But these should not distract from the fact that he commanded his battalion, albeit briefly, in dangerous and disagreeable frontline trench warfare, displaying his usual reckless bravery.

Relieved of his command in May 1916 when his unit was amalgamated with another, he returned to London and to Parliament. The following year, when Asquith was replaced by Lloyd George, Churchill was made minister of munitions, a position he held until the end of the war.

Jenkins characterizes the post–World War I period, when Churchill headed first the War Office and then the Colonial Office, as "one of the least creditable periods" of his career.[33] Best has it as the beginning of ten years of "considerable celebrity and achievement."[34] Among the events of those years were Churchill's support of the Jewish homeland in Palestine, his condemnation of the British-provoked Amritsar massacre in India, and his spirited opposition to Soviet communism (bolshevism, as he always referred to it). For Jenkins, his anti-bolshevism was "extravagant" in rhetoric and a "debacle" in practice, reinforcing the popular view of Churchill (which Jenkins shares) as a "rash military adventurer."[35] Best denies neither the rhetorical excesses nor the impracticality of a war against Russia at a time when Britain had not yet recovered from the Great War. But he endorses Churchill's own retrospective judgment of that period: "The failure to strangle Bolshevism at birth," Churchill declared in 1949, "lies heavily on us today."[36]

This episode typifies the fundamental differences between the two biographers—and between alternative views of Churchill. From the perspective of history, Best finds that Churchill was going against the grain of his time but was ultimately vindicated by history. "Eighty years later, with the horrific story of Communist Russia behind us, the reader may conclude that Churchill was not so silly after all."[37] For Jenkins, the politician, Churchill's "anti-Bolshevik crusade" was nothing more than an adventure (the words "adventure," "adventurer," "adventurism" appear repeatedly in his account)—and a failed one at that, first because it spoiled his relations with Lloyd George and ruined his chance of getting the coveted chancellorship of the Exchequer, and then because it antagonized the Labour party and trade unions, who never forgot or forgave him his bloody-minded (as it seemed to them) anti-bolshevism.

When the Liberal party began to make overtures to Labour in 1923, Churchill (who had lost his seat the preceding year) became fearful not only of a pro-Soviet policy abroad but also of a pro-socialist policy at home. "I am what I have always been," he told a former colleague, "a Tory Democrat. Force of circumstances has compelled me to serve with another party, but my views have never changed, and I should be glad to give effect to them by re-joining the Conservatives."[38] The following year he did just that. The victory of the Conservatives brought him the chancellorship of the Exchequer. In that role he earned the enmity of Labour yet again, this time when he helped suppress the General Strike of 1926. Labour was not appeased by his much more conciliatory role in the miners' strike that followed, when he supported their demands for higher wages and safer working conditions (against the interests of the owners, one of whom was his cousin, Lord Londonderry). Nor did they give him credit for introducing legislation providing for contributory (rather than means-tested) pensions, more generous funds for social services, a cut in direct taxes, and an increase of death duties. Here, and consistently throughout his career, Churchill pursued a kind of benevolent paternalism, making him favorably disposed to social reforms and wary of any social disorder that would be inimical, as he saw it, to the welfare of the people.

The election of 1929 brought in a Labour government and with it the beginning of Churchill's "wilderness years"—his own term for the ten-year period when he was in Parliament but out of office. His unrelenting opposition to dominion status for India (which the Conservative leadership supported), accompanied by his blimpish, near-racist remarks about Gandhi, earned him the reputation of arch-imperialist that was to dog him for years. Again, we have two very different views of Churchill. For Jenkins, Churchill's position on India revealed an almost incomprehensible failure to take the measure of parliamentary opinion, so that he found himself in one of the most futile "blind alleys of modern British politics." In an unusually reflective mood, Jenkins sees this as a rejection of the Lockean world of liberalism (epitomized by Gladstone and Asquith) and an embracing of the Hobbesian universe of Mussolini.[39] For Best, it reveals a Churchill whose view of the non-Western world was neither Hobbesian nor Lockean but paternalistic Toryism. Believing that good government rather than self-government was in the best interests of the Indian people, Churchill was convinced that only the Raj could provide the public services that were needed and, more important, preserve the peace between the hostile religious communities. As soon as the British left India, Churchill predicted, Hindus and Moslems would begin to slaughter each other—which was, indeed, what eventually happened.

A minor episode (in retrospect, although it did not seem so at the time) was Churchill's stubborn, almost quixotic defense of Edward VIII during the abdication crisis. The far more momentous event of those years was, of course, the threat of Nazism. Churchill was the first British political figure of any note to appreciate the gravity of that threat and to seek to counteract it. As the menace of Nazism grew, his voice became more insistent and uncompromising, until his colleagues began to regard him as a "privileged eccentric." When Chamberlain returned from Munich to proclaim "peace with honor," Churchill pronounced it, to the dismay of both his party and his constituency, "a disaster of the first magnitude."[40] A dozen hours after Hitler's invasion of Poland, Churchill was given a seat in the War Cabinet. Eight months later—on the very first day of the Blitzkrieg—he became prime minister of Great Britain.

For some historians there is a sharp break between pre- and post-1939 Churchill—between the politician in the wilderness and the statesman leading his country to victory in war. Both of these biographies belie that; it was the same Churchill, warts and all (for Jenkins, more warts than not). Best's chapter on the critical early years of the war is entitled "His Finest Hour," echoing Churchill's famous phrase, "their finest hour," in his "Battle of Britain" speech delivered just after the collapse of France. (*Their Finest Hour* was also the title of the second volume of his history of the war.) Jenkins's section on the war period bears the ambiguous title, "The Saviour of His Country and the Light of the World?" Even without the question mark, the phrases themselves sound ironic. Unlike such revisionist historians as John Charmley, Jenkins does not believe that Britain should have sought an early peace with Germany. But he is suspicious of the motives and character of the Tory politician, and Churchill remains that for him—a politician, not a statesman, certainly not a "saviour of his country."

So, too, the period of the war takes on a different aspect in the two books. Best, the military historian, focuses upon the war itself while Jenkins, the politician, never loses sight of Parliament and partisan politics. Neither quite captures the drama of those crucial days in May 1940—a fortnight in most accounts, five days in John Lukacs's book of that title—which started out so ominously and ended not in victory, to be sure, but in survival. If America and Russia helped win the war, Lukacs points out, it was Churchill, in those momentous days, "who did not lose it."[41] And that was the prelude to victory.

The victory was finally qualified, thanks to the other victors. Roosevelt and Stalin did not merely reflect the will of their countrymen; to a considerable degree they created that will. Churchill, having fulfilled his juvenile aspirations to be a soldier and a politician, was now called upon to be a diplomat as well. But his diplomatic resourcefulness was tried to the limit by the two allies who pursued their own policies and purposes as vigorously as he did his. At Yalta and again at Potsdam, he was obliged to settle for much less than he would have liked. He won the war but not entirely the peace.

Churchill won the war at least in part because of his rhetoric and oratory. Best rebukes one historian, too young to have heard Churchill's wartime speeches, for scoffing at "the myth of Churchill inspiring the nation huddled round its crackling wireless sets."[42]* It was not a myth, Best protests. People listened to the broadcasts everywhere, in homes and pubs, factories and air-raid shelters, intently, almost reverently. Those speeches had the effect not only of maintaining popular morale and the national spirit at a time when there was every reason to be demoralized and dispirited, but also of arousing Britons to their historic responsibility, a responsibility to the entire world. Best rises to the occasion in a Hegelian spirit: "His speeches set them on a world stage, somewhere few had ever dreamed of ever finding themselves, defending values important for the world at large. Their survival was to mean more than the survival of their insular selves, it meant the survival of civilization and freedom."[44] Those speeches, on the radio, in Commons, and reprinted in the newspapers (there are seven volumes of wartime speeches and another five of postwar speeches), were not mere "rhetoric." They were as much the hard facts of history, determining the course of events, as the deliberations and disputations of Parliament.

*He might have been rebuking Jenkins as well, who, while conceding that the speeches were "an inspiration for the nation" (and "a catharsis for Churchill himself"), is put off by their "stridency," "high-flown eloquence," and "self-indulgence."[43]

Churchill thought of himself, and presented himself, not only as the political head of the government but also as the spokesman of the nation. Like Disraeli, he believed in a nation that had an integral unity transcending class and political divisions, with himself as the representative of that nation. This is the meaning of the famous metaphor in his speech responding to tributes to him on his eightieth birthday: "It was a nation and a race dwelling all around the globe that had the lion's heart. I had the luck to be called upon to give the roar."[45] *The Roar of the Lion* was a fitting title to one of the volumes in his own history of the war.[*]

"Victory in Europe and Defeat in Britain," Jenkins entitles the chapter on the postwar period—as if the two events were commensurable: the victory against a Nazi terror that threatened to engulf the world, and the defeat of the Conservative party in the election at home. Even then, at the age of seventy and in ill health, Churchill did not go gently into the night. He began to write (or supervise the writing of) the six volumes on the Second World War. He continued in Parliament as a very vocal leader of the Opposition. And he remained on the world stage as a counsel of caution and alarm. Just as he had taken the initiative in warning Britain of the threat of Germany before the First World War and again before the Second, so he now warned the world of the threat of Stalin. His famous Fulton address in 1946 (delivered at the college in President Truman's home state) has been said, more often in criticism than praise, to have ushered in the cold war. The realities of that war were already evident. But it took Churchill's metaphor of an "iron curtain" descending upon the continent,

---

[*]Manchester's biography, *The Last Lion*, distorts the meaning of the metaphor. Churchill did not see himself as the lion. The British people were that; he was simply their voice.

"from Stettin in the Baltic to Trieste in the Adriatic," to galvanize the public and, more reluctantly, to rouse the leaders and foreign offices of the West. Churchill may have been out of power at home, but he was still a formidable moral—and therefore, political— force in the world.

Churchill's return as prime minister in 1951 was almost anti-climactic. In retrospect he may be judged to have been unfit for the challenges of that office. Labour was not appeased—and many Conservatives were distressed—by his conciliatory attitude to the welfare state and to a united Europe. Because the European Union has emerged as a major issue in British politics today, Churchill is now quoted on both sides of that issue. In fact, his commitment to a united Europe was qualified by his simultaneous and no less staunch commitment to the British Commonwealth and, more boldly, to the "special relationship" with the United States. Advocates of the European Union today cannot take much comfort in his remark, "I want a Europe to evolve on British lines, but, hopefully, without the British!"[46] Nor are they likely to quote his warning, in a meeting at Albert Hall intended to promote the idea of a united Europe, that it should be made "absolutely clear that we shall allow no wedge to be driven between Great Britain and the United States of America."[47] His final injunction to his cabinet, just before his retirement, was: "Never be separated from the Americans."[48]

Churchill resigned as prime minister in 1955 at the age of eighty, remaining an almost silent member of Parliament (he was reelected four years later) until his death in January 1965. His was the first great state burial for a nonroyal person since Gladstone's in 1898 (and Gladstone's was the first since Wellington's in 1852). It was a dramatic occasion. Three hundred thousand people waited in the bitter cold outside Westminster Hall where Churchill was lying in state; many thousands of others witnessed the procession to Saint Paul's and lined the banks of the Thames when the body was being conveyed to Waterloo Station for transport to Blenheim Park; and three and a half million viewers watched this extraordinary spectacle on television, culminating in the memorable sight of the great cranes along the river dipping their masts in tribute as the launch went by.

Jenkins closes his book by comparing Gladstone and Churchill, the former "the greatest Prime Minister of the nineteenth century," the latter "the greatest of the twentieth century"—and marginally better than his predecessor. "I now put Churchill," Jenkins concludes, "with all his idiosyncracies, his indulgences, his occasional childishness, but also his genius, his tenacity and his persistent ability, right or wrong, successful or unsuccessful, to be larger than life, as the greatest human being ever to occupy 10 Downing Street."[49] "10 Downing Street"—Jenkins can think of no higher tribute to his subject. It is odd praise, however, for a man whose great achievements came not in his official role as prime minister but in his self-appointed and generally accepted role as spokesman for the nation and the free world. And it is odder still to find him compared with Gladstone, who was pitted not against a tyrant bent on world conquest but against another British politician seeking office (there are even some who would question Gladstone's preeminence over Disraeli), and whose great cause was not the Battle of Britain but Home Rule for Ireland.

In his obituary of Churchill, Clement Attlee, the leader of the Labour party, rose above party fealty to pay homage to "one of the greatest men that history records."[50] So too Best accords him a historic greatness far surpassing the prime-ministership: "What he did for the good of his country and, it is not extravagant to say, for western civilization was what no other person on the political stage at those times could have done. He did what the more dogmatic critics of 'great man theory' doubt that even the greatest of men can do: he changed the apparent course of history."[51]

"Western civilization"—that is not a term in good repute today. Most academics use it, if at all, ensconced in quotation marks, as if to distance themselves from it, to deny its reality or impugn it as ethnocentric, colonialist, even racist. It is sobering to read Best's concluding remarks on a culture that may not appreciate the ideals and spirit that animated Churchill.

> One might not lament the end of "glory," but what about "chivalry" and "honour"? There must be improvement of some kind in the fact that the concept of "dying for your country" no longer provides the model of an ideal death; but there may not be much of an improvement in not knowing whether there is anything in your country worth dying for, whether you belong to this country or to that, or even whether you belong to any distinctive country at all. . . . I am persuaded that, in this later time, we are diminished if, admitting Churchill's failings and failures, we can no longer appreciate his virtues and victories.[52]

Lionel Trilling

The Moral Imagination

꿍 A recent casual, dismissive reference to Lionel Trilling recalled to me the man who was the most eminent intellectual figure of his time, certainly in New York intellectual circles but also
beyond that, in the country as a whole. So, at any rate, he appeared
to me many years ago. And so he appeared to many of his contemporaries, who thought it entirely fitting he should have received in
1972 (a few years before his death) the first of the Thomas Jeffer-
son Awards bestowed by the National Endowment for the Humanities. It was typical of the man that the lecture he delivered on
that occasion, "Mind in the Modern World," was exhortatory
rather than celebratory, cautioning us about tendencies in our culture that diminished the force and legitimacy of mind, tendencies
that were to become obvious to others only many years later. In
2005, on the centenary of his birth, it is interesting to reflect upon
the quality of Lionel Trilling's mind, a quality rare in his time and
rarer, I suspect, in ours.

I was a budding Trotskyite in college in 1940 when I came
across Trilling's essay on T. S. Eliot in *Partisan Review*. I had read
only a few of Eliot's poems; "Prufrock" was a particular favorite
among my friends at the time, much quoted and affectionately

parodied.* But I had never read Eliot's essays or the journal he edited, the *Criterion,* which had ceased publication before the outbreak of World War II. I was, however, a faithful reader of *Partisan Review,* which was, in effect, the intellectual and cultural organ of Trotskyites (or crypto-Trotskyites, or ex-Trotskyites, or, more broadly, the anti-Stalinist Left). Many years later I remembered little about Trilling's essay except its memorable title, "Elements That Are Wanted," and the enormous excitement it generated in me and my friends. Rereading it recently, I experienced once again that sense of excitement.

Trilling opened by quoting an essay by John Stuart Mill on Coleridge, written a century earlier. That essay had angered Mill's radical friends, Trilling said, because it told them they could learn more from a "religious and conservative philosopher" like Coleridge, who saw "further into the complexities of the human feelings and intellect," than from the secular and radical utilitarianism of their own mentor, Jeremy Bentham.[1] In this spirit, Trilling introduced his own radical friends, the readers of *Partisan Review,* to another "religious and conservative" thinker, T. S. Eliot. Trilling did not, he hastened to say, mean to recommend Eliot's "religious politics" to their "allegiance"—only to their "attention." He reminded them of their own precarious situation a year after the outbreak of war in Europe: "But here we are, a very small group and quite obscure; our possibility of action is suspended by events; perhaps we have never been more than vocal and perhaps soon we can hope to be no more than thoughtful; our relations with the future are dark and dubious." Of only one thing about the future could we be certain: our "pledge to the critical intellect."[2]

*In a Yiddish mock-translation by Isaac Rosenfeld (with the collusion of Saul Bellow), the verse, "In the room the women come and go / Talking of Michelangelo," became (loosely retranslated): "In the room one hears the women / Talking of Marx and Lenin."

That pledge recalled to Trilling not only Mill's invocation of Coleridge but also Eliot's "long if recalcitrant discipleship" to Matthew Arnold. (Trilling did not have to remind his readers of his own, less recalcitrant discipleship to Arnold; his book on Arnold, a revision of his doctoral dissertation, had been published the preceding year.) Trilling quoted Arnold on the function of criticism: "It must be apt to study and praise elements that for the fullness of spiritual perfection are wanted, even though they belong to a power which in the practical sphere may be maleficent."[3] The audacity of this proposal is hard to recapture now: first, the implication that there were elements that were wanted in his own intellectual circle; then, that these elements were wanted "for the fullness of spiritual perfection"; and finally, most provocatively, that these elements might be found in a thinker like Eliot, whose ideas could well be maleficent in the practical sphere. Yet it was precisely in the practical sphere—not as a poet but as a political thinker—that Trilling went on to commend Eliot to readers of *Partisan Review*.

Although *Partisan Review* had broken with the Communist party three years earlier, the journal was still committed to a radical politics and to an only somewhat reformist Marxist philosophy (of the kind espoused by Sidney Hook, most notably). But it was also committed to a modernist literary vanguard—Eliot, Joyce, Yeats, Pound, Proust—who all too often had conservative, if not reactionary, views on political and social affairs. The editors were entirely candid about the disjunction between literature and politics. Indeed, it was the Communists' insistence upon a party line in literature, as in politics, that contributed to the break from the party. This disjunction made for a tension in the journal that was a constant challenge to the ideological pieties of its readers.

What Trilling was now proposing, however, went well beyond the reassertion of this disjunction between literature and politics.

Where others found Eliot interesting in spite of his politics, Trilling found him interesting *because* of his politics: a politics not only conservative but religious, and not only religious but identifiably Christian. And this, to readers who were, as Trilling said in his usual understated manner, "probably hostile to religion" (and many of whom, he might have added, were, like himself, Jewish).[4] Where John Stuart Mill had cited Coleridge's *On the Constitution of Church and State* as a corrective to Benthamism, Lionel Trilling recommended Eliot's *The Idea of a Christian Society* as a corrective to Marxism. The Left, he said, had simplistically assumed that Eliot "escaped" from "The Waste Land" into the embrace of Anglo-Catholicism. But even if this were true, it would not be "the worst that could be told of a man in our time." Surely Marxist intellectuals, he observed, who had witnessed the flourishing and the decay of Marxism, should appreciate the intellectual honorableness of Eliot's conversion. They need not follow Eliot's path to theology, but they could emulate him in questioning their own faith.[5]

Marxism was not the only thing that Trilling (by way of Eliot) called into question. He challenged liberalism as well, because it offered, he said, no defense against totalitarianism. Totalitarianism was inherently "pagan," recognizing no authority or principle but that of the state. Liberalism, so far from providing an alternative to paganism, actually contained within itself the seeds of paganism, in its materialism and relativism. Only Christianity, Eliot argued— the "Idea" of Christianity, not its pietistic or revivalist expressions— could resist totalitarianism, because only Christianity offered a view of man and society that promoted the ideal of "moral perfection" and "the good life." "I am inclined," Trilling echoed Eliot, "to approach public affairs from the point of view of the moralist."[6]

Trilling hastened to qualify his endorsement of Eliot; he did not believe morality was absolute or a "religious politics" desirable.

But he did find Eliot's vision of morality and politics superior to that of liberals and radicals, who had contempt for the past and worshipped the future. Liberals, in the name of progress, put off the realization of the good life to some indefinite future; radicals put off the good life in the expectation of a revolution that would usher in not only a new society but also a new man, a man who would be "wholly changed by socialism." Marxism was even more dangerous because it combined "a kind of disgust with humanity as it is and a perfect faith in humanity as it is to be."[7]

Eliot's philosophy, on the other hand, whatever its defects and dangers, had the virtue of teaching men to value "the humanity of the present equally with that of the future," thus serving as a restraint upon the tragic ambition to transcend reality. It was in this sense that Eliot bore out the wisdom of Arnold's dictum. Eliot's religious politics, while maleficent in the practical sphere, contained elements wanting in liberalism—"elements which a rational and naturalistic philosophy, to be adequate, must encompass."[8]

I do not know how Trilling's radical friends reacted to this essay, but I do remember the effect it had on some radicals of a younger generation. For us it was a revelation, the beginning of a disaffection not only with our anti-Stalinist radicalism but, ultimately, with liberalism itself. Trilling has been accused (the point is almost always made in criticism) of being not himself a neoconservative, to be sure, but a progenitor of conservatism. There is some truth in this. Although he never said or wrote anything notable about the "practical sphere" of real politics (he was not a "public intellectual" in our present sense, commenting on whatever made the headlines), he did provide a mode of thought, a moral and cultural sensibility, that was inherently subversive of liberalism and thus an invitation not to conservatism but to some hybrid form of neoliberalism or neoconservatism.

The Liberal Imagination, the volume of essays Trilling published ten years later, may be the best known of his books. Oddly enough, when I looked, some years ago, for "Elements That Are Wanted" in that volume, I could not find it, although the preface clearly alluded to it. (Nor was it included in *The Partisan Reader,* a collection of essays from *Partisan Review* published in 1946.) When I remarked upon this omission to Diana Trilling, she could not account for it. The essay, under the title "T. S. Eliot's Politics," reached book form only in 1980 in *Speaking of Literature and Society,* the final volume of her edition of Trilling's *Collected Works.*[9]

A much-quoted sentence in the preface to *The Liberal Imagination* may be interpreted as Trilling's attempt to dissociate himself from conservatism: "For it is the plain fact that nowadays there are no conservative or reactionary ideas in general circulation."[10] What is not generally quoted are the qualifications that follow, which almost belie that assertion. If there are no conservative ideas, there are nonetheless conservative "impulses," which are "certainly very strong, perhaps even stronger than most of us know." For that matter, liberalism itself is more a "tendency" than a set of ideas. Goethe had said there are no "liberal ideas," only "liberal sentiments." But sentiments, Trilling observed, naturally and imperceptibly become ideas, and those ideas find their way into the practical world. *"Tout commence en mystique,"* he quoted Charles Péguy, *"et finit en politique"*—everything begins in mysticism and ends in politics. Thus liberalism is no more a party of ideas than conservatism; indeed, without the corrective of conservatism, liberal ideas become "stale, habitual, and inert."[11] The job of criticism is to restore that "first essential imagination of variousness and possibility, which implies the awareness of complexity and difficulty." Here literature has a unique role, for it is "the human activity that takes the fullest and most precise account of variousness, possibility, complexity, and difficulty."[12]

These words and variants upon them—"complexity," "difficulty," "contingency," "irony," "ambiguity," "ambivalence"—appear as a refrain throughout all of Trilling's work; they are his unmistakable signature.* In one writer after another—in Eliot, Wordsworth, Keats, Austen, Dickens, James, Hawthorne, Tolstoy, Joyce, Flaubert, Babel—Trilling found the corrective to those "elements that are wanted," elements that testify to the essential humanity of man and defy political machination or social engineering.

The last book Trilling saw into print before his death in 1975, *Sincerity and Authenticity*, seems a departure in tone and substance from his earlier work, for in it philosophers—Rousseau, Diderot, Hegel, Nietzsche, Burke, Sartre, Marx, Freud—played a starring role, mingling with his usual cast of literary figures.† This juxtaposition of philosophy and literature is exhilarating and sometimes startling. Rousseau, for example, suggests the thought: "Oratory and the novel: which is to say, Robespierre and Jane Austen." Trilling justified that odd coupling: "This, I fancy, is the first time the two personages have ever been brought together in a single sentence, separated from each other by nothing more than the conjunction that links them." But they were not, he insisted, "factitiously conjoined: They are consanguineous, each is in lineal descent from Rousseau, cousins-german through their commitment to the 'honest soul' and its appropriate sincerity."[13] ("Honest soul" refers back to yet another figure in this linkage, Hegel.)

---

*The title of the volume, *The Liberal Imagination,* is itself ambiguous, and perhaps ironic, for Trilling's criticism of liberalism was precisely its failure of imagination, a failure that had to be corrected by a large dose of literature.

†There are more than passing references to some of these philosophers in his early essays, sometimes in unlikely but revealing contexts. Rousseau and Diderot, for example, appear in "Elements That Are Wanted," Hegel and Nietzsche in essays on Wordsworth and Austen.

The final chapter of *Sincerity and Authenticity* returned to the subject that had long occupied Trilling, personally as well as intellectually. Trilling, his wife, and his son had been in psychoanalysis for many years, and he had given much thought to it as theory and as therapy. Now, in the discussion of authenticity, Freudianism presented a special challenge. Where most psychoanalysts regarded the therapeutic practice as an effort to identify and overcome the inauthentic nature of man, to make conscious what was unconscious, Trilling insisted the unconscious had its own authenticity—the "Authentic Unconscious," as the title of his chapter put it. And where others were troubled by Freud's *Civilization and Its Discontents* because it seemed to take a bleak view of human beings and their potentialities, Trilling saw it as evidence, once again, of "the essential immitigability of the human condition, . . . its hardness, intractability, and irrationality."[14]

Perhaps even more than Eliot, Arnold, or his other literary heroes, the initial and enduring inspiration for much of Trilling's work was Freud. In the first of his essays on Freud, published shortly before "Elements That Are Wanted," Trilling described the peculiar synthesis of romantic anti-rationalism and positivistic rationalism that gave Freudianism the distinctive character of "classic tragic realism."[15] Another essay, written two years later, explained that Karen Horney's revisionist mode of psychoanalysis was popular in liberal circles because it posited "a progressive psyche, a kind of New Deal agency which truly intends to do good but cannot always cope with certain reactionary forces." Freud's view of the psyche (and Trilling's), was less "flattering" but more in accord with "the savage difficulties of life."[16]

A more provocative version of this theme, "Freud: Within and Beyond Culture," was delivered as a lecture in 1955 and reprinted ten years later in the volume that took its name from it, *Beyond Culture.* Here Trilling posed the issue as biology *versus* culture: biology representing the "given," the immutability of man's nature; culture, the forces of society (or "civilization," as Freud put it) that strove to alter and overcome biology. Again Trilling challenged the dominant liberal, progressive orthodoxy, this time at a meeting of the New York Psychoanalytic Society, which represented that orthodoxy. Unlike most of his audience, who regarded any idea of a "given" as reactionary, Trilling insisted that the givenness of our biological condition was, in fact, "liberating"—liberating man from a culture that would otherwise be absolute and omnipotent. "We reflect that somewhere in the child, somewhere in the adult, there is a hard, irreducible, stubborn core of biological urgency, and biological necessity, and biological *reason* that culture cannot reach and that reserves the right, which sooner or later it will exercise, to judge the culture and resist and revise it."[17]

The issue went beyond Freud and psychoanalysis to the larger problem posed by George Orwell in *Nineteen Eighty-Four*. Reviewing that book when it appeared in 1949, Trilling pointed out that Orwell was not, as liberals liked to think, merely attacking Soviet communism. "He is saying, indeed, something no less comprehensive than this: that Russia, with its idealistic social revolution now developed into a police state, is but the image of the impending future and that the ultimate threat to human freedom may well come from a similar and even more massive development of the social idealism of our democratic culture."[18] A few years later, reviewing another book by Orwell, Trilling repeated this theme. "Social idealism," whether of the communist or democratic variety, was not the only principle that could be perverted into tyranny; so could any idea "unconditioned" by reality. "The essential point of *Nineteen Eighty-Four* is just this, the danger of the ultimate and absolute power which mind can develop when it frees itself from conditions, from the bondage of things and history."[19]

Trilling could not have anticipated the ultimate perversion of this tendency half a century later: the mutation of social engineering into genetic engineering. Today the imperious "mind" is even more bent upon that "ultimate and absolute power" as it attempts to free itself from the bondage of all conditions, things, and history—indeed from the bondage of biology itself. One can imagine a volume of essays by Trilling today entitled *Beyond Biology*.

In "Elements That Are Wanted," Trilling quoted Eliot as writing from "the point of view of the moralist."[20] He might well have made that statement of himself, understanding "moralist" in the largest sense of that term. He did not reflect much upon the kinds of moral questions, or "moral values," that occupy us today: marriage, family, sex, abortion. What interested him was the relation of morality to reality—the abiding sense of morality that defines humanity, and at the same time the imperatives of a reality that necessarily, and properly, circumscribes morality. He called this "moral realism." Even before the appearance of Orwell's novel, Trilling wrote about "the dangers of the moral life itself," of a "moral righteousness" that preens itself upon being "progressive."

> Some paradox of our natures leads us, when once we have made our fellow men the objects of our enlightened interest, to go on to make them the objects of our pity, then of our wisdom, ultimately of our coercion. It is to prevent this corruption, the most ironic and tragic that man knows, that we stand in need of the moral realism which is the product of the free play of the moral imagination.[21]

"Moral realism" is Trilling's legacy to us today—to conservatives as well as liberals. Conservatives are well disposed to that realism, being naturally suspicious of a moral righteousness that has all too often been misconceived and misdirected, confusing feeling good with doing good. That realism is derived from the disciplines conservatives habitually draw upon: philosophy, economics, political theory, and, most recently, the social sciences, which have been so valuable in disputing much of the conventional (that is to say, liberal) wisdom about social problems and policies. The element that is still wanting, however, for conservatives as well as liberals, is the sense of variety, complexity, and difficulty which comes, Trilling reminds us, primarily from the "experience of literature"— the title Trilling gave to the monumental anthology he edited.[22] It is this that gives a passion, and a reality, to the moral imagination, which, at its best, informs the political as well as the literary imagination.

Notes

Introduction

1. Lionel Trilling, *Matthew Arnold* (New York, 1949 [1st ed. 1939]), p. 182.

Adam Smith: Political Economist *cum* Moral Philosopher

1. On Marshal, see pp. 167–184 herein.
2. John Ruskin, "Fors Clavigera: Letters to the Workmen and Labourers of Great Britain," in *Works,* ed. E. T. Cook and Alexander Wedderburn (London, 1907 [1st ed., 1871–1884]), XXVIII, 516, 764.
3. E. P. Thompson, "The Moral Economy of the English Crowd in the Eighteenth Century," *Past and Present,* 1971, pp. 78–79, 89–90.
4. Dugald Stewart, *Biographical Memoir of Adam Smith* (New York, 1966 [1st ed., 1793]), p. 52.
5. Walter Bagehot, "Adam Smith as a Person" (1876), *Collected Works* (Cambridge, Mass., 1968), III, 93.
6. Joseph A. Schumpeter, *History of Economic Analysis* (London, 1981 [1st ed., 1954]), pp. 185–86. (Here, and throughout, I have Americanized the English spelling to avoid a discrepancy between the commentary and the quotations.)
7. Adam Smith, *An Inquiry into the Nature and Causes of the Wealth of Nations,* ed. Edwin Cannan (New York, 1937 [1st ed., 1776]), p. 14.
8. Ibid., p. 423.
9. Adam Smith, *The Theory of Moral Sentiments,* ed. D. D. Raphael and A. L. Macfie (Oxford, 1976), pp. 184–85. The expression appeared still earlier in Smith's essay, "The History of Astronomy," where the ancients are said not to have seen "the invisible hand of Jupiter" in such natural agencies as fire, water, or gravity (p. 185, n. 7).

10. *Wealth of Nations*, p. 651.
11. Ibid., p. 821.
12. Ibid., p. 11.
13. Ibid., pp. 78–79.
14. Ibid., p. 250.
15. Ibid., p. 128.
16. Ibid., pp. 128, 460–61, 463, 577, 609.
17. Ibid., p. 98.
18. Arthur Young, *The Farmer's Tour Through the East of England* (London, 1771), IV, 361.
19. A. W. Coats, "Changing Attitudes to Labour in the Mid-eighteenth Century," *Economic History Review*, 1958, p. 39 (quoting Hume's *Political Discourses* of 1752).
20. *Wealth of Nations*, p. 81.
21. Ibid., p. 141.
22. Ibid., p. 683. See also pp. 777 and 821.
23. Ibid., pp. 734–35. Similar remarks about the "inconveniences . . . arising from a commercial spirit" (i.e., the division of labor) appear in Smith's *Lectures on Jurisprudence* ("Report of 1766"), ed. R. L. Meek, D. D. Raphael, and P. G. Stein (Oxford, 1978), pp. 539–41.
24. *Wealth of Nations*, p. 3.
25. Ibid., p. 735.
26. Ibid., p. 737.
27. Ibid., p. 127.
28. Karl Marx, *Capital: A Critique of Political Economy* (New York, 1936), p. 398.
29. Ibid., pp. 528–29, 534.
30. Karl Marx and Friedrich Engels, *The Communist Manifesto,* ed. Samuel H. Beer (New York, 1955), pp. 28, 32.
31. Hannah Arendt, *The Human Condition* (Chicago, 1958), pp. 101ff.
32. *Wealth of Nations*, pp. 324–26.
33. Ibid., p. 385.
34. Ibid., pp. 248–49.
35. Ibid., pp. 121–22.
36. Ibid., p. 13.
37. Ibid., pp. 15–16.
38. David Hume, "Of the Original Contract," in Hume, *Political Essays* (Indianapolis, 1953 [1st ed. 1741–1742]), p. 44.

39. John Locke, *An Essay Concerning Human Understanding* (Chicago, 1952 [1st ed., 1690]), p. 390.
40. John Morley, *Diderot and the Encyclopaedists* (New York, 1978), p. 338.

Edmund Burke: Apologist for Judaism?

1. Edmund Burke, *Reflections on the Revolution in France*, ed. Conor Cruise O'Brien (New York, 1982 [1st ed., 1790]), p. 38.
2. Burke, *Reflections on the Revolution in France* (New York, Dolphin ed., 1961), pp. 60–61. (See also p. 67.)
3. Ibid., pp. 97–98.
4. Ibid., pp. 43–45. The italics are Burke's. (I have modernized the spelling.)
5. Ibid., pp. 44–45.
6. Ibid., p. 104.
7. Ibid., pp. 106–108.
8. Ibid., p. 165.
9. Ibid., p. 105.
10. Ibid., pp. 100–101.
11. Ibid., p. 174.
12. Ibid., p. 104. (See above, p. 5.)
13. Ibid., p. 115.
14. Ibid., p. 84.
15. Ibid., p. 89.
16. Ibid., p. 90.

George Eliot: The Wisdom of Dorothea

1. F. R. Leavis, *The Great Tradition* (New York, 1954 [1st ed., 1948]), p. 42, quoting Henry James, *Partial Portraits.*
2. Ibid., p. 50. See Virginia Woolf, "George Eliot," in *Collected Essays* (New York, 1967), p. 201 (reprinted from *The Common Reader,* 1st series).
3. John Emerich Edward Dalberg Acton, *Historical Essays and Studies*, ed. J. N. Figgis and R. V. Laurence (London, 1908), p. 277; *Selections from the Correspondence of the First Lord Acton*, ed. Figgis and Laurence (London, 917), p. 292 (July 9, 1885).
4. Acton, *Letters to Mary Gladstone*, ed. Herbert Paul (1st ed., London, 1904), p. 155 (December 27, 1880).
5. Henry James, review of *Middlemarch* (1873), reprinted in George Eliot, *Middlemarch* (Norton Critical Edition, New York, 1977), p. 654.

6. George Eliot, *Middlemarch* (Penguin ed., 1981 [1st ed., 1874]), p. 25. Citations below are to this edition.

7. Ibid., p. 178.

8. *New York Times Book Review*, June 12, 1994.

9. *Middlemarch*, p. 105.

10. Ibid., p. 252.

11. James (in Norton ed.), p. 654. See also C. S. Lewis: "Who can forgive Dorothea for marrying such a sugarstick as Ladislaw?" Lewis, "A Note on Jane Austen," in *Jane Austen: A Collection of Critical Essays,* ed. Ian Watt (Englewood Cliffs, N. J., 1963), p. 31.

12. *Middlemarch*, p. 880.

13. W. J. Harvey, "The Intellectual Background of the Novel: Casaubon and Lydgate," in *Middlemarch: Critical Approaches to the Novel*, ed. Barbara Hardy (New York, 1967).

14. *Middlemarch*, p. 427.

15. Ibid., p. 136.

16. Gordon S. Haight, *George Eliot: A Biography* (Oxford, 1968), p. 464.

17. *Middlemarch*, p. 243.

18. Ibid., p. 894.

19. Rosemary Ashton, *George Eliot: A Life* (London, 1996), p. 327.

20. *The George Eliot Letters*, ed. Gordon S. Haight (New Haven, 1975 [1st ed., 1954]), IV, 364 (May 14, 1867).

21. *The Diary of Beatrice Webb*, ed. Norman and Jeanne MacKenzie (Cambridge, Mass., 1983), II, 53–54 (July 25, 1894).

22. Ashton, *Eliot*, p. 330.

23. *Middlemarch,* p. 32.

24. Ibid., p. 890.

25. Ibid., p. 810.

26. Ibid., pp. 226–227.

27. Virginia Woolf, "Women and Fiction," in *Collected Essays*, II, 144.

28. Phyllis Rose, *Parallel Lives: Five Victorian Marriages* (New York, 1983), p. 237.

29. *Middlemarch*, p. 893.

30. Ibid., p. 896.

Jane Austen: The Education of Emma

1. Jane Austen, *Emma* (Everyman ed., London, 1963 [1st ed., 1815]), p. 1.

2. Ibid., pp. 5–6.

3. Ibid., pp. 7–8.

4. Ibid., p. 17.
5. Ibid., p. 23.
6. Ibid., p. 24.
7. Ibid., pp. 52–53.
8. Ibid., pp. 130–131.
9. Ibid., p. 326.
10. Ibid., p. 330.
11. Ibid., p. 77.
12. Ibid., p. 364.
13. Ian Watt, introduction to *Jane Austen: A Collection of Critical Essays,* ed. Watt (Englewood Cliffs, N.J., 1963), p. 2.
14. *Emma,* p. 3.
15. Ibid., p. 290.
16. Ibid., p. 218.
17. See the essay on Eliot, p. 16.
18. See the essay by Arnold Kettle in *Jane Austen,* pp. 119ff.
19. Essay by C. S. Lewis, ibid., p. 33.
20. Edmund Burke, "Letters on a Regicide Peace" (1796), in *The Works of Edmund Burke* (London, 1909–1912), V, 208.
21. Thomas Hobbes, *Leviathan* (Everyman ed., London 1943), p. 49.

Charles Dickens: "A Low Writer"

1. *Dickens: The Critical Heritage,* ed. Philip Collins (New York, 1971), p. 476 (*Westminster Review,* April 1866).
2. Philip Collins, "The Significance of Dickens's Periodicals," *Review of English Literature,* 1961, pp. 62–63. See, for example, Collins, *Dickens and Crime* (London, 1962); Collins, *Dickens and Education* (London, 1964); Norris Pope, *Dickens and Charity* (London, 1978).
3. Lionel Trilling, "Little Dorrit," in *The Opposing Self: Nine Essays in Criticism* (London, 1955), p. 52. On symbol-hunting in *Our Mutual Friend* and *The Waste Land,* see Trilling, "The Dickens of Our Day," in *A Gathering of Fugitives* (Boston, 1956), pp. 42–43. Philip Collins traces the emergence in literary criticism of the symbol of the prison in "Little Dorrit: The Prison and the Critics," *Times Literary Supplement,* April 18, 1980.
4. *Dickens: The Critical Heritage,* p. 502 ("Obituary Tributes," 1870).
5. *Dickens: The Critical Heritage,* p. 324 (Trollope, *St. Paul's Magazine,* July 1870; ibid., *Times,* July 11, 1870). Neither the *Times* nor Trollope was as kind to Dickens while he was alive. Reviews of Dickens's books in the *Times* were as often unfavorable as favorable. And writers like Trollope and Thackeray,

who were acutely aware of the commercial aspects of writing (and, perhaps, of Dickens as a rival), made no secret of their dislike of Dickens's books while appreciating (and envying) his appeal to the public.

6. *Dickens: The Critical Heritage,* p. 64 (Lewes, *National Magazine and Monthly Critic,* December 1837).
7. Henry Mayhew, *London Labour and the London Poor* (New York, 1968 [1st ed., 1861]), I, 250.
8. Ford, p. 79.
9. Walter Bagehot, "Charles Dickens" (1858), in *Literary Studies* (London, 1898), pp. 11, 128.
10. *Dickens: The Critical Heritage,* p. 502 ("Obituary Tributes," 1870).
11. An obvious measure of Dickens's appeal is the sale of his books. The installments of *Pickwick Papers* sold 40,000 copies a week, *The Old Curiosity Shop* 100,000, the Christmas tales as many as 250,000. The figures for his more sober books are no less impressive: 33,000 copies of *Dombey and Son* (which sold out on the first night of its issue), 35,000 of *Bleak House* and *Little Dorrit,* 50,000 of the first part of *The Mystery of Edwin Drood.* These figures represent only the original serialized parts (the weekly parts selling for a penny-halfpenny, and the monthly parts for a shilling). In the dozen years following his death, well over 4 million copies of his books were sold in England alone. These figures do not take into account the copies passed on among friends, or sold and resold by secondhand dealers, or borrowed from the circulating libraries. Mudie's lending-library complained that no set of books wore out as quickly as Dickens's. (Robert L. Patten, "The Sale of Dickens's Work," in *Dickens: The Critical Heritage,* pp. 617–620. See also the works by Patten, Richard D. Altick, Edgar Johnson, George Ford.)
    There were also numerous dramatizations of his novels, most of them unauthorized, performed in the cheap theaters frequented by the poor. *Pickwick Papers* had the distinction of being not only the most plagiarized and pirated book of the time but also the most imitated. There was a *Pickwick Abroad* and a penny-periodical *Penny Pickwick,* an *Oliver Twiss* by "Bos" and another *Oliver Twiss* by "Poz," a *Nickelas Nicklebery* and a *Nicholas Nicklebury,* a *Mr. Humfries Clock,* a *Martin Guzzlewit,* a *Dombey and Daughter.* (Montague Summers, *A Gothic Bibliography* [New York, 1964], pp. 14–15; Louis James, *Fiction for the Working Man, 1830–1850: A Study of the Literature Produced for the Working Classes in Early Victorian Urban England* [London, 1963], pp. 46, 62.)
12. *Dickens: The Critical Heritage,* p. 93 (*Metropolitan Magazine,* June 1840).
13. *Dictionary of National Biography* (London, 1888), V, 935.

14. R. H. Horne defended Dickens against this criticism in *A New Spirit of the Age* (New York, 1844), p. 18. Almost a century later, this charge was echoed by Q. D. Leavis, who associated Dickens with the other sensation-seeking novelists catering to the new reading public, an "uncultivated and inherently 'low'" class of readers brought into being by the cheap serials. Dickens was so successful, Mrs. Leavis claimed, because he shared the childish sensibility of his readers: he laughed and cried aloud as he wrote, and his upper-class characters were "the painful guesses of the uninformed and half-educated writing for the uninformed and half-educated." Only in *David Copperfield* and *Great Expectations*, she said, did Dickens rise above his public and produce novels that could genuinely be called "literature." (Q. D. Leavis, *Fiction and the Reading Public* [New York, 1965 (1st ed., 1932)], pp. 153, 157–158.) This was written in 1932. Later the Leavises reread Dickens and admitted him to the "Great Tradition," their personal literary canon. But even then they were uncomfortable with the "low" scenes, the picaresque and melodramatic "exposure" scenes, Q. D. Leavis called them. (F. R. Leavis and Q. D. Leavis, *Dickens the Novelist* [New Brunswick, N.J., 1979 (1st ed., 1970)], pp. 111ff.

15. *Dickens: The Critical Heritage*, p. 284 (*Spectator*, September 24, 1853). See also Richard C. Maxwell, Jr., "G. W. M. Reynolds, Dickens, and the Mysteries of London," *Nineteenth-Century Fiction*, 1977.

16. John Ruskin, "Fiction, Fair and Foul" (1880), in *Works*, ed. E. T. Cook and Alexander Wedderburn (London, 1908), XXXIV, 276–277.

17. *Uncollected Writings from Household Words, 1850–59*, ed. Harry Stone (Bloomington, Ind., 1968), I, 13 (March 30, 1850).

18. *The Girlhood of Queen Victoria: A Selection from Her Diaries, 1832–40*, ed. Viscount Esher (London, 1912), II, 86 (December 30, 1838).

19. Ibid.

20. Keith Hollingsworth, *The Newgate Novel, 1830–1847: Butler, Ainsworth, Dickens, and Thackeray* (Detroit, 1963), p. 159.

21. Horne, *A New Spirit*, p. 18.

22. Steven Marcus, *Dickens: From Pickwick to Dombey* (New York, 1965), p. 359. Another critic, John Bayley, also associates Oliver and Fagin: "That the two worlds are one in the mind appears even in Cruikshank's drawings, where Oliver often has a distinct look of Fagin." (*Dickens and the Twentieth Century*, ed. John Gross and Gabriel Pearson [Toronto, 1962], p. 52.)

23. *David Copperfield* (Modern Library ed., New York, n.d. [1st ed., 1849–1850]), p. 172.

24. *Oliver Twist* (Oxford ed., London, n.d. [1st ed., 1837–1838]), p. 81.

25. Ibid., pp. 179, 182.

26. Marcus, *Dickens,* p. 67. This part of Marcus's analysis is at variance with his equation of Oliver and Fagin, the pauper and the criminal. Refuting Thackeray's charge that Dickens tended to confuse virtue and vice, Marcus insists that, on the contrary, he kept them so sharply demarcated that "goodness and wickedness seem to live in quite separate regions where commerce with each other is at best minimal."

27. *Oliver Twist,* p. 29.

28. George Orwell, "Charles Dickens" (1940), in *The Collected Essays, Journalism and Letters of George Orwell,* ed. Sonia Orwell and Ian Argus (New York, 1968), I, 429–441.

29. *The Posthumous Papers of the Pickwick Club* (Oxford ed., London, n.d. [1st ed., 1836–1837]), p. 208.

30. Ibid., p. 267.

31. Orwell, "Charles Dickens," p. 440.

32. Ibid., p. 415.

33. George Gissing, *Charles Dickens, A Critical Study* (New York, 1966 [1st ed., 1898]), p. 243.

34. Louis Cazamian, *The Social Novel in England, 1830–1850: Dickens, Disraeli, Mrs. Gaskell, Kingsley,* trans. Martin Fido (London, 1973 [1st French ed., 1903]), pp. 155–157. Other critics have made the same point, Richard Aldington, for example, claiming that Dickens's "really sympathetic characters all come from the middle and lower middle classes." (*Four English Portraits* [London, 1948], p. 150.)

35. *The Old Curiosity Shop* (Oxford ed., London, n.d. [1st ed., 1840–1841]), p. 371.

36. *David Copperfield,* p. 36.

37. Orwell, "Charles Dickens," p. 415.

38. *David Copperfield,* p. 37.

39. *A Christmas Carol* (New York, 1939 [1st ed., 1843]), pp. 121, 129.

40. *David Copperfield,* p. 31.

41. *Dombey and Son* (Oxford ed., London, n.d. [1st ed., 1846–1848]), p. 268.

42. *Bleak House* (Oxford ed., London, n.d. [1st ed., 1852–1853]), pp. 390, 560.

43. *Old Curiosity Shop,* p. 111.

44. *Dickens: The Critical Heritage,* p. 153 (*The Mirror of Literature, Amusement, and Instruction,* December 21, 1844).

45. Ibid., p. 444 (Ruskin to Norton, July 8, 1870). For a more favorable estimate by Ruskin, see "Fiction, Fair and Foul," *Works,* XXXIV, 277.

46. Francis Sheppard, *London 1808–1870: The Infernal Wen* (Berkeley, 1971), p. 282.

47. Mayhew's work appeared serially in the early 1850s and was reprinted in 1861–1862 and again in 1864–1865. *Our Mutual Friend* appeared in 1864–1865. On the possible relationship between the two, see Harland S. Nelson, "Dickens's *Our Mutual Friend* and Henry Mayhew's *London Labour and the London Poor,*" *Nineteenth Century Fiction*, 1965; Harvey Peter Sucksmith, "Dickens and Mayhew: A Further Note," ibid., 1969; Richard J. Dunn, "Dickens and Mayhew Once More," ibid., 1970; Q. D. Leavis, *Dickens the Novelist*, pp. 184–186; Anne Humphreys, *Travels into the Poor Man's Country: The Work of Henry Mayhew* (Athens, Ga., 1977), pp. 178ff.

48. Dickens evidently knew Mayhew personally. He was a friend of Horace Mayhew, Henry's brother; they wrote for the same journals (although not at the same time—Dickens had been a reporter for the *Morning Chronicle* in the mid-thirties and wrote occasionally for it later); they even once appeared in the same amateur theatrical production. An avid reader of newspapers, Dickens must have come across Mayhew's work—as Mayhew must have read Dickens's novels. Mayhew's initial article in the *Morning Chronicle* (in 1849) was a report on the cholera epidemic in that notorious slum, Jacob's Island, which owed its notoriety in large part to *Oliver Twist* (which appeared a dozen years earlier). It was there, in "the filthiest, the strangest, the most extraordinary of the many localities that are hidden in London," that Bill Sikes met his gruesome death (p. 460).

49. *The Dickens Critics*, ed. George H. Ford and Lauriat Lane, Jr. (Ithaca, N.Y., 1966 [1st ed., 1961]), p. 50 (Henry James, in *The Nation*, 1865).

50. *Our Mutual Friend* (Modern Library ed., New York, 1960 [1st ed., 1864–1865]), p. 6.

51. "The Prisoner's Van" (not reprinted in *Sketches by Boz*), quoted by J. Hillis Miller, "The Fiction of Realism: *Sketches by Boz, Oliver Twist*, and Cruikshank's Illustrations," in *Charles Dickens and George Cruikshank* (Los Angeles, 1971), p. 3.

52. *Dombey and Son*, pp. 43–44.

53. Ibid., pp. 98ff.

54. The fourth volume of *London Labour* (published fourteen years after *Dombey and Son*) had an entire category corresponding to Mrs. Brown: "child stripping," an occupation of "old debauched drunken hags who watch their opportunity to accost children passing in the street, tidily dressed with good boots and clothes" (*London Labour*, IV, 281–282).

55. *Oliver Twist*, preface, p. 8; *David Copperfield*, p. 179. There is a large literature on Dickens and London, e.g., F. S. Schwarzbach, *Dickens and the City* (London, 1979); Alexander Welsh, *The City of Dickens* (Oxford, 1971); Christopher Hibbert, "Dickens's London," in *Charles Dickens 1812–1820: A*

Centennial Volume, ed. E. W. F. Tomlin (New York, 1969), pp. 73–99; Philip Collins, "Dickens and London," in *The Victorian City: Images and Realities*, ed. H. J. Dyos and Michael Wolff (London, 1973), II, 537–557; Raymond Williams, *The Country and the City* (New York, 1973), pp. 153–164.

56. *Pickwick Papers*, p. 576.

57. *Dickens: The Critical Heritage*, p. 60 (*Quarterly Review*, October 1837); p. 52 (*London and Westminster Review*, July 1837).

58. Ibid., p. 36 (letter by Mary Russell Mitford, June 30, 1837).

59. *Pickwick Papers*, pp. 675–676.

60. Marcus, *Dickens*, p. 17.

61. *Dickens: The Critical Heritage*, p. 37 (*Examiner*, July 2, 1837).

62. Ibid., p. 38 (Thackeray, *The Paris Sketch Book*, 1840).

63. Ibid., p. 34 (*Court Magazine*, April 1837).

64. Joseph Butwin, "Hard Times: The News and the Novel," *Nineteenth-Century Fiction*, 1977, p. 186 (quoting *Blackwood's Magazine*, April 1855, and *Westminster Review*, October 1854).

65. John Forster, *The Life of Charles Dickens* (2 vol. ed., London, n.d. [1st ed., 1872–1874]), II, 85 (January 20, 1854).

66. *Hard Times*, ed. George Ford and Sylvere Monod (New York, 1966 [1st ed., 1854]), p. 1.

67. Ibid., p. 11.

68. Ibid., p. 17.

69. Ibid.

70. Ibid., pp. 9, 15, 26–27, 179, 275.

71. Ibid., p. 23.

72. Ibid., p. 27.

73. To some historians, the circus represents yet another form of "social control"— the means by which the upper classes reinforced their control over the lower. See, for example, *Social Control in Nineteenth Century Britain*, ed. A. P. Donajgrodzki (London, 1977).

74. Benjamin Disraeli, *Popanilla and Other Tales,* ed. Philip Guedalla (London, 1926), p. 15.

75. *Hard Times*, p. 2.

76. Ibid., p. 125.

77. E.g., John Holloway, "*Hard Times*: A History and a Criticism," in *Dickens and the Twentieth Century*, pp. 166ff.; G. D. Klingopulos, "Notes on the Victorian Scene," in *From Dickens to Hardy* (vol. VI of *Pelican Guide to English Literature*, London, 1958), p. 44; Ivanka Kovacevic, *Fact into Fiction: English Literature and the Industrial Scene, 1750–1850* (Leicester, 1975), pp. 114ff.; Dingle Foot, introduction to Oxford ed. of *Hard Times* (1955), pp. xii ff.

78. *Hard Times,* pp. 206–207.
79. Ibid., pp. 115–116.
80. Ibid., p. 114.
81. Ibid., p. 110.
82. Ibid., pp. 120–121.
83. Ibid., p. 288.
84. Forster, *Life of Dickens,* II, 86.
85. G. Otto Trevelyan, *The Life and Letters of Lord Macaulay* (New York, 1875), II, 320 (August 12, 1854); Bagehot, *Literary Studies,* p. 157; *Dickens: The Critical Heritage,* p. 304.
86. Gissing, *Dickens,* p. 242.
87. *The Dickens Critics,* pp. 132–133.
88. Orwell, "Charles Dickens," pp. 434, 416–417.
89. G. M. Young, *Victorian England: Portrait of an Age* (New York, 1954 [1st ed., 1936]), p. 89. In another book edited by Young, the minister is identified as Baldwin Brown. (*Early Victorian England, 1830–1865* [London, 1934], II, 4n.)
90. Forster, *Life of Dickens,* I, 129.

Benjamin Disraeli: The Tory Imagination

1. Foot prided himself on being more of a Disraeli admirer than some Conservatives—than Lord Butler, for example, the prominent Conservative statesman, who wrote a less than enthusiastic introduction to a new edition of Disraeli's *Sybil.* Foot also criticized the author of a book on Disraeli's novels for being insufficiently appreciative of Disraeli's "revolutionary mind" (*Times Literary Supplement,* April 18, 1980, p. 434).
2. Paul Seabury, *Wall Street Journal,* June 23, 1981.
3. David Gelernter, "The Inventor of Modern Conservatism: Disraeli and Us," *Weekly Standard,* February 7, 2005.
4. William Flavelle Monypenny and George Earle Buckle, *The Life of Benjamin Disraeli Earl of Beaconsfield* (2 vol. ed., London, 1929 [1st ed., 6 vols., London, 1910–1920]); James Anthony Froude, *Thomas Carlyle: A History of the First Forty Years of His Life* (London, 1882), I, ix.
5. Robert Blake, *Disraeli* (London, 1966).
6. Sarah Bradford, *Disraeli* (New York, 1983), p. 75.
7. Blake, p. 149.
8. Ibid., p. 158.
9. Ibid., p. 88.
10. Robert Blake, *Disraeli's Grand Tour: Benjamin Disraeli and the Holy Land, 1830–31* (New York, 1982), p. 7.

11. Disraeli, *Tancred, or The New Crusade* (London, Longmans, Green ed., n.d. [1st ed., 1847]), pp. 370, 294.

12. Bradford, *Disraeli*, p. 186; *Tancred*, p. 149.

13. Benjamin and Sarah Disraeli, *A Year at Hartlebury, or The Election* (Toronto, 1983), p. 103.

14. Blake, *Disraeli*, pp. 4–5.

15. Cecil Roth, *Benjamin Disraeli: Earl of Beaconsfield* (New York, 1952), p. 60.

16. Blake, *Grand Tour*, p. 129.

17. Bradford, *Disraeli*, pp. 94, 113.

18. Benjamin Disraeli, *Letters*, ed. J. A. W. Gunn, John Matthews, Donald M. Schurman, and M. G. Wiebe (Toronto, 1982), II, 42n (quoting speech by O'Connell, May 2, 1835).

19. Lawrence and Elisabeth Hanson, *Necessary Evil: The Life of Jane Welsh Carlyle* (New York, 1952), p. 413 (quoting Carlyle's notebook, February 28, 1852); Monypenny and Buckle, *Life*, II, 698.

20. *Tancred*, p. 427.

21. Monypenny and Buckle, *Life*, I, 886. Lord Rothschild and others were disappointed that Disraeli did not speak in favor of later bills introduced in the House. Both Monypenny and Buckle (pp. 886–895) and Blake, *Disraeli* (pp. 260–261), reject the charge that Disraeli wavered in support of the cause and explain his failure to speak on those occasions.

22. George Hutchinson, *The Last Edwardian at Number Ten: An Impression of Harold Macmillan* (1980), quoted in *The Oxford Book of Political Anecdotes*, ed. Paul Johnson (Oxford, 1986), pp. 135–136.

23. Blake, *Grand Tour*, pp. 130–132. Isaiah Berlin, on the other hand, found any association of Disraeli with Zionism "anachronistic and not plausible." (Berlin, "Benjamin Disraeli, Karl Marx and the Search for Identity," in *Against the Current: Essays in the History of Ideas* [London, 1982], p. 270).

24. Charles Dickens, "The Chimes," in *Christmas Books* (Oxford, 1954), pp. 106–107.

25. *Coningsby, or The New Generation* (London, 1948 [1st ed., 1844]), p. 106.

26. Citations in the *Oxford English Dictionary*.

27. In a speech to his constituency before the publication of *Sybil*, Disraeli seemed to take credit for the phrase, saying that he had written about the subject before it had been discussed in Parliament. But he did not actually claim to have used the phrase, either in Parliament or elsewhere (Monypenny and Buckle, *Life*, I, 629 [August 31, 1844]).

28. *Sybil, or the Two Nations* (Penguin ed., London, 1954 [1st ed., 1845]), pp. 72–73.

29. Alexis de Tocqueville, *A Memoir on Pauperism,* trans. Seymour Drescher, ed. Gertrude Himmelfarb (Chicago, 1997), p. 60; Asa Briggs, "The Language of 'Class' in Early Nineteenth-Century England," in *Essays in Labour History,* ed. A. Briggs and J. Saville (New York, 1960), p. 48.

30. *Sybil,* p. 146.

31. Ibid., p. 104.

32. Ibid., pp. 160–166.

33. Ibid., p. 170.

34. Ibid., p. 175.

35. *Coningsby,* p. 150.

36. *Sybil,* p. 280.

37. Ibid., p. 264.

38. Ibid., pp. 240, 270.

39. Ibid., pp. 268, 284.

40. Monypenny and Buckle, *Life,* I, 214.

41. Ibid., I, 230.

42. *Letters,* II, 60–61 (July 2, 1835).

43. Blake implies as much, saying there was no hint in Disraeli's speeches or writings of the defects in Peel's policies which he was to expose in *Coningsby* and *Sybil* (p. 162), and no notable changes in Peel's policies to account for Disraeli's opposition (p. 183).

44. *Letters,* II, 62.

45. 3Hansard (Parliamentary Debates) 49:246–252 (July 12, 1839).

46. 3Hansard 188:1603 (July 15, 1867).

47. John Morley, *The Life of William Ewart Gladstone* (New York, 1903), II, 222–223 (October 30, 1866).

48. 3Hansard 182:53 (March 12, 1866).

49. *Times,* April 18, 1883.

50. Monypenny and Buckle, *Life,* I, 486 (June 7, 1840).

51. Ibid., II, 483.

52. Ibid., II, 526–527.

53. Ibid., II, 873.

54. Bradford, *Disraeli,* p. 58; *A Year at Hartlebury,* p. 104.

55. Monypenny and Buckle, *Life,* II, 68–69.

56. Ibid., II, 534.

57. Ibid., II, 534–535.

58. Blake, *Disraeli,* p. 579.

59. Bradford, *Disraeli,* p. 337.

60. Blake, *Disraeli,* p. 624.

61. James Morris, *Pax Britannica: The Climax of an Empire* (New York, 1968), pp. 177, 512.

62. Blake, *Disraeli*, p. 646.

63. *Letters*, I, 447.

John Stuart Mill: The Other Mill

1. *Autobiography of John Stuart Mill* (New York, 1924), p. 2. (This edition is based on the original manuscript left by Mill to be published after his death.)

2. *The Early Draft of John Stuart Mill's* Autobiography, ed. Jack Stillinger (Urbana, Ill., 1961), pp. 184, 66, 36.

3. *Autobiography*, p. 99.

4. F. A. Hayek, *John Stuart Mill and Harriet Taylor: Their Friendship and Subsequent Marriage* (Chicago, 1951), p. 196 (February 14–15, 1854). (The title page, as originally published, bore the subtitle *Their Correspondence and Subsequent Marriage*. An appended errata changed "Correspondence" to "Friendship.")

5. Nicholas Capaldi, *John Stuart Mill: A Biography* (Cambridge, England, 2004), p. 108.

6. *The Later Letters of John Stuart Mill: 1849–1873,* ed. Francis E. Mineka and Dwight N. Lindley (in *Collected Works of John Stuart Mill,* Toronto, 1972), I, 96 (July 13, 1852).

7. Ibid., IV, 1693 (February 2, 1870).

8. *Autobiography*, p. 75.

9. *On Liberty*, ed. Gertrude Himmelfarb (Penguin ed., London, 1974), p. 58.

10. *Autobiography*, pp. 176–177. See also Mill's preface to the reprint of "Enfranchisement of Women" in his collection of essays, *Dissertations and Discussions* (2 vols., London, 1859), II, 411.

11. See the essay by Harriet Taylor in the appendix to Hayek, *Mill and Taylor*, pp. 275–279.

12. *Autobiography*, p. 177.

13. *On Liberty*, p. 63.

14. Ibid, p. 68.

15. Ibid., p. 69.

16. *The Earlier Letters of John Stuart Mill, 1812–1848,* ed. Francis E. Mineka (in *Collected Works,* Toronto, 1963), I, 36 (JSM to Gustave d'Eichthal, October 8, 1829), italics in original. D'Eichthal was evidently not persuaded by Mill; he went on to become a prominent Saint-Simonian.

17. "The Spirit of the Age," in *Essays on Politics and Culture,* ed. Gertrude Himmelfarb (New York, 1962), pp. 8–10. These essays were not included in *Dissertations and Discussions.* In his *Autobiography,* Mill dismissed them as "lumbering" and "ill-timed," their only effect being to bring him to the attention of Carlyle who welcomed him as a "new Mystic" (p. 122).

18. *Essays on Politics and Culture,* pp. 12–17.

19. Ibid., p. 18.

20. Ibid., p. 41. Italics here, as in other quotations from Mill, are in the original.

21. Ibid., p. 50.

22. Quoted by J. H. Burns, "J. S. Mill and Democracy," *Political Studies,* 1957, p. 161.

23. *Earlier Letters,* I, 153 (May 18, 1833).

24. *On Liberty,* p. 76.

25. "Civilization," in *Essays on Politics and Culture,* p. 69.

26. Ibid., pp. 72–73.

27. Ibid., p. 165–166.

28. "Coleridge," ibid., pp. 150–151.

29. It is this edited version that appeared in the essay reprinted in *Dissertations and Discussions,* I, 419. For other changes in this essay, see Gertrude Himmelfarb, *On Liberty and Liberalism: The Case of John Stuart Mill* (New York, 1974), p. 47, n. 44.

30. *Earlier Letters,* I, 236 (to John Nichol, October 14, 1834). See also I, 172 (to Carlyle, August 2, 1833).

31. "Bentham," in *Essays on Politics and Culture,* p. 102.

32. Ibid., p. 112.

33. "Coleridge," ibid., p. 154.

34. Ibid., p. 150.

35. Ibid., p. 151.

36. Ibid., p. 149.

37. *On Liberty,* p. 125. Yet *On Liberty* itself contains a tantalizing allusion to something like the "education" propounded in the Coleridge essay. In the final chapter, after describing his own educational proposal, Mill briefly entertained the idea of a "national education" that would take citizens out of their "personal and family selfishness," habituate them to act from "public or semi-public motives," and guide their conduct so as to unite rather than isolate them. Without these habits, he added, a free constitution "can neither be worked nor preserved." These two sentences, in the middle of a paragraph on another subject, were prefaced by the offhand remark that it belonged to a "different occasion" to dwell on such matters (p. 181).

38. Mill, *A System of Logic* (London, 1949), pp. 590–591.

39. Ibid., pp. 601–603, 605. The Coleridge essay was reprinted in *Dissertations and Discussions.*

40. *On Liberty*, p. 146.

41. *Logic*, p. 586.

42. Hayek, *Mill and Taylor*, p. 122.

43. For the changes in the section on socialism, see *Principles of Political Economy: With Some of Their Applications to Social Philosophy*, ed. J. M. Robson (in *Collected Works,* Toronto, 1965), II, 975–987 (Appendix A).

44. Ibid., II, 978n.

45. Hayek, *Mill and Taylor*, pp. 134–137, 144 (February 19, 1949; March 21, 1949).

46. "Chapters on Socialism," in *Essays on Economics and Society,* ed. J. M. Robson (in *Collected Works,* Toronto, 1967), II, 705.

47. Ibid., 746–748.

48. *Utilitarianism,* in *Essays on Ethics, Religion and Society,* ed. J. M. Robson (in *Collected Works,* Toronto, 1969), p. 231.

49. Ibid., p. 232.

50. Ibid., p. 216.

51. *On Liberty*, pp. 90–93.

52. Mill, "Theism," in *Three Essays on Religion* (1st ed., 1874), in *Essays on Ethics, Religion and Society,* p. 482.

53. Ibid., p. 485.

54. Ibid., pp. 487–488.

55. Ibid., pp. 488–489.

56. "Utility of Religion," ibid., pp. 424–428.

57. Ibid., pp. 371–372.

58. Michael St. John Packe, *The Life of John Stuart Mill* (London, 1954), p. 443.

59. *Later Letters,* III, 1414 (to Henry Jones, June 13, 1868).

60. "Coleridge," in *Essays on Politics and Culture,* p. 185.

Walter Bagehot: "A Divided Nature"

1. Mrs. Russell Barrington, *Life of Walter Bagehot* (London, 1914), p. 11.

2. Bagehot, *Literary Studies* (Everyman's ed.; London, 1911), I, 67.

3. Bagehot, *Historical Essays*, ed. Norman St. John-Stevas (Anchor ed.; New York, 1965), p. vii.

4. *Literary Studies*, I, 134.

5. *Historical Essays*, p. xv.

6. Alistair Buchan, *The Spare Chancellor* (London, 1959), p. 107 (quoting letter by Bagehot, December 1, 1857).
7. *Literary Studies*, I, 31.
8. *Historical Essays*, p. 403.
9. Ibid., pp. 166–167.
10. Bagehot, *Biographical Studies* (London, 1889), p. 237.
11. Ibid., p. 219.
12. *Literary Studies*, I, 83.
13. Ibid., I, 68–69.
14. Ibid., I, 76.
15. Ibid., I, 69.
16. Ibid., I, 122.
17. Leslie Stephen, *Studies of a Biographer* (London, 1902), III, 165, 157.
18. *Literary Studies*, I, 2.
19. Ibid., I, 22.
20. Ibid., I, 14.
21. Ibid., I, 19.
22. Ibid., I, 25.
23. Ibid., I, 5, 23.
24. Ibid., I, 81–82.
25. Ibid., I, 27.
26. Ibid., I, 34.
27. Ibid., II, 273.
28. Ibid., I, 260.
29. Ibid., II, 271.
30. *Historical Essays*, p. 12.
31. Ibid., p. 73.
32. Ibid., p. 72.
33. Ibid., p. 106.
34. Ibid., p. 216.
35. Ibid., pp. 280–281.
36. Ibid, p. xvi.
37. *The English Constitution* (World's Classics ed.; London, 1952 [1st ed. 1865–1866]), pp. 6–7.
38. *Historical Essays*, p. 260.
39. Ibid., p. 253.
40. Ibid., pp. 261, 254, 248.
41. Ibid., pp. 190–191.
42. Ibid., pp. 182, 185.
43. Ibid., p. 196.

44. Ibid., p. 211.
45. Ibid., p. 193.
46. Ibid., p. 201.
47. Ibid., pp. 203, 213.
48. Ibid, p. 241.

Lord Acton: The Historian as Moralist

1. Gertrude Himmelfarb, *Lord Acton: A Study in Conscience and Politics* (Chicago, 1952), vii.
2. Himmelfarb, *Victorian Minds* (New York, 1968), 155.
3. Roland Hill, *Lord Acton* (New Haven, 2000), 407 (letter to the *Times,* November 21, 1874).
4. Himmelfarb, *Lord Acton,* p. 144.
5. Acton, "The Pope and the Council," *North British Review,* 1869, 130.
6. *Lord Acton and His Circle,* ed. Francis A. Gasquet (London, 1906), 60; (February 4, 1859), 4; (February 16, 1858).
7. "Political Causes of the American Revolution" (1861), in Lord Acton, *Essays on Freedom and Power,* ed. Himmelfarb (Boston, 1948), 246.
8. Himmelfarb, *Victorian Minds,* pp.188–89, quoting Acton manuscript, Cambridge University Library.
9. *Essays on Freedom and Power,* pp. xxxiii.
10. Ibid., p. 34.
11. Ibid., p. 45.
12. Ibid., p. 57.
13. Ibid., p. 69.
14. Ibid., p. 83.
15. Himmelfarb, *Victorian Minds,* p. 189 (quoting manuscript).
16. Ibid.
17. "Sir Erskine May's 'Democracy in Europe'" (1878), in *Essays on Freedom and Power,* pp. 150–51.
18. "The History of Freedom in Christianity," ibid., p. 84.
19. "The History of Freedom in Antiquity," ibid., p. 40.
20. "Inaugural Lecture on the Study of History" (1895), ibid., pp. 18, 25, 28.
21. Acton-Creighton Correspondence (April 5, 1887), ibid., p. 365.
22. Acton, *Lectures on Modern History,* ed. John Neville Figgis and Reginald Vere Laurence (London, 1950), 318 (March 12, 1898).
23. *Essays on Freedom and Power,* p. 19.
24. *Lectures on Modern History,* p. 317.
25. Acton-Creighton Correspondence, *Essays on Freedom and Power,* p. 364.

26. *Letters of Lord Acton to Mary Gladstone,* ed. Herbert Paul (London, 1905), 228 (January 25, 1882).

27. Himmelfarb, *Victorian Minds,* p. 184 (quoting manuscript).

28. "Döllinger's Historical Work" (1890), in *History of Freedom,* p. 434.

29. Himmelfarb, *Lord Acton,* pp. 153–54 (quoting manuscript).

30. Himmelfarb, *Victorian Minds,* pp. 194–95.

31. Ibid., pp. 193–94 (quoting manuscript).

32. Hill, p. 413.

33. *New York Times,* March 13, 2000, pp. A1, 10.

34. *Letters to Mary Gladstone,* p. 314 (December 18, 1884).

Alfred Marshall: "The Economics of Chivalry"

1. W. S. Jevons, "The Future of Political Economy," *Fortnightly Review,* 1876, pp. 619-31.

2. Quoted by Beatrice Webb, *My Apprenticeship* (London, 1971 1st ed., 1926]), 190.

3. Alfred Milner, "Reminiscences," introduction to Arnold Toynbee, *Lectures on the Industrial Revolution of the Eighteenth Century in England* (London, 1937 [1st ed., 1884]), xxv.

4. Joseph Schumpeter, *History of Economic Analysis,* ed. Elizabeth Boody Schumpeter (New York, 1954), 830.

5. Quoted by John Maynard Keynes, "Alfred Marshall," in *Essays in Biography* (London, 1951 [1st ed., 1933]), 208.

6. Marshall, *Memorials,* ed. A. C. Pigou (London, 1925), 71 ("Reminiscences" by F. Y. Edgeworth).

7. Keynes, p. 138.

8. Stefan Collini, Donald Winch, and John Burrow, *That Noble Science of Politics: A Study in Nineteenth-Century Intellectual History* (Cambridge, 1983), 331.

9. Quoted by Keynes, p. 138.

10. Marshall, *Memorials,* p. 422 (Marshall to A. L. Bowley, March 3, 1901).

11. Marshall, *Principles of Economics* (9th ed, London, 1961 [1st ed., 1980]), 404, 778. See also 38, 368.

12. Henry Sidgwick, *The Principles of Political Economy* (London, 1883), 12. This was Sidgwick's definition of the "science" of political economy, the subject of the first two books of his work. The "art," or practical application, of political economy, in the third book, dealt with some of the ethical concerns that Marshall featured more prominently.

13. Marshall, *Principles,* p. 1.

14. Ibid., p. 43.

15. Keynes, p. 136.

16. Marshall, *Principles*, pp. 9–10.

17. Marshall, *Memorials*, p. 285 ("Some Aspects of Competition") (1890).

18. Joseph A. Schumpeter, *Ten Great Economists* (New York, 1965), 104.

19. Marshall, *Principles*, p. 17.

20. J. F. K. Whitaker, *History of Political Economy* (London, 1977), 187 (quoting a talk by Marshall, "The Aims and Methods of Economic Study," October 9, 1877).

21. Marshall, *Principles*, p. 243.

22. Ibid., p. 90.

23. Marshall, *Official Papers* (London, 1926), 205.

24. Keynes, pp. 137–38.

25. Marshall, *Memorials*, p. 83 (quoted by A. C. Pigou, "In Memoriam; Alfred Marshall").

26. Marshall, *Principles*, pp. 1–3.

27. Marshall, *Memorials*, pp. 144–50 ("Where to House the London Poor," 1884).

28. Marshall, *Official Papers*, pp. 199, 203, 211, 233, 239, 244–47.

29. Ibid., p. 244.

30. Marshall, *Principles*, pp. 3–4.

31. Ibid., pp. 105–7.

32. See above, chapter on Adam Smith herein.

33. Marshall, *Principles*, pp. 261–63.

34. Marshall, *Memorials*, p. 118 ("The Future of the Working Classes," 1873).

35. Ibid., pp. 115, 102.

36. Ibid., p. 103.

37. Marshall, *Memorials*, pp. 330, 343 ("The Social Possibilities of Economic Chivalry," 1907).

38. Marshall, *Principles*, pp. 718–20.

39. Ibid., pp. 208-9.

40. Ibid., p. 721.

41. Marshall, *Memorials*, p. 345 ("Economic Chivalry").

42. Ibid., p. 444 (letter to Helen Bosanquet, September 28, 1902).

43. Ibid., p. 334 ("Economic Chivalry").

44. Marshall, *Principles*, p. 713.

45. Marshall, *Memorials*, p. 291 ("Some Aspects of Competition," 1890).

46. *Times*, March 24, 1891.

47. Marshall, *Memorials*, p. 462 (letter to Lord Reay, November 12, 1909).

48. Ibid., p. 334 ("Economic Chivalry").

49. Ibid., p. 342.

50. Marshall, *Principles*, p. 763.

51. *Manchester Guardian*, Auust. 29, 1890.

52. *Athenaeum*, October 24, 1891.

53. *Times*, July 24, 1890.

54. *Pall Mall Gazette*, July 19 and 20, 1890.

55. Schumpeter, *History of Economic Analysis*, p. 835.

56. Marshall, *Memorials* ("Economic Chivalry"), p. 336.

John Buchan: An Untimely Appreciation

1. *Mr. Standfast* (Penguin ed.; London, 1956 [1st ed., 1919]), p. 312.

2. *Greenmantle* (Penguin ed.; London, 1956 [1st ed., 1916]), p. 127; *John Macnab* (Penguin ed.; London, 1956 [1st ed., 1925]), pp. 123, 143.

3. *Greenmantle*, p. 269.

4. *Mountain Meadow* [English title: *Sick Heart River*] (Boston, 1941), p. 155; *Greenmantle*, pp. 41, 22; *Prester John* (New York, 1938 [1st ed., 1910]), p. 111.

5. *Augustus* (Boston, 1937), p. 4.

6. *Greenmantle*, p. 171.

7. *John Macnab*, pp. 194–195, 139, 53.

8. *Homilies and Recreations* (London, 1926), pp. 29–30.

9. Richard Usborne, *Clubland Heroes* (London, 1953).

10. *Mountain Meadow*, pp. 23–27.

11. *The Three Hostages* (Penguin ed.; London, 1956 [1st ed., 1924]), pp. 25, 48; *Mountain Meadow*, p. 32.

12. *Mountain Meadow*, p. 7.

13. *Mr. Standfast*, pp. 234, 341.

14. *Montrose* (World's Classics ed.; London, 1957 [1st ed., 1928]), pp. 16, 422.

15. *Mr. Standfast*, p. 36.

16. *Memory Hold-the-Door* [American title: *Pilgrim's Way*] (London, 1940), pp. 211–212.

17. *Homilies*, p. 27.

18. *Prester John*, p. 38.

19. Ibid., p. 365.

20. *Three Hostages*, p. 97.

21. Joseph Conrad, *The Nigger of the Narcissus* (New York, 1960), pp. 43, 56.

22. *Thirty-Nine Steps* (Penguin ed.; London, 1956 [1st ed., 1915]), p. 17.

23. *Three Hostages*.

24. Ibid., p. 17.

25. Private letter to me by a participant in the ceremonies.

26. *Memory*, p. 153.

27. Ibid., p. 67.
28. Ibid., p. 239.
29. *Oliver Cromwell* (London, 1934), p. 303.
30. *John Macnab*, p. 233.
31. Ibid., pp. 136–137.
32. *Memory*, p. 95.
33. Ibid., p. 174.
34. Ibid., p. 130.
35. Ibid.
36. *Cromwell*, pp. 486, 502.
37. *Memory*, p. 62.
38. *Cromwell*, p. 523.
39. *Huntingtower* (Penguin ed.; London, 1956 [1st ed., 1922]), p. 130.
40. *Memory*, p. 300.
41. *Three Hostages*, p. 15.
42. Ibid., p. 61.
43. *Greenmantle*, p. 130.
44. *Three Hostages*, p. 229.
45. *Cromwell*, p. 355.
46. This Postscript appeared as a footnote in the republished version of this essay in *Victorian Minds* in 1968.

The Knoxes: A God-Haunted Family

1. N. G. Annan, "The Intellectual Aristocracy," in *Studies in Social History: A Tribute to G. M. Trevelyan* (London, 1955), pp. 241–287.
2. Philip Toynbee, "Lord Russell and Lord Amberley," *New Republic,* January 21, 1967.
3. Penelope Fitzgerald, *The Knox Brothers* (Melrose, Mass., 2000 [1st ed., London, 1977]).
4. Ibid., pp. 3–6, 17.
5. Ibid., pp. 8–9.
6. Ibid., p. 12.
7. Ibid., pp. 26–29.
8. Ibid., pp. 29–32.
9. Ibid., p. 35.
10. Ibid., p. 105.
11. Ibid., pp. 56, 61.
12. Ibid., p. 83.
13. Ibid., p. 126.
14. Ibid., p. 93.

15. Ibid., p. 151.
16. Ibid., p. 236.
17. Malcolm Muggeridge, review of first ed. of *The Knox Brothers*, in *Times Literary Supplement,* October 28, 1977, p. 1256.
18. Fitzgerald, *Knox Brothers*, p. 52.
19. Ibid., p. 109.
20. Evelyn Waugh, *Monsignor Ronald Knox* (Boston, 1959), p. 72.
21. Fitzgerald, *Knox Brothers*, pp. 108–110.
22. Ibid., p. 93.
23. Ibid., p. 91.
24. Ibid., p. 132.
25. Ibid., p. 165.
26. Waugh, *Monsignor Ronald Knox*, p. 189.
27. Fitzgerald, *Knox Brothers*, p. 254.
28. Waugh, *Monsignor Ronald Knox*, p. 313.
29. Fitzgerald, *Knox Brothers*, p. 166.
30. Ibid., pp. 143–144.
31. Ibid., p. 47.
32. Ibid., p. 238.
33. Muggeridge review, p. 1256.
34. Fitzgerald, *Knox Brothers*, p. 43.
35. Jane Austen, *Emma* (Oxford World's Classics ed., New York, 1999), p. v.
36. *New Yorker,* February 7, 2000, p. 80.
37. Ibid., p. 85; *New York Times* obituary, May 3, 2000, p. A23.
38. *New Yorker,* p. 82.
39. Fitzgerald, *Knox Brothers*, p. 245.
40. A. S. Byatt, "Morals and Metaphysics," *Prospect,* August/September 2000, p. 66.
41. Annan, "Intellectual Aristocracy," p. 286.

Michael Oakeshott: The Conservative Disposition

1. Lionel Trilling, *The Liberal Imagination: Essays on Literature and Society* (New York, 1950), p. ix.
2. Peregrine Worsthorne, "Notebook," *The Spectator* (March 11, 1978), p. 5.
3. "The Activity of Being an Historian" (1955), in *Rationalism in Politics and Other Essays* (London, 1962), pp. 137ff. A later volume, *On History and Other Essays*, published in 1983, contains three essays on history—not on historical events or persons but on the "philosophy of history" (a term Oakeshott might have rejected). These essays exhibit the same kind of skepticism about historical "truths," generalizations, or abstractions that is evident in

his treatment of political philosophy. For Oakeshott's view of history—the writing of history and the actuality of history—see Gertrude Himmelfarb, "Does History Talk Sense?" in *The New History and the Old: Critical Essays and Reappraisals* (Cambridge, Mass., 1987).

4. "Political Education" (1951), Rationalism in Politics, p. 132.
5. Josiah Lee Auspitz, "Bibliographical Note," *Political Theory*, August 1976, pp. 295–296.
6. "Rationalism in Politics" (1947), in *Rationalism in Politics*, pp. 1–2.
7. Ibid., p. 4.
8. Ibid., p. 11.
9. Ibid., p. 19n.
10. "On Being Conservative" (1956), ibid., p. 169.
11. Ibid., pp. 172–173.
12. Ibid., p. 184.
13. Ibid.
14. Ibid., p. 195. (See Edmund Burke, *Reflections on the Revolution in France* [New York, 1961], p. 110.)
15. Ibid., pp. 193, 186, 194.
16. Ibid., p. 196.
17. Ibid., pp. 193–195.
18. *Experience and Its Modes* (Cambridge, England, 1978 [1st ed., 1933]), pp. 294–295, 308.
19. *On Human Conduct* (Oxford, 1975), pp. 81, 83, 86.
20. Ibid., p. 81.
21. *Religion and the Moral Life* (Cambridge, England, 1927), p. 13; "The Importance of the Historical Element in Christianity," *Modern Churchman*, 1928–1929, pp. 360–371.
22. "The Tower of Babel" (1948), in *Rationalism in Politics*, pp. 61–62.
23. Ibid., p. 65.
24. "Introduction to *Leviathan*," in *Hobbes on Civil Association* (Berkeley, Calif., 1975), p. 73.
25. Ibid., pp. 5–6.
26. "The Voice of Poetry in the Conversation of Mankind" (1959), in *Rationalism in Politics*, pp. 197ff.

Winston Churchill: "Quite Simply, a Great Man"

1. G. R. Elton, *Political History: Principles and Practice* (New York, 1970), pp. 70–71.
2. *Washington Post,* October 7, 2001, p. A15.

3. Martin Gilbert, *Churchill: A Life* (New York, 1991), p. 690.

4. *Washington Post,* October 7, 2001, p. A15.

5. *New York Observer,* September 24, 2001, p. 1.

6. Guy Eden, "Churchill in High Office," in *Churchill by His Contemporaries,* ed. Charles Eade (London, 1953), p. 63. (Guy Eden was a parliamentary journalist reporting what Churchill said to him on May 11, 1941.)

7. (London) *Times,* April 25, 1995, p. 3; (London) *Daily Mail,* April 26, 1995.

8. *Washington Times,* April 26, 1995, p. 17, quoting from the (London) *Daily Telegraph.*

9. John H. Plumb, "The Dominion of History," in *Winston Churchill: Resolution, Defiance, Magnanimity, Good Will,* ed. R. Crosby Kemper III (Columbia, Mo., 1996), p. 65.

10. Geoffrey Best, *Churchill: A Study in Greatness* (London, 2001); Roy Jenkins, *Churchill: A Biography* (New York, 2001). (Jenkins's book is 1,002 pages in the English version and 736 in the American.)

11. Best, *Churchill,* p. ix.

12. Jenkins, *Churchill,* p. xiii.

13. Best, *Churchill,* pp. x, xii.

14. Isaiah Berlin, "Winston Churchill in 1940" (written in 1949), in *Personal Impressions,* ed. Henry Hardy (London, 2001), pp. 12, 22. The expression "saviour of his country" was common at the time. Best (p. x) cites A. J. P. Taylor's use of the term in his *English History: 1914–1945* (Oxford, 1965), p. 4. See also Michael Ignatieff, *Isaiah Berlin: A Life* (New York, 1998), p. 197.

15. Jenkins, pp. xiv–xv.

16. Jenkins, *Gladstone* (London, 1995), p. xiv.

17. Both men, Jenkins reminds us, changed parties (ibid., p. 89); a casual remark by Churchill recalls a not very similar one by Gladstone (pp. 108–109); a political crisis in 1916 over an obscure question of property rights in Nigeria evokes the memory of the Home Rule controversy in 1886 (p. 316), as does the debate in the House of Commons after the failure of the Norway campaign in May 1940 (p. 577); Churchill's "brooding" about the dangers of the H-bomb was reminiscent of Gladstone's vexations about increased naval expenditures (p. 884). There are also repeated comparisons of their age at various stages of their careers, their health, their marital relations, their diversions, and, finally, their funerals. In place of Gladstone, Jenkins sometimes introduces his own personal and parliamentary experiences: his contesting of a by-election in 1981 recalls Churchill's in 1924 (p. 391); his disagreement with the leadership of his party reminds him of Churchill's situation in 1939 (p. 537); a debate during his term as chancellor of the Exchequer resembles one Churchill was involved in early in the war (p. 599).

18. Winston S. Churchill, *Lord Randolph Churchill* (London, 1906), I, 222–223; II, 461, 214, 282–284.

19. William Manchester attributes this to Disraeli himself. (See *The Last Lion: Winston Spencer Churchill,* vol. I, *Visions of Glory, 1874–1932* [New York, 1983], p. 177.) Leslie Stephen attributed it to David Hume (*History of English Thought in the Eighteenth Century* [New York, 1962 (1st ed., 1876)], I, 289). On its source in Shaftesbury, see Gertrude Himmelfarb, *The Roads to Modernity: The British, French, and American Enlightenments* (New York, 2004), p. 39.

20. Winston S. Churchill, *A History of the English-Speaking Peoples* (New York, 1990 [1st ed., 1957]), III, 100. (Much of this section of the *History* is derived from his earlier work, *Marlborough: His Life and Times* [1933–1938].)

21. Jenkins, *Churchill,* p. 5.

22. Ibid., p. 10.

23. Ibid., p. 8; Winston Churchill, *My Early Life: 1874–1904* (New York, 1996 [1st ed., 1930]), p. 5.

24. Best, *Churchill,* p. 6.

25. Gilbert, *Churchill,* p. 23.

26. Jenkins, *Churchill,* p. 95.

27. Ibid., p. 87.

28. Ibid., p. 147.

29. R. F. Foster, *Lord Randolph Churchill: A Political Life* (Oxford, 1981), pp. 165–166.

30. Best, *Churchill,* p. 28.

31. Jenkins, *Churchill,* p. 250.

32. Ibid., p. 291; Best, *Churchill,* p. 77.

33. Jenkins, *Churchill,* p. 345.

34. Best, *Churchill,* p. 93.

35. Jenkins, *Churchill,* p. 351.

36. Best, *Churchill,* p. 93.

37. Ibid., p. 97.

38. Robert Blake, "Churchill and the Conservative Party," in *Winston Churchill,* ed. Kemper, p. 149.

39. Jenkins, *Churchill,* pp. 437, 457.

40. Ibid., pp. 156–157.

41. John Lukacs, *Five Days in London: May 1940* (New Haven, Conn., 1999), p. 190.

42. Best, *Churchill,* p. 186.

43. Jenkins, *Churchill,* pp. 567, 591, 612. In the 250 pages on this period, there are only half a dozen paragraph-length extracts from Churchill's talks (radio broadcasts and speeches in Commons) and about 50 from other sources.
44. Best, *Churchill,* p. 187.
45. Martin Gilbert, "The Origins of the 'Iron Curtain' Speech," in *Winston Churchill,* ed. Kemper, p. 49.
46. Lord Amery, "Memories of Churchill and How He Would Have Seen the World Today," ibid., p. 241.
47. Martin Gilbert, *Churchill and America* (New York, 2005), p. 381.
48. Ibid., p. 437.
49. Jenkins, *Churchill,* p. 912.
50. Best, *Churchill,* p. 334.
51. Ibid., p. 330. See also Lukacs on those critical days in May when Churchill "saved Britain, and Europe, and Western civilization" (Lukacs, *Five Days,* p. 2).
52. Best, *Churchill,* pp. 335–336.

Lionel Trilling: The Moral Imagination

1. Lionel Trilling, "T. S. Eliot's Politics" (1940), in *Speaking of Literature and Society,* ed. Diana Trilling (New York, 1980), p. 156. This essay originally appeared in *Partisan Review,* September/October 1940 under the title "Elements That Are Wanted."
2. Ibid., pp. 157–158.
3. Ibid., p. 158.
4. Ibid., p. 157.
5. Ibid., p. 158.
6. Ibid. p. 163.
7. Ibid., p. 168.
8. Ibid., p. 169.
9. This essay has since been reprinted in Trilling, *The Moral Obligation to Be Intelligent: Selected Essays,* ed. Leon Wieseltier (New York, 2000).
10. Trilling, *The Liberal Imagination: Essays on Literature and Society* (New York, 1950), p. ix.
11. Ibid., pp. ix–xi.
12. Ibid., p. xv.
13. Trilling, *Sincerity and Authenticity* (Cambridge, Mass., 1972), p. 68.
14. Ibid., pp. 156–157.
15. Trilling, "Freud and Literature" (1940), in *The Liberal Imagination,* p. 57.

16. Trilling, "The Progressive Psyche" (1942), in *Speaking of Literature and Society,* p. 185.

17. Trilling, "Freud: Within and Beyond Culture" (1955), in *Beyond Culture: Essays on Literature and Learning* (New York, 1965), p. 115.

18. Trilling, "Orwell on the Future" (1949), in *Speaking of Literature and Society,* p. 253.

19. Trilling, "George Orwell and the Politics of Truth" (a review of *Homage to Catalonia,* 1952), in *The Opposing Self: Nine Essays in Criticism* (New York, 1978; 1st ed., 1955), p. 146.

20. Trilling, *Speaking of Literature and Society,* p. 163.

21. Trilling, "Manners, Morals, and the Novel" (1947), in *Liberal Imagination,* pp. 221–22.

22. Trilling, ed., *The Experience of Literature: A Reader with Commentaries* (New York, 1967).

Index